Readings & Responses

Rod Quin

Pearson Australia
(a division of Pearson Australia Group Pty Ltd)
707 Collins Street, Melbourne, Victoria 3008
PO Box 23360, Melbourne, Victoria 8012
www.pearson.com.au

Copyright © Pearson Australia 2009
(a division of Pearson Australia Group Pty Ltd)
First published 2003
Reprinted 2003 (twice), 2004, 2006, 2007, 2008, 2009, 2010 (twice), 2011 (twice),
2012 (twice), 2013

Designed by Pierluigi Vido and Lucy Adams
Edited by Janet Mau
Cartoons by Connah Brecon
Prepress work by The Type Factory
Set in Poppl-Laudatio
Produced by Pearson Australia
Printed in Malaysia, VVP

National Library of Australia
Cataloguing-in-Publication data

Quin, Rod.
Readings & responses.

Includes index.
For Year 12 English students.
ISBN 978-0-7339-2479-8

1. English literature – Study and teaching (Secondary). 2.
Language arts (Secondary). I. Title.

820.712

Pearson Australia Group Pty Ltd ABN 40 004 245 943

Contents

Preface

To the student

Readings and Responses reflects a number of beliefs about how you can become better at English.

First is the belief that becoming better at English means becoming a critical user of language, someone who thinks about language and deliberates on how they use it and respond to it, rather than someone who just uses or responds to language without thinking.

Second is the belief that you will learn best if you are presented with challenging, worthwhile knowledge and activities, rather than watered down knowledge or trivial busy work. Some parts of this book may be difficult at first and you might come across some 'big' words, but that is what learning is all about—conquering new ideas and expanding your ability to talk about ideas.

Third is the belief that one of the most effective ways of helping you learn is by giving you models and examples of the tasks you might be required to undertake in English. This book includes examples of work by those who have gone before you. When you read these work samples, examine not just what they say but how they say it. Examine them critically and thoughtfully. The work samples are not examples of perfect work. Some of them contain glitches. There are ways in which they could be improved. But by reading them and thinking about them you will be learning how to improve your own work.

Fourth, this book is based on a spiral curriculum approach. This approach is the opposite of explaining a concept once and assuming you've got it. You know that approach doesn't work from your own experience of education. A spiral curriculum approach is based on the idea that our understanding of a concept develops as we are exposed to it over and over again. Just because there's a chapter or section on a particular concept in this book doesn't mean the concept does not appear elsewhere. The key concepts in this book crop up over and over again in different ways and in different words. The index can help you find different references to a concept.

Dedication

This book is dedicated to the wonderful students and ex-students of Balcatta Senior High School and especially the graduating students of 1997, 1998, 1999, 2000 and 2001, who taught me what I needed to know to write this book.

Rod Quin

Acknowledgements

The publishers would like to thank the following for permission to reproduce material in this book.

For Images:
Austral International, pp. 45, 51.
Australian Picture Library, pp. 5, 24, 63, 90, 95, 99, 167, 177.
Becker Entertainment, pp. 193, 199, 200bl.
The Body Shop, p. 154.
The Bridgeman Art Library International, *Portrait of a Young Woman*, c.1550, by the Master of the Female Half Lengths in the Kunsthistorisches Museum, Vienna, p. 161.
Cooke, Kaz. Reproduced with permission of Allen & Unwin, pp. 146–52.
Fowles, John. Copyright © 1963. Cover from *The Collector* by John Fowles. Used by permission of The Random House Group Ltd, pp. 183–4.
Kobal Picture Library, pp. 92, 192, 195, 198, 200tl, 208, 211.
Smith, Sean. Copyright © *The Guardian Newspaper*, p. 102.

For Textual Extracts:
Atwood, Margaret. Used by permission of The Random House Group Ltd, pp. 185–6.
Barnouw, Erik. *Documentary: a history of the non-fiction film*, 2nd revised edition. Copyright © 1974, 1983, 1993. Used by permission of Oxford University Press, Inc., pp. 79, 83–7.
Barsam, R.M./Indiana Press 1975, pp. 88–9.
Berardinelli, James, pp. 51–2, 195, 208.
Biddulph, Steve. *Manhood*, Finch Publishing, Sydney, 3rd edition, 2002, pp. 128–31.
Bryson, Bill. Extract from *Down Under* by Bill Bryson, published by Black Swan, a division of Transworld Publishers. All rights reserved, pp. 113–8.
Cooke, Kaz. Reproduced with permission of Allen & Unwin, pp. 146–52.
Daily Mail, pp. 153–5.
Donaghy, Bronwyn, HarperCollins Publishers Australia, pp. 27–8.

Elton, Ben. Copyright © Stand Up Limited, 1997, Simon & Schuster Publishers, pp. 67–8, 164.
Fowles, John. Copyright © 1963. *The Collector* by John Fowles. Used by permission of The Random House Group Ltd, pp. 183–4.
Frost, Robert. Random House UK, p. 14.
Gray, John. Copyright © 1992. Reprinted with permission of HarperCollins Publishers Inc., p. 126.
Ibsen, Henrik, translated by Peter Watts (Penguin Books, 1965). Copyright © Peter Watts 1965, pp. 36–9.
Macoll, R.M. © 2000, *The Washington Post*. Reprinted with permission. pp. 62–3.
Marks, Michelle. *The Age*. pp. 64–5.
McLeish Kenneth and Valatic Ltd. The extract from *Medea* by Euripides is copyright © 1994. Reproduced by courtesy of the publisher Nick Hearn Books, London 1994, pp. 39–43.
O'Rourke, P.J./Macmillan London, pp. 119–20.
Pearl, Cyril. Excerpt from *The Best of Lennie Lower* (EET Imprint, Sydney, 1995), pp. 65–7.
Spencer, Megan/Miami Movies, pp. 107–10.
Suzuki, David. Reproduced with permission of Allen & Unwin, pp. 138–40.
Thurber, James. © The Thurber Estate 1945, p. 2.
Weekend Australian Newspaper, pp. 134–6.
Winton, Tim. Reproduced with permission of Penguin Books Australia, pp. 162, 174–6, 179.
Wolf, Naomi. Extract from *The Beauty Myth*, published by Chatto & Windus. Used by permission of The Random House Group Ltd, pp. 141–5.
Wolfe, Tom. 'The Last American Hero', in *The Purple Decades*, Berkley Publishing Group, New York, 1982, pp. 126–7.

Every effort has been made to trace and acknowledge copyright. However, should any infringement have occurred, the publishers tender their apologies and invite copyright owners to contact them.

Constructing readings

Many people assume that reading is a passive activity. They think that all they have to do is look at a text and the ideas expressed in the text will somehow appear in their heads. This is wrong. Many people think that reading is a one-way process, where ideas flow from the text to the reader but not the other way. This is also wrong. Many people think that the task of a reader is to work out the one, true meaning of the text. This, too, is wrong.

If all these assumptions are wrong, what is the truth about reading? The truth is that reading is an active process. Reading involves readers applying a wide range of tools to a text. These include:

- personal experiences
- understandings and beliefs about the world
- attitudes and values
- previous reading experiences
- knowledge about the context of the text, such as who produced it and in what circumstances
- knowledge of reading conventions
  - approach to the text (discussed on pages 10–11).

We use these tools whether we are reading a book, a film or a still image. They are not like mining tools, which enable a reader to extract a meaning from a text. Rather, they are like manufacturing tools, which enable a reader to construct meanings with the raw materials of the text. Because we know that reading is an active process, it is now common to talk about readers 'constructing readings' of texts.

Think about what is involved in making meaning from one of the first sentences many children read: 'The cat sat on the mat'. To be able to construct a reading of this sentence, children first need to have some experience or knowledge of cats and how they behave, mats and how they are used and what it means to be 'on' something as opposed to 'under' it, 'over' it or 'in' it. In addition, they need to know particular reading conventions, such as the ones that say the letters 'c-a-t' stand for the particular creature they

know as a cat and the letters 's-a-t' a particular action they are familiar with. Even with this knowledge, different children will probably draw on their individual experience to make different meanings from the sentence by visualising different sorts of cats—black and skinny, white and fluffy, and so on—and different sorts of mats.

Activity

Discuss with other students the mental picture that occurs to you when you read the sentence 'The cat sat on the mat'.

What possible reasons are there for any differences?

The meaning of the sentence 'The cat sat on the mat' might also vary depending on the reader's attitudes towards cats and mats. For cat-lovers, the sentence may conjure up a lovely feeling of warmth, cosiness and domesticity. For cat-haters, the feeling may be one of disgust at the thought that such a revolting animal was even in the house in the first place, let alone sullying the mat with its foul habits.

The meaning a reader constructs of the sentence will also vary according to his or her understanding of the context in which the sentence occurs. Most children realise that the text exists to help them learn to read and that's all. If they thought that the sentence was written in a different set of circumstances, they might construct a different meaning.

Activity

Discuss the contexts in which the sentence 'The cat sat on the mat' could be interpreted as:
- a reprimand
- an expression of wonder
- a boast
- an exclamation of shock.

When you were first learning to read, reading was a very consciously active process. You might have had to slowly sound out each word and then think about what it referred to. You also had to relate the words in a sentence to each other to produce a meaningful sentence, one that actually said something and made sense to you.

You are now a more proficient reader, but you might have noticed that when you encounter an unfamiliar or difficult text your reading slows down and you have to actually stop and think to make sense of what you are reading.

Apart from these encounters with difficult texts, reading may mostly seem like a fairly passive activity which you do without much conscious effort. But that is because you have become so good at reading by this stage of your education. It is like riding a bicycle. Once you have gone through the hard work of concentrating on learning how to do it, it becomes fairly automatic. When reading becomes automatic, it can be described as unreflective or uncritical reading. It is still not passive, however.

The difference between riding a bicycle and reading, is that most bicycles are pretty much the same. As you progress through school, the texts you read and the readings you are required to make of them become increasingly complex. In order to deal with these you need to engage in some of the consciously active practices you engaged in as a child.

What does all this mean for the work you will do in English this year? It means that when you are confronted with the task of writing or speaking about a text you should focus not on trying to work out or guess a right answer, but on applying the tools of reading described earlier to the raw material of the text, with the purpose of constructing an interpretation or argument, or, in other words, a reading. An important aspect of this process is actively drawing on your store of experiences, understandings, beliefs, experience of other texts and understandings of reading conventions to construct readings.

The more critically active you are as a reader and the more you consciously participate in the construction of meaning, the better you will become at reading and the wider variety of texts you will be able to construct readings from. You will also enjoy reading more and you might even recapture some of the excitement and interest in reading you had as a child.

WORK SAMPLE

Reading of *Star Wars*

This work sample is a transcription of an oral presentation by a Year 12 student to her English class. In her talk she explains how she was able to become involved in *Star Wars* by relating the film to her own experience as a student, her understandings of the world and her exposure to certain ideologies. In doing this, she is explaining how she constructed a reading of the text.

Topic for this work: Even though they are obviously fictional, many texts can seem powerfully real.

Every one of us here today shares a common goal. You could say that we are all on a quest—our task being to finish our education so we can embark on our future. The basic idea of a quest is that you must accomplish a certain task and ours is simply to get through Year 12. Now, in the film Star Wars the central character is on a quest just like ours except that his quest is to believe in himself so he can become a Jedi pilot. Although it might surprise you I was able to see how the quest portrayed in Star Wars could be applied to the world in which we live, and in particular could be applied to our very own quest to finish our education.

You see, both quests are about the growth into maturity we all experience in life. _Star Wars_ offered me a plausible understanding of the learning process that comes with accomplishing a quest and despite the fact that _Star Wars_ is centred around a population at war in another galaxy, on a thematic level I thought it was one of the most powerfully real films I've seen.

I know that you're all thinking there's no way a film about 'a galaxy far, far away' could be the slightest bit realistic but in terms of what _Star Wars_ says about the world in which we live it offers us a powerful sense of realism. It is able to do this by drawing on a number of social ideologies that we are familiar with. _Star Wars_ is able to encourage us to suspend the disbelief we have towards the obviously fictional aspects of the film, such as the robots and the spaceships, and instead become involved with its ideological position.

One of the main ways _Star Wars_ was able to do this, was by presenting me with a very traditional way of thinking about good versus evil. You see _Star Wars_ encouraged the idea that we all have a dark side and that every person is in a constant battle with this 'evil' nature of theirs. By offering us this ideology, _Star Wars_ taps into the deep seated fear we all have of our evil consciences and there couldn't be a better way to enhance our involvement with the film, since we all like to blame our evil conscience for leading us astray and for making us do evil things.

The central character in _Star Wars_ spends most of the film trying to resist the lure and the temptation of the dark side and by the end we feel like we are right there with him chanting in his ear, 'Come on Luke, you can't give in to the dark side!' When his good side finally does triumph over the dark side we breathe a sigh of relief by being assured that good wins the battle. _Star Wars_ reassures us that good is stronger than evil, an ideology that appeals to our sensibilities.

To further enhance its involvement, _Star Wars_ takes an unfamiliar plot about a battle between a population living in another galaxy and presents it in terms of plots from other genres that are usually seen as more realistic than science fiction. The sets of _Star Wars_ resemble those well known scenes of the Wild West and the characters move about like Tarzan or war heroes. _Star Wars_ blends the science fiction genre with a combination of mythology, samurai spiritualism, quest and cowboy genres which are all very familiar to us so there's more chance we will become involved in the plot. I could also attribute the involvement I had with _Star Wars_ to the fact that the film reminded me of a typical war film. The characters displayed those war-like heroics we all know so well, just like we have seen in the films _The Thin Red Line_ and in _Saving Private Ryan_. By reminding me of a war film, _Star Wars_ offered me the familiar ideology that you become a hero and a real man by fighting for what you believe, even if it means going to war.

The central character in _Star Wars_ is a guy around our age, and as I explained earlier, he is also on a quest just like we all are! In Luke's growth into maturity, we can identify with the frustration he shows when he thinks his goal is unobtainable. Don't we all get frustrated and become overwhelmed when trying so desperately to achieve a certain goal? Luke Skywalker is the classic cowboy, or that courageous hero we all love to love. However, the fact that he still needs guidance and advice, proves that he is not at all invincible and seems like a typical human after all. Luke seeks the advice and wisdom he needs from the character Obi Wan Kenobi. Obi Wan Kenobi is the classic Merlin type of character, someone who passes on their wisdom to an eager young person. In fact he is the perfect Mr Myagi from <u>The Karate Kid</u> movies. His sole job is to pass on the wisdom to the central character. By offering me a humble and wise character to pass on his wisdom, <u>Star Wars</u> encouraged me to agree with the advice about life that this character gives to believe in yourself and always persevere.

From *Star Wars*

Despite the fact that many characters in <u>Star Wars</u> were not even human some had behaviours we know are very human-like. An unusual example of psychologically real characters are those two robot characters—the tall gold metal one and the little R2D2 robot that looks like a vacuum cleaner. Both these characters are obviously fictional, but they bicker like old women, get frightened, whinge and have silly little arguments. There couldn't be a better way to enhance the audience's involvement than by using two robots to demonstrate very human characteristics.

There were several elements of <u>Star Wars</u> that enhanced my involvement with the film in addition to the way it borrowed from familiar genres and the way it presented me with psychologically realistic characters. However, the main reason why <u>Star Wars</u> proved powerfully real to me was because of the ideologies it offered me on a thematic level. <u>Star Wars</u> focused on ways of thinking that are common to many people, emphasising some bits of advice I'm sure you're all familiar with, that 'You must believe in yourself' and that 'You must never give up'. These two bits of advice are summed up by the best known line in the film, 'May the force be with you' or in other words 'Believe in yourself'.

Work supplied by Laura Kuuse

Activities

1 Make a set of notes on the experiences, understandings or beliefs about the world that the author of the work sample says influenced her reading of *Star Wars*.

2 Make a list of other films or books where a reader might draw on similar experiences, understandings or beliefs to relate to the text.

WORK SAMPLE

Reading of *Medea*

In this work sample, produced in an examination, the writer describes how she was able to construct a reading of the character of Medea, in the play of the same name, as a hero by relating the play to her exposure to the then popular idea of 'girl power', the pressures on her to conform to certain gender roles and her reading of other texts. For a taste of *Medea* see pages 39–43.

Topic of this essay: Like other texts, a play encourages specific attitudes and values through its construction of heroes and villains.

Medea was evil, she was bad, she was my favourite. Due to the construction of Medea I was able to recognise certain values and attitudes and appreciate their relevance to today's society. Medea was considered a sorceress because she acted upon instinct and emotion and defied her gender construction which was why I liked her character.

Euripides wrote Medea two thousand years ago exploring the issue of male dominance. I believe that Medea was a spice girl who was way ahead of her time. In a way Euripides was experimenting by endorsing 'girl power' when constructing Medea and by showing how people react when they see a woman fighting for her rights.

When first reading Medea I found myself unconsciously relating her to people that I could recognise in society. It also allowed me to see that even two thousand years after Medea was written we still live in a very patriarchal society and while people such as Euripides have challenged these values their challenges seem to have had little effect.

When I think of Medea and how she fought for her love for Jason and was then abandoned I thought of Nora in Henrik Ibsen's A Doll's House. Both characters were villains in the eyes of the male characters but heroes to women like me but sadly both were banished by society and even their families, simply for basing their actions on their emotions and what they believed was right rather then acting according to their gender.

The actions taken by Jason, Medea's husband, might seem heroic to some, but I can't see what is heroic about leaving your wife for a younger woman. Medea wouldn't stand for this so she took action in a similar way to Nora: both women stood up and claimed that women were not puppets or little girls or even toys that could be tossed away and replaced simply because their novelty had worn off or they had become too old.

The values and attitudes portrayed in <u>Medea</u> are those of male dominance and female resistance. The play asks us to question why in some societies it is considered okay to leave your wife for a better opportunity yet if the situation was reversed the woman would be named a whore.

To me Medea was a hero. Although I couldn't justify her killing her children for revenge, I can relate to the frustration felt by her when Jason announced he was leaving her and then tried to announce that it was for her own good. On reading that I thought, 'Give me a break!' and this made me not only sympathise with Medea but also empathise with her situation.

Medea fought the battle of girl power and lost due to the patriarchal nature of society at the time. But she encouraged me to continuously ask why I should have to live in a society where I have to have kids and I have to get married. I realise that no one is forcing me—well actually my mum is—but if this means reinforcing the patriarchal nature of society to some extent then I will challenge this to the best of my ability. In other words I will fight for girl power.

I believe if there were more Noras, female politicians or world leaders women would have a greater chance. However I will never forget the Medea who fought the battle against Jason and society and lost but changed my values which I believe was an achievement.

You see, until we can overcome this cliché of Boys Rule and Girls Drool, and cook and clean etc ... then girls like Medea and Nora and me will keep fighting for girl power.

Work supplied by Anita Tancevski

Influences and limitations on readings

Because reading involves the interplay between the reader's resources and a text, different readers often construct different readings of the same text.

It is also possible for individual readers to construct more than one reading of a text. You might have experienced this if you have read a book or watched a film more than once and picked up different ideas the second or third time around.

Pointing out that texts can be read in a range of different ways might tempt you to see reading as a process where 'anything goes' or something like an unplanned chemical experiment where a whole lot of different unknowns are thrown together with unpredictable results. This would be a mistake because it ignores a number of important factors that influence and limit the readings that readers construct of texts.

First, reading is a socially controlled process. The shared reading conventions in a society determine the boundaries of the readings that can be made of texts. This means that it is actually possible to describe some readings as simply incorrect or mistaken. To return to our earlier example of 'The cat sat on the mat', a reader who visualises a dog sitting in an armchair has simply got it wrong in terms of the reading conventions of current society. This means that to be able to construct readings effectively you need to have as wide an awareness as possible of the reading conventions available within your society. One of the functions of this book is to help you develop this awareness.

Second, members of most societies share many similar experiences, understandings, beliefs, values and reading conventions. Producers of texts usually think about the audience for whom they are writing and create their texts in such a way that they will connect with the resources their audiences bring to the text. So the readings that members of a society construct of a text are influenced by the way the text is constructed, and as a result are often fairly similar. The way in which a text is constructed to connect with common experiences, understandings, beliefs, attitudes or reading conventions is sometimes called reader positioning and is examined in more detail later in this book.

Reminder card

Tools and resources readers apply to a text:
- personal experiences
- understandings and beliefs about the world
- attitudes and values
- previous reading experiences
- knowledge about the context of the text, such as who produced it and in what circumstances
- knowledge of reading conventions
- approach to the text.

WORK SAMPLE

Readings of *Brave New World* and *The Handmaid's Tale*

In this work sample, produced in an examination, the writer describes how texts draw on commonly held experiences and attitudes to allow readers to relate to them.

Topic of this essay: How can texts set in another time and/or place be relevant to Australian teenagers of the present?

Somehow novelists manage to produce works that, although their settings bear little resemblance to modern lifestyles, people can relate to. Two books which have been successful in doing so are The Handmaid's Tale by Margaret Atwood and Brave New World by Aldous Huxley. Both of these texts are set in the future. That people can relate to these two texts means that there must be similarities of a sort between these fictional worlds and the world we live in today. These similarities can exist in the form of characters, the situations that the characters are involved in and the issues and events portrayed in the novels.

Characters are always a strong influence in a text because the reader is a character in a way. If a character in a text is experiencing similar problems to those of the reader then there is a strong possibility that the reader will relate to the text. In _Brave New World_ the main character, Bernard Marx finds that because he is not physically perfect, he does not fit in. In a world like ours where physical perfection is in utmost demand, a reader who regards him/herself as having flaws in physical appearance might find something to relate to and perhaps comfort them while reading of Bernard's troubles. In the same way, someone who feels they are being suppressed or held back by someone may find a way of relating to Offred. Offred is the main character in _The Handmaid's Tale_, and has come from a successful lifestyle to become a female slave, purely a means of reproduction.

Problems are not the only way that readers can relate to characters. If a character is placed in an environment similar to the reader then he/she may also find something to relate to. Bernard Marx is an expert in human reproduction and everyday does the same job in exactly the same way. To most teenagers this is precisely what school feels like, a never-ending routine of attending school for ten weeks to receive a measly two weeks holidays. Many teenage readers are likely to sit up and think, 'I know how you feel'. Offred, on the other hand, is treated like an irresponsible daughter. She is sent to pick up the groceries, allowed no privileges and not allowed to socialise. Again there may be some teenage girls who experience the same strict rules and so can relate to her.

In the dystopia, _The Handmaid's Tale_, women are treated as inferior to the male caste of the human race. Women have been treated much the same way for centuries in our own world. Although treated as inferiors, they were shown respect but were not allowed important jobs. This similarity to our own past could result in readers relating to the story as many believe that history is cyclical and what was will be again. Another similarity between _The Handmaid's Tale_ and our history is that minority groups or handicapped groups have been shunned and in the case of World War Two, even locked up and killed. In _The Handmaid's Tale_ Offred's own mother is locked up in a camp because of her age. Again this similarity to our history may result in people relating to the texts.

Much of people's emotions, time and effort are put into protecting or fighting for rights. In our society, students are often violently and emotionally supportive of protests and fights. Two of the biggest and on-going protests are for women's rights and freedom of speech. Both of these are represented in _Brave New World_ and _The Handmaid's Tale_ in large degrees. In Huxley's work freedom of speech figures largely, as in his world, perfection can be sustained only by the elimination of dissent. Thus no one may speak out against the world leaders. This is represented in the same way in Atwood's book. Atwood's book also shows a *rise and fall of the rights of women. As we fight for these rights, so do the people in the books and so we can find something to relate our world to in the novels.*

In conclusion, relationships between the world of Australian teenagers of today and those worlds represented in the novels can be found easily. By looking at the characters in texts, we can identify problems, environments and lifestyles which readers can relate to. In the same way, issues, events and histories can also become aspects of a text to which a reader can relate. If a relation to the text can be found, then the reader is much more likely to enjoy the text and think about it, rather than throw it on the 'too hard' heap or 'too boring' heap.

Work supplied by Christopher Lee

Activities

1 Make a set of notes on the experiences and attitudes mentioned by the author of the work sample.

2 Make a list of other films or books that appeal to similar experiences and attitudes.

Approaching the text: reading practices

The fact that the readings are influenced and limited by socially controlled reading conventions and textual construction might lead you, and in fact has led others, to conclude that constructing a reading is a totally controlled, stimulus–response style of activity where readers simply respond to a carefully constructed text by drawing on the experiences, understandings of the world and reading conventions provided by society and appealed to by the text. The reason why this is not necessarily the case is contained in the last bullet point in the list of resources available to the reader on page 8—approach to reading the text.

You can choose how you approach a text and thus control the readings you construct. Here are some examples:

- Rather than continuing to read in ways you have become used to and practise automatically, you can practise different ways of reading, such as reading on different levels or reading for representation.
- Rather than simply responding to a text, you can examine how the text is constructed in order to encourage you to respond in this way.
- Rather than reading in the manner encouraged by the dominant ideas, beliefs and reading conventions of society, and appealed to by the text, you can explore the consequences of applying alternative ideas, beliefs and reading conventions.

These approaches are sometimes called different 'reading practices', and can produce very different readings of texts.

It is true that many readers do not choose how they approach a text. They read uncritically, responding to the way the text has been constructed using the dominant understandings of the world and the dominant reading conventions they have learnt from their society that are appealed to by the text. This is because they have not learnt alternative reading practices and are acting in the absence of choice.

Once you have learnt different approaches to reading, you may sometimes still choose to read uncritically, allowing yourself to simply be absorbed in a film or book and allowing it to just 'flow' over you. That's fine, but the difference will be that you will be acting from choice.

Some students resist the idea of critically active reading and adopting different reading practices. This is because it can be difficult at first. You will find, however, as with all learning, that it will become easier as you become more proficient.

Arguing for readings

If readings depend on the reader and the approach they adopt to the text and it is possible to construct very different readings of the same text, then you may be asking how it is possible to actually assess readings of a text.

In the world outside educational institutions, it does not really matter very much. No-one is going to mark you on your interpretations of films, books or articles. It is only in educational institutions that it is thought necessary to formally assess readings and give them a mark. Even here, however, what happens is not all that different to what happens in the outside world. The key factor by which your readings will be judged is how convincing they are. This in turn depends on such things as:

- how well you express yourself
- how well you use evidence from the text and elsewhere to support your explanation or argument
- how logical your explanation or argument seems to your audience.

Making your readings convincing does not mean that you are necessarily trying to convince your audience that yours is the correct reading or one that they should accept. Rather, it means showing that your reading is a valid one within a certain framework.

This leads to one more important criterion by which readings are assessed in schools: the extent to which it makes sense within the framework of a particular discussion. Most of the time you will be constructing your readings of texts in response to a specific topic. The extent to which your reading addresses the requirements of the topic will affect how it is assessed. This means nothing more than what you have no doubt heard time and again from teachers: 'Make sure you answer the question!'

Ultimately, your readings will be assessed not so much on the readings they offer but on the understandings they display about how readings can be constructed.

Activity

Discuss which of the three work samples in this chapter you think is the 'best' and your criteria for deciding this.

Getting better

Constructing readings is difficult when you do not have sufficient tools at your disposal or the tools you have are blunt. To become better at constructing readings, you need to expand the range of tools available to you and keep them sharp. Among other things this means:

*   expanding the range of texts you can draw on
*   expanding your knowledge of reading conventions
*   practising reading in different ways.

That's what the rest of this book is designed to help you do.

Texts can be read on a number of levels. On one level a text can be read in terms of what it is specifically and most obviously about on the surface. On other levels it can be read in terms of the more general ideas or issues it deals with. Another way of explaining this is to say that you can read a text in terms of the particular characters or situations it presents but you can also read it in terms of people, life or ideas in general. These other levels of reading are sometimes described as the thematic or ideological levels. The term ideology refers to systems of beliefs, values or ways of thinking about the world.

Many students find the concept of levels of reading very difficult. They find it hard to see the more general levels of meaning that other people, usually their teacher, discover when reading a text. They may even secretly suspect it is all a load of pretentious nonsense. There are two ways to overcome this problem.

First, it is important to realise that these more general levels of meaning are produced by readers relating the text to their understandings of the world in which they live. The general levels of meaning are not simply in a text, although sometimes a text may include signs that point us in the direction of these more general levels.

Second, it is also important to realise that people may disagree about the other levels of meaning of a text. This is not surprising because the more general levels of meaning arise from the interaction of text and reader, and not all readers are the same. They bring different experiences, beliefs, values and approaches to a text. Because of this, when you are writing or talking about the more general level of meanings of a text, it is more appropriate to say that it *can be read as being* about certain topics or issues rather than saying that it *is* about these topics or issues.

WORK SAMPLE

Reading of 'The Road Not Taken'

This work sample is a journal entry produced by a Year 8 student in response to the poem 'The Road Not Taken' by the American writer Robert Frost. It has been included because it provides a very straightforward example of what is meant by levels of reading and because it shows very clearly the way in which reading on more general levels of meaning involves readers relating the text to the world in which they live.

The Road Not Taken

Two roads diverged in a yellow wood,
And sorry I could not travel both
And be one traveller, long I stood
And looked down one as far as I could
To where it bent in the undergrowth;

Then took the other, as just as fair,
And having perhaps the better claim,
Because it was grassy and wanted wear;
Though as for that the passing there
Had worn them really about the same,

And both that morning equally lay
In leaves no step had trodden black.
Oh, I kept the first for another day!
Yet, knowing how way leads on to way,
I doubted if I should ever come back.

I shall be telling this with a sigh
Somewhere ages and ages hence:
Two roads diverged in a wood and I—
I took the one less travelled by,
And that has made all the difference.

Robert Frost

Topic for this work: **Explain your interpretation of this poem and its relevance to your experience.**

'Two roads diverged in a yellow wood.' What a great line!! I think this poem is about a man who is trying to express the way he feels when he has to make a specific choice. I really enjoyed hearing this poem because I feel as though I can relate to it!!

We all have to make decisions: some are minor like what sox to wear in the morning or whether to have cereal or toast for breakfast!! These sorts of decisions don't take too much thinking about. But in our lifespan we will come across more serious decisions such as whether to smoke or whether or not we should say 'yes' to getting married.

A very important choice I've had to make is if I want to live with my mum or with my dad.

I had to consider everything like if my dad would be able to drive me to and from my dancing etc etc. This was definitely not a choice of who I loved more. It was more than that. Once I had made up my decision I had to think about if seeing my dad just on weekends was enough.

Decisions aren't easy but it's something we are all in the same boat about.

Work provided by Belinda DiLorito

Activity

In this work sample, the student mentions some very specific examples from her own life to which she can relate the poem. What other examples from life might different readers be able to draw on in order to construct a reading of the poem? Discuss this with other students.

Robert Frost, the author of 'The Road Not Taken', said:

There are many other things I have found myself saying about poetry, but the chiefest of these is that it is metaphor, saying one thing and meaning another, saying one thing in terms of another.

As this indicates, many poems are written with the expectation that they will be read on more than one level. This is also true of many other types of text.

One such type of text with which you may be familiar is the fable. Fables are simple stories that use animals to make a comment on humans and how they behave or illustrate beliefs about how they should behave.

CASE STUDY

1

Aesop's fables

The earliest fables we have on record are Aesop's fables from ancient Greece. Below are four examples. Aesop's fables usually conclude with a sentence that sums up the moral of the fable. In the first two reproduced here, the moral has been included. In the last two, the moral has been omitted.

The Wolf and the Lamb

Once upon a time a Wolf was lapping at a spring on a hillside, when, looking up, what should he see but a Lamb just beginning to drink a little lower down. 'There's my supper,' thought he, 'if only I can find some excuse to seize it.' Then he called out to the Lamb, 'How dare you muddle the water from which I am drinking?'

'How can that be?' said the lamb. 'If the water is muddy up there, I cannot be the cause of it, for it runs down from you to me.'

'Well, then,' said the Wolf, 'why did you call me bad names this time last year?'

'That cannot be,' said the Lamb. 'I am only six months old.'

'I don't care,' snarled the Wolf, 'if it was not you it was your father,' and with that he rushed upon the poor little Lamb and ate her all up. But before she died she gasped out: 'Any excuse will serve a tyrant.'

The Ant and the Grasshopper

In a field one summer's day a Grasshopper was hopping about, chirping and singing to its heart's content. An Ant passed by, bearing along with great toil an ear of corn he was taking to the nest.

'Why not come and chat with me,' said the Grasshopper, 'instead of toiling and moiling in that way?'

'I am helping to lay up food for the winter,' said the Ant, 'and recommend you to do the same.'

'Why bother about winter?' said the grasshopper. 'We have got plenty of food at present.' But the Ant went on its way and continued its toil. When the winter came the Grasshopper had no food and found itself dying of hunger, while it saw the ants distributing every day corn and grain from the stores they had collected in the summer. Then the Grasshopper knew: It is best to prepare for the days of necessity.

The Hare and the Tortoise

The Hare was once boasting of his speed before the other animals. 'I have never yet been beaten,' said he, 'when I put forth my full speed. I challenge any one here to race with me.'

The Tortoise said quietly, 'I accept your challenge.'

'That is a good joke,' said the Hare; 'I could dance round you all the way.'

'Keep your boasting till you've beaten,' answered the Tortoise. 'Shall we race?'

So a course was fixed and a start was made. The Hare darted almost out of sight at once, but soon stopped and, to show his contempt for the Tortoise, lay down to have a nap. The Tortoise plodded on and plodded on, and when the Hare awoke from his nap, he saw the Tortoise just near the winning-post and could not run up in time to save the race. At this point the Tortoise said: ...

1

The Boy Who Cried Wolf

There was once a young Shepherd Boy who tended his sheep at the foot of a mountain near a dark forest. It was rather lonely for him all day, so he thought upon a plan by which he could get a little company and some excitement. He rushed down towards the village calling out 'Wolf, Wolf,' and the villagers came out to meet him, and some of them stopped with him for a considerable time. This pleased the boy so much that a few days afterwards he tried the same trick, and again the villagers came to his help.

But shortly after this a Wolf actually did come out from the forest, and began to worry the sheep, and the boy of course cried out 'Wolf, Wolf,' still louder than before. But this time the villagers, who had been fooled twice before, thought the boy was again deceiving them, and nobody stirred to come to his help. So the Wolf made a good meal of the boy's flock, and when the boy complained, the wise man of the village said: …

Activities

1. Write down what you believe would be an appropriate concluding moral for the last two fables. Discuss what you have written with other students.
2. In suggesting particular morals, fables promote particular beliefs or ways of thinking. In a critical literacy approach to English, identifying these beliefs is only the first step. You also need to decide whether you agree with these beliefs. Take each of the morals and critically evaluate them, discussing whether you think they are true. For instance, the fable of the hare and tortoise seems to suggest that determination and effort will win out over natural ability. To what extent do you think this is always true and reflects what happens in the real world?

2

CASE STUDY

The use of fables did not die out with the ancient Greeks. Fables have been used throughout history to comment on the human world. The following fable was written by an American journalist, James Thurber, and published in 1940. On one level, you can draw direct parallels between the story and political events in Europe. At that time, the Nazi regime in Germany was persecuting minority groups and threatening neighbouring countries. On another level, you can read the story as about all forms of political persecution and aggression throughout history. On still another, you can read the story as a comment on the type of bullying and intimidation you might come across in your everyday social life.

2

'The Rabbits Who Caused All The Trouble' by James Thurber

Within the memory of the youngest child there was a family of rabbits who lived near a pack of wolves. The wolves announced that they did not like the way the rabbits were living. (The wolves were crazy about the way they themselves were living, because it was the only way to live.) One night several wolves were killed in an earthquake and this was blamed on the rabbits, for it is well known that rabbits pound on the ground with their hind legs and cause earthquakes. On another night one of the wolves was killed by a bolt of lightning and this was also blamed on the rabbits, for it is well known that lettuce-eaters cause lightning. The wolves threatened to civilize the rabbits if they didn't behave, and the rabbits decided to run away to a desert island. But the other animals, who lived at a great distance, shamed them, saying, 'You must stay where you are and be brave. This is no world for escapists. If the wolves attack you, we will come to your aid, in all probability.' So the rabbits continued to live near the wolves and one day there was a terrible flood which drowned a great many wolves. This was blamed on the rabbits, for it is well known that carrot-nibblers with long ears cause floods. The wolves descended on the rabbits, for their own good, and imprisoned them in a dark cave, for their own protection.

When nothing was heard about the rabbits for some weeks, the other animals demanded to know what had happened to them. The wolves replied that the rabbits had been eaten and since they had been eaten the affair was a purely internal matter. But the other animals warned that they might possibly unite against the wolves unless some reason was given for the destruction of the rabbits. So the wolves gave them one. 'They were trying to escape,' said the wolves, 'and, as you know, this is no world for escapists.'

Moral: Run, don't walk, to the nearest desert island.

James Thurber, 'The Rabbits Who Caused All The Trouble'
in *Fables For Our Time and Illustrated Poems*, 1940.

Activities

For discussion:

1. What comments can this story be read as making on:
   - scapegoating
   - the responses of bystanders to persecution and aggression
   - the manipulation of language?
2. What parallels can you find between the story and
   - political events besides those of 1930s Europe
   - events you have witnessed in your own life?

While fables are clearly intended to be read on more than one level, you can apply the way in which you read fables—as fictional stories that have something to say about the world in which you live—to other types of text. It can be argued that all the stories that members of a society tell each other, fictional or otherwise, are ways of exploring and saying something about the shared world in which they live. A society's stories reflect its worries, hopes, fears, anxieties, beliefs, aspirations and desires.

The development of the science fiction genre in the twentieth century, for example, can be read as reflecting people's concerns about the growth of technology and their ability to control it. Other types of text might reflect people's concerns about crime, sexual relationships, the struggle between the individual and society and so on.

It is not only fictional texts that can be read in this way. The nonfiction book *Anna's Story* by Bronwyn Donaghy, for example, tells the story of the death of a fifteen-year-old Sydney girl from the drug ecstasy in 1995. It can also be read, however, as expressing the anxieties and worries that many adult Australians have about teenagers in general and the extent to which teenagers can be controlled and trusted.

One of the major reasons why you enjoy reading certain books or watching particular films and why you become involved in their narratives is because they deal with matters of concern or interest to you. This is why, for example, films that deal with the frustrations, difficulties and joys of establishing sexual relationships, such as *10 Things I Hate About You*, are so popular with teenagers, but not terribly popular with the over-fifties.

In many texts, the resolution to the narrative offers the audience the idea that the difficulties or conflicts presented can be overcome in ways that the audience finds satisfying. In a way, they work like the morals to Aesop's fables. This is especially true of many Hollywood movies. Not all texts, however, offer their audiences such comforting resolutions.

The work samples below provide examples of the way in which many texts can be read, like fables, on more than one level.

WORK SAMPLE

Reading of *The Truman Show*

This sample is a transcript of an oral presentation by a Year 12 student to her class. In the presentation, the student offers a reading of the film as a comment on certain trends in modern society.

Topic for this work: Even though they are obviously fictional, many texts can seem powerfully real.

Every day, from the moment Truman Burbank was born for the next thirty years he has been the unwitting star of the longest running and most popular documentary soap opera in history. The perfect town of Seahaven he calls home is actually a massive sound stage. Truman's friends and family are all actors. He lives every moment of his life under the gaze of five thousand TV cameras.

Truman's unsettling but humorous world is unlike anything previously created on film. It speaks directly to our innermost fears and frustrations. Truman is not only preyed upon by the network of cameras and actor spies, he is trapped in his own life—held down in the surreal existence in which he has been forced to spend the last thirty years.

The Truman Show is a story that reveals an essential truth about what is happening to society in the twentieth century. It is about how the media and corporations have begun to surround us and dominate our existence. From a control centre in Seahaven's moon Christof, the creator of Truman's world, stage manages events, creating the world that Truman and we find ourselves living inside, a stage-set that we discover is largely controlled by media corporations.

The world is entering public debate over the way the media manipulates public opinion and has such control over society's moral values and ideologies. This change has occurred due to the media becoming so powerful. Our concern for this change has been voiced through the creation of The Truman Show. Thus, the movie offers a metaphor for our own situation. The media environment Truman lives in is our own media environment in which things such as news, politics, advertising and current affairs are increasingly influencing us in terms of style, taste and fashion. Like our media environment, it is convincing in its realism with lifelike simulations and story lines, from his advertisement-dominated world to the powerful Christof who controls him much like media propaganda controls our lives.

Truman's fear of leaving this world is like our own reluctance to break our relationship with the media as we discover that a lot of our morals and values are influenced by opinions presented through media sources. Christof represents the large media corporations which surround us with this influence and power.

The movie isn't only a satire on TV and media but about the morality of the audience. We are the ones who make this system possible the movie tells us. The movie highlights the willingness of the audience to exploit Truman so they can enjoy his life as entertainment.

Voyeurism is becoming one of the major growth industries of the 90s—the chance to watch the private lives of others. The voyeuristic urge is growing and as technology improves, the line between public and private becomes increasingly blurred.

As we are allowed to explore Truman's life so closely we identify with him on a personal level and find it easier to be drawn into his world. The show presents us with a psychologically sympathetic character with whom the reader can empathise and identify especially through shared moral values. As the narrative shows his growth from a child to manhood the audience develops a bond with his character—an audience connection is developed through the narrative and genre. This audience involvement is another strong element of the movie which encourages the audience to reflect on his traumas, relating them to aspects of their own life.

The movie also draws on the 'unknown identity' genre. This is one where a character discovers that they're not the person they always thought they were. You may recognise this genre in movies such as _The Matrix_ where the main character discovers that he and his existence through the world around him is false, that his whole life has not been what he thought it was. This genre may also reflect inbuilt fears from the audience. We see stories every day of people finding out they were adopted as a child. That is why it is familiar to us and we are able to recognize Truman's position and relate it to events within our own lives. This familiarity makes it easier to connect with Truman's character, sympathising for his situation and being able to side with him against the media which dictates his life.

Truman's hunt for freedom also reflects aspects of our own life. This is a second genre which is often seen in other movies, and it also raises the idea of freedom as an important societal value represented by Truman's ability to overcome his greatest fear and risk death to achieve freedom. Movies similar to this include _Gattaca_ which is a futuristic film in which every man fights to preserve individuality against the threat of new technology. Individuality is a strong aspect of personal freedom. Truman's desire for freedom reflects our own desires for individuality.

The Truman Show is strong in thematic relevance, reflecting issues from within our own lives. As one reviewer pointed out, _The Truman Show_ depicts us. We are the villains, victims and heroes of _The Truman Show_. Truman's story reflects the anxieties and hopes that grip us all.

Work supplied by Rachel Thomas

Activity

Make notes on this work sample, listing the aspects of the modern world that the student sees reflected in _The Truman Show_. Discuss the extent to which you agree with the student's views about the way in which the film reflects attitudes in the modern world.

WORK SAMPLE

Reading of *Popcorn*

This work sample is an assignment produced by a Year 12 student.

Topic for this assignment: In presenting a fictional world novels often reflect and comment on the real world.

They're mad, they're wild, they're out of control. Wayne and his scrawny girlfriend Scout are blazing across the United States, massacring innocent strangers. They're on a killing spree, like something we would expect to see in a violent, Hollywood movie. So as no surprise, Wayne and Scout are doing just that—they're 'acting' out their favourite movie, bringing a fictional world to reality. Ben Elton's novel <u>Popcorn</u> is centred around Wayne and Scout's ruthless mission of murder and destruction, their goal being to capture the film's director, Bruce Delamitri.

Now, I know you're thinking that Wayne and Scout's mission sounds completely far fetched, but it only scrapes the surface of <u>Popcorn</u>'s excessively fictional nature, the novel becoming more and more hard to believe as you read on.

<u>Popcorn</u> is clearly designed to be fictional, going completely over the top and employing all the necessary Hollywood 'requirements'. It's got fancy Oscar parties, cocaine-sniffing celebrities, playboy centrefolds, a hostage situation—you name it! The novel is just like one of those excessively unrealistic Hollywood films. I lost count of the number of times that <u>Popcorn</u> left me thinking, 'Yeah right, what next?' However, by being so similar to a typical Hollywood film, we are encouraged to see that most of the films around today are terrible interpretations of reality.

You see, <u>Popcorn</u> reflects our most common beliefs and concerns about the world today. It does this on three thematic levels. First, it reflects our strong fear of the increasing amount of violence in our society, and our belief that the entertainment industry must be held partly responsible for some of this violence. Second, it mirrors our beliefs that the media has little concern for morality and about presenting the public with a truthful interpretation of reality. On a final thematic level, <u>Popcorn</u> reflects our most common ways of thinking about the rich and famous, including how we all think they live and how we expect them to behave.

By reflecting our beliefs, <u>Popcorn</u> encourages us to suspend the disbelief we have towards the novel's obviously fictional nature, and instead become involved with what it has to say about the world in which we live. By using this technique, <u>Popcorn</u> makes us wonder whether we should see people like Wayne and Scout as victims of the entertainment industry or simply as a couple of horrid people who murder by no fault but their own. As I asked myself this question, I realised just how relevant this way of thinking is to our society today.

Popcorn reminds us how real the idea of impressionable young people going on a 'killing-spree' is in the world today. Just look at that recent schoolyard massacre in Denver, where out of the blue two young boys walked into their school, killing their classmates. It's plain to see the similarities between the fictional killers in *Popcorn*, and those two boys in Denver. In both the fictional world of *Popcorn* and in the reality of that Denver high school, we are reminded of the increasing amount of violence in the world today, and in both situations we are left trying to work out who should be held responsible for such horrific crimes.

It's plain to see that *Popcorn* also reflects the criticism we have towards the media and the entertainment industry, by the way the novel highlights the flaws and imperfections of the media and Hollywood's elite. This technique not only provides plenty of light-hearted humour to an otherwise serious novel, but it also enhances the involvement we have with *Popcorn's* thematic positions. The novel depicts the media as a bunch of shallow, egotistical people, who have no concern about morality.

By presenting us with this satire of the media, *Popcorn* also reflects our concerns about the media being able to 'construct' reality, in order to achieve a desired response. You see, the novel constantly reminds us of its fictional status, pointing out that the novel itself is all a big 'construction'. Ben Elton employs this technique, not only to show us how clever he is, but to show us how easily we can be misled by Hollywood and the media. Certain characters in *Popcorn* actually brag about how easy it is for the media and the entertainment industry to 'design' films, television or the news, to provide 'entertainment' for a certain audience. This aspect of the novel, reflects our beliefs that the media is more concerned about finding that 'juicy' bit of gossip, than maintaining their morality.

The media and the entertainment industry are not the only ones who are criticised in *Popcorn*, as the novel offers a broad criticism of every person who has ever read, watched, or listened to any form of the media's gossip. By offering us this open criticism of society, *Popcorn* makes an extremely relevant comment on our way of life, which further enhances our involvement with the novel.

Popcorn asks us all to take a close look at ourselves before we start blaming the media for having no concern for morality, pointing out we are the ones who support the media, so therefore we are all partly responsible for the media's actions. The novel suggests that if we didn't give the media so much attention, they wouldn't be so desperate for that 'juicy' story, and begin invading people's privacy or stooping to other low levels. *Popcorn* opens our eyes to the fact that we are just as bad as the media, seeing that we are the ones buying the gossip magazines and laughing at those sneaky pictures of celebrities caught with their pants down.

Popcorn is not one of those typical novels that constructs certain characters who we are supposed to admire, or become involved with. In fact, *Popcorn* does the complete opposite. It asks us to treat the characters critically, ensuring that we stand back from each character. However, it's not that difficult to despise the characters in <u>Popcorn</u>, seeing that most of them are shallow, self-centred celebrities, or other members of Hollywood's silicone society. <u>Popcorn</u> ridicules all those television personalities, morning talk show hosts, movie stars and other celebrities who we usually idolise, encouraging us to see that our so-called 'heroes', are not that great after all.

<u>Popcorn</u> presents us with characters that we can't help criticising, like Bruce Delamitri, who's an arrogant, chauvinistic pig, and his shallow wife and his spoilt brat of a daughter. <u>Popcorn</u> depicts these characters, along with the rest of Hollywood's rich and famous, as a bunch of superficial people, who couldn't care less about what's going on in the world if their images or their careers are at stake. News readers and talk show hosts in particular cop a lot of criticism in the novel, an example being the way <u>Popcorn</u> refers to two characters as perfect Ken and Barbie stereotypes, this technique reflecting our belief that the media seems to have lost their concern for morality in layers of make-up and hairspray.

Of course we all know that <u>Popcorn</u> portrays its characters, the media and the entertainment industry, in an exaggerated and fictional manner. However, the novel doesn't necessarily have to present us with a world that is completely true, it simply has to offer us a world we can find plausible, and this it does very effectively. You see, although the fictional world depicted in <u>Popcorn</u> is not necessarily realistic we are still able to find this world plausible, and become involved with the ideas reflected by the novel.

Ben Elton

By constantly moving between different fictional worlds, <u>Popcorn</u> makes it difficult for us to distinguish between what is 'real', and what is not. It jumps from the 'unrealistic' scenes from one of Bruce's violent films, into the 'reality' of Bruce's life. By employing this technique, we can't be sure if <u>Popcorn</u> is presenting us with 'reality', or if all the violence and murder is just a film being retold. By employing the typically post-modernist technique of blurring fiction with reality, Ben Elton is able to make a very effective point, that we can relate to all the Hollywood-like killing sprees in our world today. You see, Ben Elton wants us to ask: If we are so easily confused by a novel

that blurs fiction with reality, should we blame murderers like Wayne and Scout, for copying their favourite film? <u>Popcorn</u> made me think that perhaps Wayne and Scout were misled by the entertainment industry after watching one too many violent films.

If I had to choose just one reason why I found <u>Popcorn</u> so effective, I would have to say that it was simply because the novel made such a relevant point about all the violence and murder in our world today. This is an issue that not only concerns me, but also the rest of society. <u>Popcorn</u> made me take a closer look at what has been happening around me, and wonder whether we should be so critical of those two schoolboys in Denver. After all, perhaps these two boys would never have had the idea to kill all their classmates, if Leonardo DiCaprio didn't make it seem okay in the film <u>The Basketball Diaries</u>. Let's put Leo in jail! But is the media to blame for the amount of violence in the world today? After putting down <u>Popcorn</u>, I am still unsure, although I can't help wondering whether all these young murderers in our society today simply can't distinguish between what is real and what is not.

Work supplied by Laura Kuuse

Activities

1. Brainstorm a list of films, books or other texts that can be read as dealing with the following subjects or issues:
   - fear of technology
   - the difficulties of sexual relationships
   - the problems of family life
   - discrimination
   - oppression
   - the conflict between the individual and society.
2. Make a list of other common topics or issues often dealt with in modern texts.

Representation

One important way of reading a text on more than one level is through the concept of representation. When you read in terms of representation, you look at the way particular aspects of the world in which you live are represented in the text. When you read for representation, you read critically, keeping in mind that the ideas in a text are just one set of possible ideas about the subject you are focussing on.

The study of representation often focuses on members of particular social groups, such as females, males, teenagers, children, older people, ethnic and racial groups or social classes. Texts can also be read, however, in terms of their representation of more abstract concepts such as love, friendship, family life, technology, science, work and so on. The list of potential topics is endless, limited only by your imagination and interests.

You can examine representation in a single text from a number of different angles. For example, in the book *Anna's Story* by Bronwyn Donaghy, which tells the story of the death of a fifteen-year-old Sydney girl from the drug ecstasy in 1995, you can examine representation by looking at the way the text represents Anna herself and the events surrounding her death. But this is only one possible angle. You can also examine how it represents:

- teenagers in general
- ecstasy
- drugs in general
- rave parties
- rock music
- parenting
- and so on.

CASE STUDY

The following passage is from a chapter of *Anna's Story* entitled 'Wicked Risks'. As you read the passage, focus on how it represents teenagers, and think about the extent to which you agree with this representation.

Anna's Story

'Anna Wood was about as unlucky as it's possible to be,' said Dr Simon Clarke, a consultant physician in adolescent medicine at Westmead Hospital in Sydney.

'Kids are out getting blind drunk every night of the week and most of them don't get killed. Hundreds of people are taking ecstasy every weekend and they're not all dying.

'These days, a lot of drunken kids are saved from death by the drink driving laws. Illegal drugs, naturally, are not governed by such laws. Drugs are made by morons who only have to get one radical wrong in the mix to produce poisons which may result in death or permanent brain damage. Nobody knows what's in them. Nobody knows what they might do.

'Anna Wood took the same risk that thousands of other teenagers do. She had been out dancing before. She would have seen people all around her, high on ecstasy and apparently having a marvellous time. How could she have known what a dangerous game she was playing?'

Why kids take chances

Needless to say, some kids take bigger risks than others. But one way or another, almost all adolescents do it. They have to take risks to win the respect of their peers, to prove they are mature, to break through the safety barrier which parents have erected around them since the day they were born.

Some kids skydive. Some abseil from rocks in remote bush. Some take boards out into an unguarded ocean and pit themselves against the waves.

Some play football—in terms of potential injury, probably the silliest thing they can do; in terms of the glory they can achieve, a risk worth taking.

Some go out onto a concert stage and risk failure.

Some run away from home—and risk not being found.

Some take drugs—and risk death.

Taking risks is a natural part of growing up. Breaking down the barriers of childhood, doing things they've never done before, going places they've never been—this is all part of the process that's involved in establishing themselves as independent individuals.

Almost all teenagers long for new experiences. Within reason, and despite their inevitable anxiety, most parents wouldn't want it any other way.

Dr David Bennett, Head of Adolescent Medicine at the Royal Alexandra Hospital for Children in Sydney, said it was natural for a majority of young people to want to try out new skills, to test the limits of their abilities, to compete, to challenge, to rebel.

3

'Kids who are in the frenzied grip of pubertal hormones, who are bursting at the seams with energy, are usually very impulsive when it comes to looking for thrills,' said Dr Bennett.

'They often do things on the spur of the moment, with little thought for the consequences. In fact, it's not necessarily true that they don't care about what might happen. The truth is that they don't *know* what might happen. They are too immature to think things through the way adults do.

'Too many adolescents have not received adequate information about dangerous risks, such as taking drugs and drinking. They simply don't know enough about it.'

For many reasons, adolescents, more than any other group, are likely to believe they are immortal—that 'it', whatever 'it' may be, won't happen to them.

You can't just talk them out of doing silly, impractical, dangerous and life-threatening things. Parents are no longer the only influence on their lives. For better or worse, the peer group and the community shape their behaviour and their beliefs.

'Our society teaches that sex, alcohol and purchasing power lead to the good life,' said David Bennett. 'So why should we be surprised that teenagers are the only age group whose health status has not improved in the past forty years?'

In fact, Dr Bennett believes there are clear indications that the health of adolescents in our society is deteriorating. Drug and alcohol abuse, depression and suicide, violent crime, eating disorders, and unsafe sexual behaviour occur with depressing regularity and at enormous cost to the community.

Bronwyn Donaghy, *Anna's Story*, Angus and Robertson, Sydney 1996, 97–100.

Activities

1 Discuss your responses to the way teenagers are represented in the passage. In particular, discuss the descriptions of teenagers as:
- 'kids'
- 'in the frenzied grip of pubertal hormones'
- 'too immature to think things through the way adults do'
- 'more than any other group, ... likely to believe they are immortal—that "it", whatever "it" may be, won't happen to them'
- not being able to be talked out of 'doing silly, impractical, dangerous and life-threatening things'.

2 Discuss the impressions of teenagers created by the following statements:
- 'Kids are out getting blind drunk every night of the week'
- 'She would have seen people all around her, high on ecstasy and apparently having a marvellous time. How could she have known what a dangerous game she was playing?'

3 To what extent do you think the ideas about teenagers represented by the descriptions and statements in questions 1 and 2 are:

- true of yourself
- true of other teenagers you know
- true of teenagers in general?

WORK SAMPLE

Reading of *The Wog Boy*

The following work sample, produced by a Year 12 student in an examination, discusses the representation of ethnic groups in the film *The Wog Boy*. If you have not yet seen the film, it would be a good idea to do so before reading the work sample.

The work sample has been included because, in addition to being an example of the discussion of representation, it shows the variety of readings it is possible to construct of the same text. In response to this topic, it is possible to offer a reading of *The Wog Boy* as a text that challenges ethnic stereotypes by showing how a member of a marginalised group triumphs over members of more powerful groups. It is also possible to construct a reading of the film as a heartwarming and inspiring story that reassures the audience by promoting the ideology that the underdog is able to triumph over prejudice and win through in the end. Instead, this student has chosen to read resistantly and focus on the way the film cements existing stereotypes.

Topic for this essay: Texts are more effective when they disturb, challenge or make us question our existing attitudes and values.

What does the term effective mean? Does it mean 'entertain', 'successfully engage audiences', 'persuade audiences to feel a particular way' ... if this is the definition of effective then the film The Wog Boy is an effective text. However, the film is effective, not through the way it disturbs, challenges or questions our existing ideologies, but rather through the way it endorses and cements stereotypes of ethnic and Anglo-Saxon Australians. Thus the film achieves success by further polarising ethnic minorities in Australia and endorsing divisions which have existed in Australia since the 1950s.

The main aim of the film is to get cheap laughs from audiences, and it does this primarily through the use of stereotypes of ethnic Australians, or to use the correct term 'Wogs'. Through the characters of Mr and Mrs Karamitsis, Theo and Dominic and of course Frank and Steve, the age old stereotype of ethnic Australians being extremely stupid, socially corrupt and interested only in sex and cars, is endorsed. The way Mr Karamitsis came to Australia with just one shoe and also the way both parents get the word uniform confused and send their child to school in the full Greek national costume constructs ethnic Australians in accordance with the stereotype which portrays them as completely stupid.

Similarly Theo, the compensation seeking Greek, and Dominic, the pharmacist who deals drugs in his spare time, are characters who portray the commonly held misconception that ethnic Australians are morally corrupt and somehow involved in illegal operations. Similarly, the main characters Steve and Frank also represent common stereotypes of ethnic Australians, Steve, through his sickening love for his car, and Frank for his famous 'Hall of Fame', are constructed as only being interested in sex and cars, exactly how common stereotypes construct young ethnic men.

Now I'm not going to lie and say that these characters weren't very funny, they were hilarious in fact, thus they were extremely effective. However their effectiveness was not due to them challenging existing ways of thinking but rather they served the main purpose of the film by endorsing negative cultural stereotypes, thus further alienating them from mainstream Australian society.

The characterisation of Anglo-Saxon Australians is also based on the social stereotypes which society has constructed. The characterisation of the two policemen and the school boys adhere to the construction of Anglo-Saxon Australians as being uptight, conservative and racist. The policeman Bazza, particularly the old man, and his ridiculous adherence to rules and regulations, construct Anglo Saxons as being 'by the book' and almost right wing. This idea of conservatism is further portrayed through the characterisation of the school-boys. Their racist sayings 'Wog boy, wog boy', are examples of how Anglo-Saxon Australians are often portrayed as racist and intolerant of others. Interestingly all Anglo-Saxon Australians in the film have fair skin and freckles. Now while this may seem insignificant it is indicative of how all the Anglo-Saxon characters in the film adhere to the physical stereotype which exists in society.

Thus and again, the film is effective as the use of stereotypes fulfils its main aim of attracting laughs but rather than challenging pre-existing values and attitudes, the film's effectiveness is essentially the way it endorses and privileges old-fashioned ideologies.

But while these stereotypes seem hilarious, they actually work to further polarise divisions among cultural groups in Australia. Thus the film is effective in two ways … getting loads of laughs but also preventing Australia from one day existing as one unified society.

Work supplied by Samantha Bellini

Activity

Discuss the extent to which you agree with this reading of *The Wog Boy*.

CASE STUDY

The following passage is the opening of the short story entitled 'Rodney Darling' by Roland Pertwee. It is set in England in the first half of the twentieth century.

Focus questions

1 What ideas about and attitudes towards children are represented in the passage?
2 What other texts can you think of that present similar ideas about children?
3 What texts can you think of that present ideas about children that conflict with those in this text?

'Rodney Darling'

At 6.30 a.m. Rodney sat up in bed and examined yesterday's scars in a slant of early sunshine, and saw that they had grown brown knobs in the night. By royal command of parents Rodney was forbidden to get up until seven o'clock, but the more insistent commands of youth decreed otherwise. Picking up the loud-ticking alarm clock from the chair beside the bed, Rodney moved the hands into the required position, closed his eyes, opened them again, and lo! it was time to get up.

'Oo—Oo—Oo!' he sang, in the high treble of childhood.

A locomotive entering a tunnel and a small boy entering upon a new day make much the same noise.

From the adjoining room Rodney's father, rudely awakened, hammered on the partition wall and shouted: 'Stop that row.'

Rodney emitted one more 'Oo'—a little one—to prove independence, and attacked the business of dressing. With an hour's start over the earliest of the grown-up contingent the need to wash did not assert itself.

Rodney's father had views about washing—tiresome views of boys stripped to the waist, soaping vigorously and splashing their limbs with cold water. Rodney had promised always to wash in that way, but since his father was almost certain to have fallen asleep again, there was a good case against doing so. However, to be on the safe side, he crossed to the bathroom, ran a tap and splashed about with a back brush.

With his free hand he put on a pair of stockings with large holes in the toes and heels (which was forbidden) and some shoes which were not a pair. Returning to his bedroom Rodney fetched his cap from under the bed and, pushing open the casement, threw it at a starling who was sitting in a rain gutter.

The starling flew away, but the cap remained in the gutter—for ever. As Rodney pulled on his shirt and undervest in one—and his pants and breeks in one (which on hygienic grounds was forbidden) he decided that the true explanation of the loss of the cap was that some boy had dropped it down a well. A 'mos' enormous' boy had done this; practically a giant—and mad at that.

Rodney did not brush his hair, according to rule, as who should say, half an hour later, hair being what it is, that he had failed to do so?

As he tiptoed towards the stair-head he had the ill luck to kick one of his father's brogues, which behaved noisily.

His mother's voice was lifted to inquire:

'Have you brushed your teeth, Rodney darling?'

'Yes, Mum,' he called back, which was true, as in the course of a long life seldom a day missed with this duty neglected.

A moment later Rodney was free in the garden.

The garden gleamed with silver, pearl and grey, for the dairymaids of dawn had not yet completed their task of skimming the dew from the grass.

Rodney shuffled across the lawn, leaving a wake of Friday's footsteps for Crusoe to find.

He was glad to get his feet wet before anyone could stop him. That kind of being wet is much nicer than soap-and-water wet. It is almost as good as paddling. The dew between his toes made squelching noises very pleasant to hear.

The advantage of being up before the rest of the house lies in immunity from restraints of all kinds. In that hour of freedom forbidden doors are open and forbidden practices flourish.

Rodney waded round to the garage, rolled in through an open window and turned on the headlights of his father's car. These, after ten minutes pleasantly spent basking in their rays, he left burning. It was better so, for, in Rodney's hearing, his father had complained that the batteries were very low. A little judicious expenditure of current would mean that his father would have to swing the engine—a practice he disliked above all others, but which afforded to the watcher and the listener much delight and education.

Returning to the house Rodney made his way to that holy of holies, the gun room, where are to be found and explored more forbidden mysteries than elsewhere. Rodney desired to satisfy himself whether or not he could put together a twelve-bore gun. The answer was in the negative. In making the attempt the gun bit him. Dropping the barrels upon the stone floor Rodney executed a nimble but agonized fandango. Prudence demanded that this should be performed in silence, despite the fact that blood and loose skin were involved. As, on some future date, a fresh attempt upon the gun was indicated, Rodney had no choice but to postpone the noisier side of lamentation. Had the wound been of a more serious character, he might have declared his fault, and so have organized his grief as to persuade sympathy to outweigh reproof.

But Rodney was no fool. He could assess the emotional value of cut or bruise or graze to a nicety. Wrapping his injured thumb with a piece of oily rag, he put back the gun in its case, and taking his father's dry-fly rod from the rack, returned to the garden and marched off to that side of the house where was a blank ivy-clad wall much affected by building sparrows.

Unhappily the lowest nest was beyond reach of the point of the rod, and what might have been an illuminating ornithological investigation came to nothing at all.

On running back to the gun room, the restless rod point stuck in the ground and, before Rodney could stop himself, nine feet of tapering split cane arched perilously. But beyond a slight fracture at the extreme tip the damage done was not worth mentioning—or, at any rate, it was not worth Rodney's while to mention.

Here was no deceit, but good common sense, for fathers are apt to attach too much importance to trifling misadventures, and should be supplied with as little material as possible for developing this fault.

Rodney's offer to carry the milk-can from the float to the back door did not result in the loss of more than a pint. Rodney's mind was eager of enlightenment, and only a day or two before someone, in his hearing, had told of the mysteries of centrifugal force. Rodney wished to put these claims to the proof and satisfy himself whether a full measure could be swung round and round over one's head without a drop being spilt. He was highly shocked that a grown-up—one of those persons who expect rigid truthfulness from the young—could have been guilty of circulating such a baseless and unwarrantable rumour. However, as Rodney was well aware, there is a proverb deprecating all show of emotion over milk casualties, and in the event of questions as to shortage being asked he felt himself armed with the perfect answer.

The minutes run swiftly when there is no one about to interfere with the manner in which they are spent. It seemed no time at all before the ring of the breakfast bell.

Responding to appetite Rodney forgot all about turning off the car's headlights.

'Rodney *darling*,' his mother said. 'Oh, Rodney, you are in a pickle! *And* your shoes! Upstairs and change them. Quick as lightning.'

Rodney said, 'Oh, I don't have to' three times before complying. This was a point of personal honour.

On the half landing he met his father, who looked as if he might be difficult. But Rodney's father only said:

'Brush your hair,' and went on down.

An accomplished hair-brusher can, with average luck, contrive one lick of smooth hair without disturbing the pleasant disorder underneath. Also he can manage three or four partings. Rodney's appearance when he came to table presented a thin veneer of tidiness and cleanliness—just sufficient to pass muster—but no more.

His father's appraising eye, although square-lidded with a conventional frown, did not conceal a gleam of tolerant good humour.

'Dirty little type,' he mumbled, and returned to the perusal of a propped-up newspaper.

Rodney made a lower-lip at his mother.

A lower-lip signifies. ''Tisn't fair, Mum. Is it fair?'

His mother said:

'You look lovely, darling.' Then. 'You are a bear, Jack. He's only a little boy.'

'All right—all right,' said Rodney's father, but without ill humour.

Rodney attacked his Breakfast Crisps, brown, bread-crumby-looking things with cold milk over them. These he shared impartially with his shirt-front, the carpet, the table-cloth and the facial scenery adjoining his mouth.

As there seemed to be no likelihood of conversation, Rodney embellished what otherwise would have been a dangerous silence with loud, sploshy noises and a fine clatter with his spoon.

Presently his father picked up his cue—

'Must you eat like a pig—?'

—And his mother hers—

'Jack, you can't notice everything.'

'Damn it,' said his father. 'One can't notice anything else.'

'Don't swear in front of Rodney. I will not have it.'

'And I will not have the boy behaving like—'

'They are off,' said Rodney to himself, and while his parents completed the course he devoured his egg and painted the neighborhood with blackcurrant jam unobserved.

'Say your grace, darling,' said his mother in her hurt voice.

So Rodney shut his eyes and thought nothing at all for a quarter of a second, then bolted.

This business of meals was a great tribulation. Standing in the sunlight wondering what he would do next, Rodney reflected that grown-ups are harder to handle at table than anywhere else. However, one must eat.

A lusty voice called upon him to return and fold his napkin 'properly.' Rodney moved out of earshot like a ghost. Under cover of the laurels he licked his lips. They tasted pleasantly sweet—reminiscently flavoursome. It is folly to use a napkin—folly and waste of good food. A napkin is an obstinate piece of furniture which refuses to be folded in its own creases. Under the table is the proper place for a napkin. Once there it affords an opportunity for a nice grovel during a meal. Feet look awfully funny without any bodies to them. Perhaps after all the napkin is a friend in disguise. Who knows?

Beyond the laurel screen was the lane and along the lane a little girl was walking. As she walked she sang for pleasure of the sun.

Rodney knew she was a little girl because she did not sing words, or any known tune. She sang 'Oo, Oo, Oo' like other children.

Rodney was moved to cry out:

'Shut up, fat fool!'

The little girl threw a flint over the hedge and went her ways.

Witnessing the enormous size of the flint, terror seized Rodney. In imagination he envisaged the disastrous results to himself had he been struck by such a missile. The peril had passed, but it called for advertisement.

Picking up the flint Rodney rushed with it houseward in panic.

'Oo, Mum, Oo!' he cried.

His father, brows knit, black avised, came forth from the garage. His face shone with sweat. He was holding the starting handle.

'Rodney!'

'Oo! Mum!' cried Rodney, for he had remembered.

'RODNEY!'

Useless to ignore that tone. The main line was blocked.

'Come you here,' said the voice inexorably.

'Oo! Dad! Look! Oo!' He held the flint aloft.

'Never mind that. You've been messing about with my lights—'

'A great man—' Rodney began.

'Now listen to me, you young devil—'

It was touch and go. Rodney employed the past terror to illustrate the present.

'A great man frew it at me,' he shrieked.

'What's this?' cried Rodney's father. 'What do you say? Chucked that flint? Where is he—who was he—?'

Like a streak of lightning he was out through the garden gate. The switch had worked. The limited express was shunted on to a siding—the main line was clear. Rodney vanished into the landscape.

He did not emerge until he heard the sound of his father's car chugging up the hill that led away from the house.

Roland Pertwee, 'Rodney Darling', *Fish are Such Liars*, William Blackwood and Sons in *Modern Short Stories*, compiled by A. Lewis Clayfield, Angus and Robertson, 1966, 146–52.

Activities

1 Write answers to the focus questions and then discuss your answers with other students.

2 Turn your attention to the representation of adults: How does the passage represent adults and their management of children?

CASE STUDY

5

The first of the following passages is from the play *A Doll's House* written by Henrik Ibsen in 1879. It is set in Norway. The second passage is from the play *Medea* written by Euripides in ancient Greece in about 431 BC.

Focus question

How are marital relations and the roles of husbands and wives represented in each of the passages?

A Doll's House

A comfortable room, furnished inexpensively, but with taste. In the back wall there are two doors; that to the right leads out to a hall, the other, to the left, leads to Helmer's study. Between them stands a piano.

In the middle of the left-hand wall is a door, with a window on its nearer side. Near the window is a round table with armchairs and a small sofa.

In the wall on the right-hand side, rather to the back, is a door, and farther forward on this wall there is a tiled stove with a couple of easy chairs and a rocking-chair in front of it. Between the door and the stove stands a little table.

There are etchings on the walls, and there is a cabinet with china ornaments and other bric-à-brac, and a small bookcase with handsomely bound books. There is a carpet on the floor, and the stove is lit. It is a winter day.

> *[A bell rings in the hall outside, and a moment later the door is heard to open. Nora comes into the room, humming happily. She is in outdoor clothes, and is carrying an armful of parcels which she puts down on the table to the right. Through the hall door, which she has left open, can be seen a PORTER; he is holding a Christmas tree and a hamper, and he gives them to the MAID who has opened the front door.]*

NORA: Hide the Christmas tree properly, Helena. The children mustn't see it till this evening, when it's been decorated. [*To the PORTER, taking out her purse*] How much is that?

PORTER: Fifty ore.

NORA: There's a krone. No, keep the change.

> *[The PORTER thanks her and goes. NORA shuts the door, and takes off her outdoor clothes, laughing quietly and happily to herself. Taking a bag of macaroons from her pocket, she eats one or two, then goes cautiously to her husband's door and listens.]*

Yes, he's in. [*She starts humming again as she goes over to the table on the right.*]

HELMER [*from his study*]: Is that my little skylark twittering out there?

NORA: [*busy opening the parcel*]: It is.

HELMER: Scampering about like a little squirrel?

NORA: Yes.

HELMER: When did the squirrel get home?

NORA: Just this minute. [*She slips the bag of macaroons in her pocket and wipes her mouth.*] Come in here, Torvald and you can see what I've bought.

HELMER: I'm busy! [*A moment later he opens the door and looks out, pen in hand.*] Did you say 'bought'? What, all that? Has my little featherbrain been out wasting money again?

NORA: But, Torvald, surely this year we can let ourselves go just a little bit? It's the first Christmas that we haven't had to economise.

HELMER: Still, we mustn't waste money, you know.

NORA: Oh, Torvald, surely we can waste a little now—just the teeniest bit? Now that you're going to earn a big salary, you'll have lots and lots of money.

HELMER: After New Year's Day, yes—but there'll be a whole quarter before I get paid.

NORA: Pooh, we can always borrow till then.

HELMER: Nora! [*He goes to her and takes her playfully by the ear.*] The same little scatterbrain. Just suppose I borrowed a thousand kroner today and you went and spent it all by Christmas, and then on New Year's Eve a tile fell on my head, and there I lay—

NORA [*putting a hand over his mouth*]: Sh! Don't say such horrid things!

HELMER: But suppose something of the sort were to happen …

NORA: If anything as horrid as that were to happen, I don't expect I should care whether I owed money or not.

HELMER: But what about the people I'd borrowed from?

NORA: Them? Who bothers about them? They're just strangers.

HELMER: Nora, Nora! Just like a woman! But seriously, Nora, you know what I think about that sort of thing. No debts, no borrowing. There's something constrained, something ugly even, about a home that's founded on borrowing and debt. You and I have managed to keep clear up till now, and we shall still do so for the little time that is left.

NORA [*going over to the stove*]: Very well, Torvald, if you say so.

HELMER [*following her*]: Now, now, my little song-bird mustn't be so crestfallen. Well? Is the squirrel sulking? [*Taking out his wallet*] Nora … guess what I have here!

NORA [*turning quickly*]: Money!

HELMER: There! [*He hands her some notes.*] Good heavens, I know what a lot has to go on housekeeping at Christmas time.

NORA [*counting*]: Ten—twenty—thirty—forty! Oh, thank you, Torvald, thank you! This'll keep me going for a long time!

HELMER: Well, you must see that it does.

NORA: Oh yes, of course I will. But now come and see all the things I've bought—so cheaply too. Look, here's a new suit for Ivar, and a sword too. Here's a horse and a trumpet for Bob; and here's a doll and a doll's bed for Emmy. They're rather plain, but she'll soon smash them to bits anyway. And these are dress-lengths and handkerchiefs for the maids … Old Nanny really ought to have something more …

HELMER: And what's in *that* parcel?

NORA [*squealing*]: No, Torvald! You're not to see that till this evening!

HELMER: Aha! And now, little prodigal, what do you think you want for yourself?

NORA: Oh, me? I don't want anything at all.

HELMER: Ah, but you must. Now tell me anything—within reason—that you feel you'd like.

NORA: No … I really can't think of anything. Unless … Torvald …

HELMER: Well?

NORA [*not looking at him—playing with his waistcoat buttons*]: If you *really* want to give me something, you could—well, you could …

HELMER: Come along—out with it!

NORA [*in a rush*]: You could give me money, Torvald. Only what you think you could spare—and then one of these days I'll buy something with it.

HELMER: But, Nora—

NORA: Oh, *do*, Torvald … please, please do! Then I'll wrap it in pretty gold paper and hang it on the Christmas tree. Wouldn't that be fun?

HELMER: What do they call little birds who are always making money fly?

NORA: Yes, I know—ducks-and-drakes! But let's do what I said, Torvald, and then I'll have time to think of something that I really want. Now, that's very sensible, isn't it?

HELMER [*smiling*]: Oh, very. That is, it would be if you really kept the money I give you, and actually bought something for yourself with it. But if it goes in with the housekeeping, and gets spent on all sorts of useless things, then I only have to pay out again.

NORA: Oh, but, Torvald—

HELMER: You can't deny it, little Nora, now can you? [*Putting an arm round her waist*] It's a sweet little bird, but it gets through a terrible amount of money. You wouldn't believe how much it costs a man when he's got a little song bird like you!

NORA: Oh, how *can* you say that? I really do save all I can.

HELMER [*laughing*]: Yes, that's very true— 'all you can'. But the thing is, you *can't*!

NORA [*nodding and smiling happily*]: Ah, if you only knew what expenses we skylarks and squirrels have, Torvald.

HELMER: What a funny little one you are! Just like your father—always on the look-out for all the money you can get, but the moment you have it, it seems to slip through your fingers and you never know what becomes of it. Well, I must take you as you are—it's in your blood. Oh yes, Nora, these things are hereditary.

NORA: I wish I'd inherited more of papa's good qualities.

HELMER: And I wouldn't want you to be any different from what you are—just my sweet little song bird. But now I come to think of it, you look rather— rather—how shall I put it?—rather as if you've been up to mischief today.

NORA: Do I?

HELMER: Yes, you certainly do. Look me straight in the face.

NORA [*looking at him*]: Well?

HELMER [*wagging a finger at her*]: Surely your sweet tooth didn't get the better of you in town today?

NORA: No … how could you think that?

HELMER: Didn't Little Sweet-Tooth just look in at the confectioner's?

NORA: No, honestly, Torvald.

HELMER: Not to taste one little sweet?

NORA: No, of course not.

HELMER: Not even to nibble a macaroon or two?

NORA: No, Torvald, really; I promise you.

HELMER: There, there, of course I was only joking.

NORA [*going to the table on the right*]: I wouldn't do anything that you don't like.

HELMER: No, I know you wouldn't—besides, you've given me your word.

Henrik Ibsen, 'A Doll's House' in *A Doll's House and Other Plays*, Penguin, London 1965, 147–52.

Medea

Medea is set in the city of Corinth. Jason and Medea are husband and wife. The chorus is a group of Corinthian women. The following passage occurs part of the way through the play. Before the scenes portrayed in the play, Jason, a Greek, had led an expedition on the ship *Argo* to the distant land of Colchis in search of the fabled golden fleece. Medea was the daughter of Aietes, king of Colchis. She fell in love with Jason and helped him slay a dragon that guarded the fleece and steal the fleece from her father. Medea then escaped from Colchis with Jason, eventually taking refuge in Corinth, where they had two children. Soon after, Jason decided to marry Glauke the daughter of Kreon, king of Corinth. In anger, Medea cursed the royal family and in response Kreon ordered her to be banished from Corinth, along with her children. The following scene occurs immediately after this.

Enter JASON.

JASON. This isn't the first time. I've seen it, often.
  Lost temper ruins everything.
  You could have stayed here, kept your home,
  If you'd accepted the decisions of your betters.
  It's your own fault they throw you out.
  This talk of yours, it's smoke to me, it's straw.
  Call me what names you like, the vilest man alive.
  But rant against the king …
  You're lucky exile's your only punishment.

5

I tried to calm him, to make him let you stay.
But you wouldn't hold your tongue,
You would talk treason. So out you go.
Even so, d'you know why I've come?
To do my best for those I love.
I won't see you penniless;
I won't see the children starve.
Banishment's hard enough, God knows.
I know. Hate if you must,
I care no less for you because of that.

MEDEA. Who could be worse than you?
What names can I call you—a man
Who is no man at all? You've come!
How dare you come, you vomit—
D'you think it noble, think it brave
To savage those you love, then *visit* them?
How did you screw yourself to such a pitch?
Still, here you are—
I'll cast my heart, and watch you wince.

First things first. I saved your life—
They know it, every Greek who sailed with you,
The good ship *Argo*'s noble crew,
When you came to yoke fiery bulls
In the field of death and sow those dragon's teeth.
The serpent, unsleeping guardian
Coiled round the Fleece, I killed.
I made your reputation,
Betrayed my father, my royal house,
Ran after you to Iolkos, Peleias' land*—
More passionate than clever then!—
And for your sake procured his death:
Most horribly, at his own daughter's hands.
A second royal house destroyed.
So I did. And you, what did you do?
Betrayed me, vileness, snatched another wife.
I gave you children. If not,
I'd have understood your lust—for sons.
But this? Kiss promises goodbye—
The gods are dead you swore them by.
This hand of mine,
The one you held so hard,
And crawled between these knees! I'm foul
With your foul touch and all my hopes destroyed.

Well, Jason, you love me. Advise me:
I trust you, rely on you—
To cheat me with every word you say.
Where shall I go? To my father's house,
The father I betrayed to follow you?
To Peleias' daughters?
How they'll welcome me, their father's murderer!
So it stands with me. I made enemies
Of those I loved, for you, hurt those
I had no need to hurt, for you—
And in return, you make me the envy of all Greece.
Can't you hear them? 'What a husband!
How lucky she is! I'd trust him anywhere!'
They have their proof,
The dazzling wedding-gift you give yourself:
Your sons, their mother who saved your life,
Banished, made tramps. O Zeus, you give
Clear signs to mark true gold from dross—
Why no hallmarks to tell true men from men?

CHORUS. What anger worse, or slower to abate,
Than lovers' love when it has turned to hate?

JASON. I see I must steer carefully,
Must play the skilful captain, trim sail
And run before your storm of words.
First, then, your towering services to me.
You overdo it. Aphrodite helped me:
It was she—no other—who saved our ship.
No one denies your witchery—
But it was Aphrodite's weapon, passion,
That made you save my skin.

So let's not overestimate your services.
And you've not done so badly out of them—
Quite frankly, more than you gave, you've got.
You came from God knows where to Greece,
And here you learned what justice is.
The Greeks respect you, appreciate your skills—
Would you be famous if you'd stayed
On that hill of yours in the sky's backyard?
I prefer the glitter to the gold.
I'd rather be sung about than sing.

So much for what you did for me.
You brought it up and—there it is.
Now about my marriage, this royal alliance

That rubs you raw. I'll show how good it is
For all of us—me, you and the children too.
Will you listen? We were on the run, from Iolkos—
Exiles, outlaws, freighted with disaster—
What better safeguard could I find than this,
To marry the king's own daughter? I call it luck!
I know what grates on you. Bed. You think
I tired of you, I lusted for younger flesh.
You're wrong. I don't want her;
I don't want shoals of children.
Our sons, yours and mine, are enough for me.
I want security, prosperity—
Who steps aside, takes time, for beggars?
I want our sons in peace and harmony
With new royal brothers,
One happy family for evermore.
You don't need more children. I do.
They'll help the ones we had.

Now do you see? The point of it?
How can you? You're raw with jealousy.
Oh, women are all alike:
If they're happy in bed, they're happy everywhere.
If that goes wrong, then offer them the Moon,
They throw it at your head. Sex!
We need another way to get us sons. No women then—
That way all human misery would end.

CHORUS. Neat words, Jason, neatly said.
    But pardon me, what you do
    Is far from just: deserting her.

MEDEA. Neat? Neat? Does no one see but me?
    This jailbait plays philosopher.
    Double-dealing, double penalty.
    Can he do what he likes if he wraps it up
    In fancy phrases? (spits) Ptah! You're not so clever.
    Such a tongue—and one little point undoes you:
    If this marriage was so sensible,
    Why not tell me before you started?
    Why hide it? The one you love—remember?

JASON. How well you'd have taken it,
    The idea of it. Look at you:
    You can't control your fury as it is.

MEDEA. As it is, you're getting old.
    Your 'foreigner' embarrasses you.

JASON. Will you get this straight? I marry
    Not for sex, hot for the royal bed,
    But as I said: to care for you,
    To make royal brothers for our sons,
    To protect us all.

MEDEA. Protection that tastes of death!
    What security repays a broken heart?

JASON. Must you take personally what helps us all?
    Why greet good luck by calling it the opposite?
    You'll change. I know you'll change.

MEDEA. You know so much. Just where you're going.
    And I? Exiled, betrayed, alone.

JASON. You brought it on yourself.

MEDEA. What did I do? *I* took a wife and let her down?

JASON. You cursed the royal house.

MEDEA. And yours.

JASON. This gets us nowhere.
    If you or the children need anything,
    Cash for the journey, ask.
    I'll be generous—letters to people
    Who'll take you in. My dear, be sensible.
    No more anger. You've everything to gain.

MEDEA. I need no friends of yours to take me in.
    I'll take none of your favours.
    They're tainted, foul. I spit on them.

JASON. Gods, will You witness this?
    I've done all I could—for you, for them—
    But what's good for others is no good to you:
    You kick our help aside. You're mad.
    What but worse can come of this?

MEDEA. Go in. You're hot. Your brand new bride—
    Get to her room, don't waste your time out here.
    Go marry! With God's good help
    Your honeymoon will soon turn sour.

Exit JASON.

* Iolkos, Peleias' land. On their escape from Colchis Jason and Medea first took refuge on the island of Iolkos, of which Peleias was king. Medea helped Jason murder Peleias in the hope that Jason might take his place.

Euripides, *Medea*, Nick Hearn Books, London 1994, 14–20.

Activity

Discuss the extent to which the roles and behaviours of characters in the passages reflect your understandings and beliefs about the appropriate roles and behaviours of husbands and wives.

Foregrounding

Reading for representation allows you to examine and draw attention to aspects of a text that the text itself does not seem to draw attention to or that might seem unimportant when read from a different approach. In other words, representation allows you to throw the spotlight on certain ideas or assumptions that might otherwise be ignored or glossed over when reading the text. This process of throwing the spotlight on certain aspects of a text is referred to as foregrounding.

While texts might foreground certain topics or issues, readers can choose to foreground other topics or issues. For example, the title of *The Wog Boy* and the opening scenes invite the audience to focus on the ethnicity of the main character, but it is quite possible to ignore this and focus on the portrayal of gender in the film or the representation of politics and politicians—hypocritical, self-serving manipulators in this case—or the representation of public servants—lazy, time-wasters in this case.

Foregounding is a useful reading practice because it enables you to construct a reading of the text in terms of what you choose and what you think is important.

The key idea is that texts cannot be easily slotted into categories according to what they are about. What they are about is what you as the reader choose to focus on.

WORK SAMPLE

A reading of gender in *The Wog Boy*

Below is an extract from an assignment by the student who produced the work sample above on *The Wog Boy*. In this case, however, she has chosen to foreground the representation of gender in the film.

Topic for this essay: To what extent do films reflect the attitudes and values of the society in which they are produced?

The construction of women in The Wog Boy is heavily influenced by social stereotypes. Raylene, Celia and Annie are representations of the cultural myths which say successful women are sexual predators, the female protagonist must be asexual, and young, adolescent Australian blondes are only interested in having sex with various partners. Raylene, the woman tipped to be the first female prime minister, is portrayed as successful, deceiving and willing to do anything to further her success and wealth. But along with determination and commitment, sexual immorality and a tendency to prey on younger men are included in the characterisation of Raylene, thus she adheres to the common stereotype which labels all headstrong women as having a large sexual appetite. Celia and Annie, despite being sisters, are representative of the two opposing models of femininity, according to cultural stereotype. These two characters, especially in terms of sexual prowess, reflect the archetypal conflict between good girl and bad girl. Celia, the one who has a better job and a more economically comfortable lifestyle, is pretty much asexual, displaying traits of frigidity and control despite her good looks and appeal, and only once does she succumb to the forces of attraction. Annie on the other hand is the conventional 'slut'. Her large sexual appetite and her tendency to be quite 'easy' are portrayed as very negative, as it is the given justification of her not being employed, financially secure or respected. Interestingly, Annie like the male character Frank has a 'hall of fame' on which she keeps records of all her sexual partners. Frank however, is glorified and constructed as a hero because of his ability to attract and lure girls to the bedroom; Annie, however, is constructed as a static character, one that is only there to attract laughs, and which doesn't have any strong status in the film or in society. Thus the film bases its representation of women on the rigid stereotypes and double standards which patriarchal society has constructed. Not only does the film therefore, enforce divisions between ethnic and Anglo-Saxon Australians, it also endorses a hierarchical division between men and women.

From *The Wog Boy*

Work supplied by Samantha Bellini

Reading intertextually

4

Reading intertextually means relating a new text to other texts you have encountered. You have always done this and you still do. When you were learning to read a sentence such as 'The cat sat on the mat', you automatically related this sentence to other cats and other mats you had read about. You also related it to cats and mats you had encountered in real life: it is important to understand that real cats and real mats are also texts you 'read' and then use to help you read other texts.

Basically, reading intertextually reflects the process you use when you encounter any new experience: you deal with it by relating it to, or trying to slot it into, the understandings of the world you have developed from previous experiences. The new experience might be easily accommodated within your existing framework of understanding, or it might challenge your existing framework of understanding and require you to modify this framework.

Here is a concrete example to clarify what this means. Imagine that when you were younger you had grown up believing dogs to be friendly. One day you see an enormous dog bounding towards you. You are a bit worried because you have never encountered a dog of this size before. But you put your hand out palm down to greet it, as you have been taught. In other words, you use your existing framework of understanding to handle the unfamiliar situation. The dog licks your hand. Your framework of understanding is reinforced. Now imagine the next day the same thing happens, but this time the dog bites you. Because of this experience, you will have to revise your framework: some dogs are friendly and some are not.

The same thing happens with reading. The texts you encounter can reinforce your understandings of the world or they can challenge them, requiring you to modify your thinking. As this example indicates, it is important to remember that when you talk about frameworks for understanding the world, you are referring to attitudes as well as knowledge. The texts you encounter interact not just with your understanding of the world, but with your understanding of

reading. They may reinforce your understanding of reading conventions and practices, or they may require you to modify or expand them.

There is another important point to make here. When you find it difficult to read a text, it could be because you are unable to fit the text into your existing understandings or attitudes about the world or your existing understandings of reading. That is, it is difficult to read the text because the ideas are unfamiliar to you or because the way the words are used is unfamiliar to you.

Intertextuality is an integral and unavoidable part of reading. Much of the time you do it without thinking about it. In the final years of high school, however, you are asked to think more deeply about intertextuality and articulate how intertextuality works in the meanings you make with texts.

Why intertextuality is important

There are three reasons an understanding of intertextuality is important. First, you can use it to help you to construct a reading of a text. You can make connections with other texts to help you make sense of the text you are reading.

Second, you can use your understanding of intertextuality to examine how a text might be attempting to position you by encouraging you to draw unreflectively on ways of thinking you have encountered in other texts.

Third, an understanding of intertextuality builds up your understanding of ideologies. By examining the way various texts reflect, reinforce or challenge ideas in other texts, you can examine the circulation and construction of ideas, beliefs and attitudes in society.

One other point: you can also use intertextuality to help explain your readings. You can refer to other texts to help explain what you mean.

Activity

Examine the work samples on *Star Wars* and *The Truman Show* on pages 3–5 and 19–21 and discuss how the authors have used other texts to help explain their readings.

Common subjects

One of the easiest ways to read a text intertextually is to compare it with other texts dealing with the same subject. You can compare a war movie like *Saving Private Ryan* with other texts dealing with war such as *The Thin Red Line, Platoon, Born on the Fourth of July, Dear America: Letters Home from Vietnam, All Quiet on the Western Front* and *Apocalypse Now*. With a little bit of thinking, you can also make comparisons between texts that might at first appear quite different, but could be read as dealing with the same subject. For instance, you could include *Braveheart, Star Wars,* or *Tomorrow When the War Began* in the list of texts dealing with war.

If you are studying a text dealing with life in prison, you might be able to make comparisons with texts such as *The Shawshank Redemption* or *Letters from the Inside*.

If your text is dealing with relations between people of different races, you might be able to make comparisons with texts such as *Mississippi Burning, Things Fall Apart, Wildcat Falling* or *To Kill a Mockingbird*.

The point of making these comparisons is to help you better understand and talk about the way in which the specific text you are studying deals with the subject. The aim is to be able to write sentences like the following:

- *Star Wars* offers a sanitised view of war unlike the full-on portrayal of violence we receive in *Saving Private Ryan*.
- Compared with *To Kill a Mockingbird* and *Mississippi Burning*, where African-Americans are portrayed as relying on the supposedly superior intelligence and good will of white Americans, *Shaft* portrays an African-American who is able to look after himself.
- In *Schindler's List*, members of the German forces are caricatured embodiments of evil whereas in *Das Boot*, we see them as human beings like us caught up in a situation beyond their control.
- The film *187* rejects the view of teachers as charismatic individuals who can change the world portrayed in films such as *Dead Poets Society* and *Dangerous Minds*.
- Like *The Catcher in the Rye, Looking for Alibrandi* portrays the teenage years as a time of uncertainty and struggle to define one's own identity.
- In *Fatal Attraction*, extra-marital affairs by males are blamed on unstable women rather than seen as the responsibility of the male concerned, a view reinforced in films such as *Disclosure*.

Activities

1. Make a list of the major texts you are studying this year and brainstorm for each one a list of other texts that can be read as dealing with the same subject.
2. Take each major text and discuss the differences and similarities between its treatment of the subject and the other texts' treatment of the same subject.
   - What different aspects of the subject does each text focus on?
   - What differences and similarities are there in the way the subject is presented?
   - Write some sentences comparing the treatment of the subject in each major text with the texts on your list.

Representations and foregrounding

In comparing texts on the same subject, you are basically reading them in terms of representation. You can also use the concept of representation to compare texts that you might not say are actually dealing with the same subject but which contain representations of similar ideas or people. In other words, you can foreground particular representations to read texts intertextually.

This means that you can compare representations in widely differing texts. For example, you can compare the representations of women in whatever text you are studying with any text that has at least one female character or that discusses females. These might include texts as diverse as *101 Dalmatians, Beauty and the Beast, Alien, The Handmaid's Tale, Brave New World, Secret Men's Business, Real Gorgeous* and *No Sugar*. This approach would also allow you to add texts such as *The Bone Collector*, which is ostensibly a detective thriller, and *Dangerous Minds*, which is ostensibly about education, to a comparison of representations of race.

You can also compare representations of men, children, teenagers, older people, families, violence, science, education and so on in widely varying texts, even where these subjects may feature in only a minor way.

Activities

1. Choose one of the following subjects and then choose or find any four texts that include an example of the subject:

fathers	families	work	cars
brides	homes	neighbours	medicine
sportsmen	schools	drugs	indigenous people
teenage girls	friends	teachers	Australians

2. Discuss the differences between the representations of the subject in each text.
3. Write some sentences comparing the representations of the subject in each text.

Archetypal narratives

Television producer Aaron Spelling has been reported as saying that there are only five stories and they've all been told but that the trick is to tell them in a new way. He may not be right about the number of basic stories that exist, but he is pointing out an essential truth: that most texts, especially narratives, are reworkings of stories that have been told before in one way or another.

If you cut most stories down to basics, you start to see interesting similarities between stories that on the surface appear to have nothing in common.

- An individual is suffering under an oppressive regime but finds a way of exerting power or asserting individuality within the system: *The Handmaid's Tale* and *The Shawshank Redemption*, but also *Braveheart, Good Morning Vietnam* and *The Outsider*.
- A young person is faced with a challenge but with the help of an older mentor learns to face the challenge and achieve success: *Star Wars* and *Karate Kid*.

When you cut a story down to basics, you find the archetypal narratives on which they are based. Some texts might be based on a number of different archetypal narratives. A useful trick for discerning archetypal narratives in a story is to compare them with well-known fairy tales or myths.

You can also compare characters in terms of their similarity to well-known archetypes such as the wicked stepmother, the prince who comes to the rescue, the clever servant who proves he is smarter than his master, the evil seductress or the fool who is really wise.

Examining the use of archetypes in texts is not simply a game of spot the archetype. The aim is to examine the manner in which they are used in specific texts and, as with all intertextual approaches, to examine the ways different texts reflect, reinforce or challenge ideas in other texts and in society.

Activities

1 Brainstorm a list of texts that feature elements of the archetypal narratives found in:

- The Ugly Duckling: a person considered plain, ugly or inferior in some way develops into someone whom others admire or respect
- Hansel and Gretel: children have to cope with the harsh realities of the world after being abandoned by or losing their parents
- Beauty and the Beast: a fearsome character is transformed into someone nice because of the actions or love of another person.

a Discuss the underlying ideologies or beliefs promoted by these archetypal narratives.

b Discuss any similarities and differences between the examples in their use of the archetype, such as the nature of the characters, the difficulties they face, how they overcome them, and the setting.

2 Come up with some archetypal narratives similar to other fairy stories or myths.

Allusion

Some texts make deliberate allusions, or references, to other texts, inviting us to read the text in the light of these other texts. For example, the film *Freeway* is a deliberate reworking of Little Red Riding Hood in which a young woman leaves home to find herself being stalked by a killer. It's not hard to miss the intertextual reference given that the young woman, played by Reese Witherspoon, leaves home dressed in red to visit her grandmother; the killer, played by Kiefer Sutherland, is called Bob Wolverton; and the girl's boyfriend is called Chopper. (*Freeway* is rated R in Australia.)

6

CASE STUDY

Review of *Freeway*

What happens when you cross the Brothers Grimm with David Lynch, and throw in a little Quentin Tarantino for good measure? The result, or something very much like it, can be found in Matthew Bright's brilliant, incisive satire, *Freeway*, which updates the children's story 'Little Red Riding Hood' in new, surprising, and very adult ways. Anyone who never appreciated this fable may revise their opinion after watching *Freeway*.

The film works—and does so manifestly—because its intentions are clearly delineated. Using black humor, blood, and a pair of tremendous performances, *Freeway* hones in on its targets and calculatedly skewers them one-by-one. First up is America's welfare system. Then the judicial system. Then the penal system. And, when you put all the pieces together, you realise that *Freeway* is making a penetrating statement about the general populace's endless

From *Freeway*

fascination with the lurid and violent. And, unlike Oliver Stone's *Natural Born Killers*, which was torpedoed by interference from the director's ego, *Freeway* drives home the point effectively. This movie is both grimly funny and thought-provoking.

Reese Witherspoon plays a modern-day, white trash Red Riding Hood by the name of Vanessa. She has what might be termed 'domestic problems'. Her mother (Amanda Plummer) is a prostitute and her stepfather (Michael T. Weiss) is a drug addict. When the cops bust both of them, Vanessa faces another round of foster care. So, instead, she runs off to find her paternal grandmother, who lives in Northern California. Her boyfriend (Bokeem Woodbine) gives her a gun as a going-away present. Shortly after she gets on the I-5, her clunker of a car breaks down. A passing motorist by the name of Bob Wolverton (Kiefer Sutherland, the wolf—or Wolverton—in sheepish clothing) gives her a lift.

As they drive north, she starts opening up to him, relating her sad life's story. His intentions are anything but altruistic, however, and their little trip leads to a violent off-highway confrontation. This critical event takes place well before *Freeway's* halfway point, and opens the door for a number of surprising plot developments.

As incisive as *Freeway's* story is, the film wouldn't be nearly as successful without terrific turns by the two leads. Reese Witherspoon, a young actress with a few impressive performances behind her (*The Man in the Moon*, *A Far Off Place*), displays an aptitude for acting naturally and believably, no matter how outrageous her circumstances are. She captivates with her nonstop energy, culling our sympathy and enabling us to see the world through Vanessa's eyes. No less effective is Kiefer Sutherland, playing a truly creepy villain with a pitch that is perfect for this kind of off-kilter motion picture. There's no doubt that he's the big, bad wolf.

Freeway contains several great moments, many of which work equally well as social commentary and comedy. For example, one particular black cop (Wolfgang Bodison) is out to get Vanessa until he realises that her boyfriend is black. Thereafter, he's her staunchest defender. Then there are the supposedly-upright people in this film—Wolverton, his wife (played by Brooke Shields), a prison matron, and others—all of whom hide at least one twisted, dark secret. This cynical view of human nature is what fuels the films of David Lynch and the Coen brothers, and it's very much in evidence here in Bright's directorial debut.

Red Riding Hood references abound, from the opening credits (which depict the Grimm story in drawings) and a TV cartoon to one of the film's last lines ('what big teeth you have'). In addition to already-noted differences between the fairy tale and *Freeway*, there's one other factor that deserves mentioning. In this 'Little Red Riding Hood', the wolf makes one huge mistake—he picks a girl who certainly doesn't need a woodcutter to do her butt-kicking for her.

James Berardinelli 1997, 'Freeway: a film review', *Reelviews*, http://movie-reviews.colossus.net/movies/f/freeway.html

Activities

1. Discuss the way in which the reviewer describes how the story of Red Riding Hood has been used in this film:
   - What variations have been made?
   - What attitudes to contemporary American society does the film encourage because of these variations?
2. In addition to reading the film *Freeway* in terms of Little Red Riding Hood, this reviewer reads it in terms of other films and the work of particular directors. Discuss the similarities and differences he finds between *Freeway* and these other texts.

Titles and epigraphs

An epigraph is a quotation at the beginning of a book. Titles and epigraphs often take the form of allusions to other texts. You can use these allusions, usually after some research, to provide a framework for constructing a reading of the text. Below are some examples.

CASE STUDY

7

Of Mice and Men

John Steinbeck's *Of Mice and Men* takes its title from the poem 'To a Mouse' by Scottish poet Robbie Burns:

> The best-laid plans o' mice an' men
> Gang aft agley,
> An' lea'e us nought but grief an' pain
> For promis'd joy.

In modern English the first two lines could be translated as 'the best laid plans of mice and men often go astray'. The title can thus be read as highlighting the uncertainty of life and portraying humans as having no more control over their fate than animals.

Eva Luna

Isabel Allende's novel *Eva Luna* opens with an epigraph from *A Thousand and One Tales of the Arabian Nights*, 'Then he said to Scheherazade: "Sister for the sake of Allah, tell us a story that will help pass the night …".' *The Arabian Nights* tells the story of a king who demands that each night a new young woman of the kingdom be provided for him to have sex with, after which he has her killed. Scheherazade manages to survive by making up a story to entertain the king each night but refusing to finish the story until the following night. The king lets her live to hear the end of the story the following night, but she also begins a new story. Eventually the king falls in love with Scheherazade and marries her. The epigraph thus allows you to read the book as celebrating the power of women to subvert male tyranny through imagination and narrative.

You can also read the title in terms of its reference to Eve and the moon, centring on women and their power as the originators of life.

Cloudstreet

The novel *Cloudstreet* begins with this epigraph:

> Shall we gather at the river
> Where bright angel-feet have trod …

The words come from a hymn written in 1864 by Robert S. Lowry.

Shall we gather at the river,
Where bright angel feet have trod,
With its crystal tide forever
Flowing by the throne of God?

Refrain

Yes, we'll gather at the river,
The beautiful, the beautiful river;
Gather with the saints at the river
That flows by the throne of God.

On the margin of the river,
Washing up its silver spray,
We will talk and worship ever,
All the happy golden day.

Refrain

Ere we reach the shining river,
Lay we every burden down;
Grace our spirits will deliver,
And provide a robe and crown.

Refrain

At the smiling of the river,
Mirror of the Savior's face,
Saints, whom death will never sever,
Lift their songs of saving grace.

Refrain

Soon we'll reach the shining river,
Soon our pilgrimage will cease;
Soon our happy hearts will quiver
With the melody of peace.

Refrain

Robert Lowry

Lowry explained how he came to write the hymn:

One afternoon in July, 1864, when I was pastor at Hanson Place Baptist Church, Brooklyn, the weather was oppressively hot, and I was lying on a lounge in a state of physical exhaustion … My imagination began to take itself wings. Visions of the future passed before me with startling vividness. The imagery of the apocalypse took the form of a tableau. Brightest of all were the throne, the heavenly river, and the gathering of the saints … I began to wonder why the hymn writers had said so much about the 'river of death' and so little about the 'pure water of life, clear as crystal, proceeding out of the throne of God and the Lamb.' As I mused, the words began to construct themselves. They came first as a question of Christian inquiry, 'Shall we gather?' Then they broke in chorus, 'Yes, we'll gather.' On this question and answer the hymn developed itself. The music came with the hymn.

Robert Lowry 1864, quoted in *The Cyber Hymnal*,
www.cyberhymnal.org/htm/s/w/swgatriv.htm, 1996.

Knowing the source of the epigraph allows you to construct a reading of *Cloudstreet* as a portrayal of life as a journey of doubts and uncertainties but also as an expression of faith in the successful conclusion of this journey in a state of happiness and contentment. Knowing that the singing of hymns is an act in which members of a common faith express and reinforce the sharing of their beliefs and common values means that you can also read *Cloudstreet* as a celebration of community.

The Christian origins of the epigraph in *Cloudstreet* can also allow you to construct parallels between aspects of *Cloudstreet* and Christian stories. For example, in the sub-plots of Rose and Quick, both characters undergo a journey like that of the prodigal son in the Bible, turning their backs on home and family only to experience pain and unhappiness and eventually realising that what they are searching for is to be found in what they had left.

Anna's Story

The book *Anna's Story* by Bronwyn Donaghy tells the story of the death of a fifteen-year-old Sydney girl from the drug ecstasy in 1995. It uses epigraphs at the beginnings of various sections and chapters. These take the form of quotations from Lewis Carroll's *Alice in Wonderland* and *Through the Looking Glass*. For readers who know the story of Alice, these references invite a comparison between Anna and Alice. They can be read as constructing Anna as an innocent, curious young girl confronted by a strange world which she can barely comprehend. The first reference states:

> In fancy they pursue
> The dreamchild moving through a land
> Of wonders wild and new.

This constructs Anna as a 'dreamchild': innocent, curious, not fully aware and not fully responsible. The words 'they pursue' can be seen as portraying her as somewhat elusive, someone who is getting away from her parents who are struggling to understand her and manage her.

A third intertextual reference occurs at the beginning of chapter 12 entitled 'Wicked Risks':

> In another moment down went Alice after it, never once considering how in the world she was to get out again.

This constructs Anna as childlike and not aware of the consequences of her actions—someone who is not sufficiently mature to be considered responsible. This idea is reinforced by the quote at the beginning of chapter 13:

> However this bottle was not marked 'poison' so Alice ventured to taste it, and finding it very nice … she soon finished it off. 'What a curious feeling!' said Alice.

7

Readers could be expected to know that just because something is not marked poison does not mean that it is safe. This, along with the other intertextual references construct Anna, and by implication teenagers in general, as people driven by curiosity who are not mature enough to be aware of the consequences of their actions.

CASE STUDY

8

The Grapes of Wrath

Like other aspects of a text, titles and epigraphs might be capable of more than one reading. John Steinbeck's *The Grapes of Wrath* portrays the plight of poor Oklahoma farmers in the 1930s who are forced to sell their farms by banks interested only in the financial bottom line. With a few meagre possessions they travel to California where they become victims of discrimination and exploitation. The title is taken from a song 'The Battle Hymn of the Republic', written in 1862 during the American Civil War.

Mine eyes have seen the glory of the coming of the Lord
He is trampling out the vintage where the grapes of wrath are stored,
He has loosed the fateful lightning of His terrible swift sword
His truth is marching on.

Glory! Glory! Hallelujah!
Glory! Glory! Hallelujah!
Glory! Glory! Hallelujah!
His truth is marching on.

I have seen Him in the watch-fires of a hundred circling camps
They have builded Him an altar in the evening dews and damps
I can read His righteous sentence by the dim and flaring lamps
His day is marching on.

I have read a fiery gospel writ in burnish'd rows of steel,
'As ye deal with my contemners, So with you my grace shall deal;'
Let the Hero, born of woman, crush the serpent with his heel
Since God is marching on.

He has sounded forth the trumpet that shall never call retreat
He is sifting out the hearts of men before His judgment-seat
Oh, be swift, my soul, to answer Him! be jubilant, my feet!
Our God is marching on.

In the beauty of the lilies Christ was born across the sea
With a glory in His bosom that transfigures you and me:
As He died to make men holy, let us die to make men free,
While God is marching on.

Julia Ward Howe

The song was written in support of soldiers fighting for the northern states in the American Civil War, one of the aims of which was the abolition of slavery. It expresses a belief that God is on the side of the singers, certainty in the morality of combatting discrimination and oppression, and faith in the eventual victory of the forces of goodness over evil. While not particularly good poetry, the song continued to be popular after the war, often sung on national occasions and even at football games. It became a general expression of Americans' beliefs about themselves as a nation.

The use of a quotation from the song as the title of Steinbeck's novel allows for at least four readings. First, you can read the novel, like the song, as an expression of faith in the eventual abolition of oppression and discrimination. Second, you can read it as a reminder that the battle against oppression and discrimination needs to continue. Third, you can read the use of the quotation ironically and the novel as pointing to the hypocrisy of American society in singing such a song when oppression and discrimination still exist. Fourth, you can read the novel as a warning, expressing the view that America may be sowing the seeds of another war.

The Handmaid's Tale

Perhaps the prize for using epigraphs that make intertextual allusions should go to Margaret Atwood, author of *The Handmaid's Tale*, who uses three:

> And when Rachel saw that she bare Jacob no children, Rachel envied her sister, and said unto Jacob, Give me children, or else I die.
> And Jacob's anger was kindled against Rachel; and he said, Am I in God's stead, who hath withheld from thee the fruit of the womb?
> And she said, Behold my maid Bilhah, go in unto her, and she shall bear upon my knees, that I may also have children by her.
>
> Genesis, 30:1-3

> But as to myself, having been wearied out for many years with offering vain, idle, visionary thoughts, and at length utterly despairing of success, I fortunately fell upon this proposal…
>
> Jonathan Swift, 'A Modest Proposal'

> In the desert there is no sign that says, Thou shalt not eat stones.
>
> Sufi proverb

The first allusion is a story from the Bible about a woman, Rachel, who has failed to conceive and suggests to her husband, Jacob, that he should impregnate Rachel's maid in order to produce children that Rachel and Jacob will raise as their own. First, the allusion can be read as suggesting that the idea of women using other women to bear children for them, a scenario presented by *The Handmaid's Tale*, has a long history and is not as far-fetched as it might have seemed to readers when the book was first published in 1985. Since that time of course surrogate pregnancy has become more common, so the epigraph proved quite prescient (forward-looking).

If you think about the epigraph a bit more, you can read it as criticising the ideology that women can only find purpose for their existence in having children. Rachel's statement, 'Give me children or else I die' seems extreme to say the least.

8

Further, the epigraph can also be read as suggesting that the pressure on women to raise children is so great that it can lead them to exploiting other women to achieve this aim, in this case Bilhah. This interpretation might frame the manner in which you respond to Serena Joy and the other wives in the novel who use handmaids to have children for them. It can allow you to interpret the novel as presenting the wives, not as evil, but as victims of this ideology. Alternatively, it might allow you to read the novel as criticising them for going along with this ideology to the extent of exploiting others such as Offred.

You can read the epigraph in another way: as a criticism of men. When Rachel approaches her husband about their lack of children, his immediate response is to deny that it could possibly be his fault. This reading can provide a framework for interpreting the commander and men in general in the novel.

The second epigraph comes from Jonathan Swift's 'A Modest Proposal'. This was a pamphlet produced in eighteenth-century England. At the time there was famine in Ireland, which was then a colony of Britain. In the pamphlet Swift suggested that the way to deal with the famine was to use the children of the Irish as food. Before you become too horrified by this idea, you need to realise that Swift was being ironic. He was satirising the attitudes of the English towards the Irish. By writing a pamphlet in which he acted as if he thought his English audience would take this idea seriously, he was actually criticising the audience for their treatment of the Irish as inferior life-forms. This knowledge allows you to read the use of this quotation as an epigraph in *The Handmaid's Tale* as asking the readers not to read the novel as a far-fetched tale that could never happen, but use it to look at their society and think about some of its attitudes towards women.

The final epigraph, the Sufi proverb, is more obscure and has been interpreted in a number of ways. Some people have interpreted it to mean that it is not necessary to forbid that which is undesirable. In terms of *The Handmaid's Tale*, the proverb can be read as pointing out that the society of the novel attempts to enforce conformity with its rules, not by spelling out the rules, but by making the consequences of breaking them so horrific as to be not worth even contemplating. You may be able to think of other interpretations.

Activity

Below are the titles of some texts that make allusions to other texts, such as books or films, or to historical events. Discuss the readings they might invite of the texts of which they are the titles. In some cases you may need to do some research. A book of quotations would be especially useful.

Novels	Films	Nonfiction
Brave New World	*Independence Day*	*Junk Male*
	Pulp Fiction	*Reviving Ophelia*
	Play It Again, Sam	

WORK SAMPLE

Intertextual reading of *Starship Troopers*

This work sample was produced by the author of this book as an example for his Year 12 English class. It provides an example of an intertextual reading.

Topic for this talk: Our enjoyment and understanding of a text can be enhanced when we are able to make connections with other texts. Discuss with reference to one or more texts.

'People who fight monsters should beware that in the process, they do not become monsters themselves.' This statement by the philosopher Nietzsche succinctly captures one of the main understandings I took from the film Starship Troopers. *I was able to enjoy the movie on a number of levels and develop this understanding because of the connections I was able to make between* Starship Troopers *and a wide range of other texts.*

On one level I enjoyed Starship Troopers *as an action adventure film. The film portrays a war between humans and giant bugs from another galaxy. While this may sound a bit far-fetched and childish, I still found myself being caught up in this rather silly plot because it was combined with a number of other plots from genres which are usually seen as more realistic than science fiction and relate more closely to the world in which we live. In the opening scenes, the film drew on the conventions of the teen romance and soap operas such as* Beverly Hills 90210. *I may not be a teen now, but I was once, and I am still even extremely romantic on occasions. More importantly the use of the teen romance genre was a way of making the unfamiliar—a war against bugs—familiar by placing it within a genre known to me. The film also drew heavily on the conventions of other genres I am familiar with, such as the military training camp genre, most recently seen in* GI Jane *but also used in* Full Metal Jacket, *and other war movies. In fact, I kept thinking of* Saving Private Ryan *while watching. Fighting bugs in outer space was made to seem not very different from fighting Germans in France in 1944.*

Another way in which Starship Troopers *enhanced my involvement and enjoyment was by providing me with a central character, Johnny Rico, that I could identify with, not because he is anything like me but because he is the sort of character I have learnt to sympathise with from other texts. Rico is not initially a hero or special. He does not do particularly well in school. He makes mistakes in training camp. He has to battle to succeed. He is the archetypal underdog whom we have all learnt to identify with and prefer to become involved with in movies. The characterisation of Rico draws on an archetype featured in countless texts:* Star Wars, The Karate Kid, *John Marsden's* The Journey *and* The Hurricane *to name just a few.*

Perhaps the main way in which the film enhanced my involvement was by offering me a classic story of good versus evil. What better way to provide involvement and enjoyment than to give the audience someone to side with and someone to hate and be afraid of. And what better enemy to create for an audience than giant bugs! I mean bugs do not exactly get a good press in our society.

In addition to its involvement of me at an action adventure level, Starship Troopers involved me at a thematic level. I was able to see that it had something to say about the world in which I live. While I was enjoying seeing the bugs killed it occurred to me that this film was actually a satire on nationalism and gung-ho militarism. While initially siding with the humans against the bugs, I gradually began to realise there were certain things about the humans' appearance and behaviour that I recognised and didn't like. The humans were behaving exactly like the Nazis I had seen in films like Triumph of the Will, countless war movies—think Schindler's List—and newsreel footage of Germany in the thirties. I decided that the filmmakers were using images I recognised to make a point. There were shots of massed uniformed troops spouting exactly the same slogans, shots composed exactly like those in Triumph of the Will. The uniforms of the troops were very similar to Nazi uniforms. The way in which the bodies of the dead bugs formed pyramids was eerily reminiscent of the pyramids of dead bodies found in Nazi concentration camps after the second world war which I have seen in history books. In addition the way in which the troops shouted slogans such as 'The only good bug is a dead bug' reminded me of the unthinking attitudes which accompanied the destruction of the American Indians and which I have seen in many old Westerns. Making this connection allowed me to see that Starship Troopers was providing me with a warning about the dangers of getting carried away in hating an enemy, of seeing an enemy as less than human. Even if the enemy is a bug!

Starship Troopers has been described as a cross between Melrose Place and Triumph of the Will. That basically sums up why I enjoyed the movie and why I developed the understandings I did.

Activity

Present a four-minute talk on one of your favourite books or films on the same topic as the work sample.

Irony

5

Irony means saying one thing and meaning another, which is often the opposite of the apparent meaning. Irony is an extremely important convention to understand; if you don't realise that a text is ironic, you will misinterpret it totally.

Irony is almost impossible to teach directly. Often you see it immediately or you don't see it at all. Not surprisingly, many students become frustrated and angry when they are told that they have not understood a text because they have missed the irony. The way to get better at recognising irony is by looking at many examples. That is what this chapter is intended to provide you with.

Irony often occurs when authors or producers do not intend what they say to be taken seriously. It is usually easy to pick up when someone is being ironic in conversation. Often the tone of voice is the give-away. It may be over-exaggerated: 'Oh, I sooo want to have an outfit like yours, Cassidy. That orange goes sooo fantastically well with the purple and green.' On the other hand, the tone may be one of understatement: 'Good one, Jake,' said abruptly as the car mounts the curb. Sometimes body language is the clue that someone is being ironic. The clue may be a wink or a smile.

Irony depends very heavily on context and shared values. You will usually realise someone is being ironic when what they say seems so out of kilter with your values and beliefs about what is appropriate that you have to assume they can't be serious. The comment on Cassidy's outfit, for example, can only be understood as ironic if you share the view that a mixture of orange, green and purple clothes is unfashionable.

The best defences against not recognising irony are to:

- take into account anything you know of the context of the text, especially the author and intended audience and your understandings of the values of each
- acquaint yourself with lots of examples of irony
- be aware that irony is always a possibility.

When I said I really liked you I was being ironic.

PUTDOWN ST

Irony is often used as a form of humour, as a way of making fun of someone or something. Because irony depends on shared values and beliefs, it is always possible that some readers, those not sharing these beliefs and values, will not appreciate the humour. Cassidy, for example, was probably far from amused about the comments on her clothes. So, as a reader or a viewer, you do not have to accept that the irony is funny or accept the preferred reading of the text.

CASE STUDY

9

'Dear Britney, Like, wow, one more time, baby'

The following passage appeared in 2000 in an American newspaper largely targeted at a middle class adult audience.

The Washington Post, 17 May 2000, p. CI.

NEWSPAPER ARTICLE

Dear Britney, Like, wow, one more time, baby

David Segal

'OMIGOD, omigod, omigod.

Oh. My. God.

Got your new album. Love it! Seriously, it just rawwwwwks, you know? After your first one, I was like, no way she can top this. Ever, ever, ever. No way. Well, way! Oops … I Did It Again is sooo amazing. Where do I begin? I love how the album is basically the same beat, the whole way through. You could Tae Bo to this thing and never miss a punch. On most albums, the beats are all mixed up—slow song, fast song, mid-tempo song.

It's confusing! With Oops it's like your drum machine got stuck or something, but in a cool way. And the album sounds a lot like your first one, Baby One More Time, so there's nothing tricky to learn.

And you look faboo on the cover. You were so right to drop that whole Catholic-school slut thing you had working on your debut. Don't get me wrong, it was really cool and sooo many kids totally ripped it off and everything. I bet you scandalised a lot of nuns.

You go, girl!

But this new look is excellent. Are those leopard-skin pants you're wearing in the promo shot? And how about that slinky suede vest with the brass buckles? Want one! Even better is that latex red jumpsuit from your new video, the one where you, like, spin through space. I love how they play it all the time on MTV. It's like, I WANT MY BRITNEY TV!

Even your album title is cool. And gutsy. I mean, there are going to be sooo many smarty-pants out there saying stuff like, 'Yeah, she put out another stinky album!' Or people will call it Britney's Second Boo Boo, or some other dumb joke. Ignore them. You're an artist! This album is totally going to debut at No. 1 this week, knocking off *NSYNC No Strings Attached.

And it'll do that because of the music. People forget that about you. Oh, they say, she's a ditz. She's a Mouseketeer. She lip-syncs in concert. She stole her moves from Janet Jackson. Even her breasts are fake. (As if!)

Well, wait till they get a load of Oops. The title track, and first single, is great.

The chorus sounds exactly like Abba doing an aerobics video. Hey, they can't sue you, right? I mean Abba is from like Sweden or something, so they probably don't even have lawyers in this country. And they're old, so they probably won't even hear this song.

Even if they sue, big whup. You're way better. Your voice is all moaning and stuff, and the music sounds like it came right out of a machine. (Are there any live musicians on this album? Message me.) Lyrics-wise, some guy thinks you're more than friends and you're like NOT! 'It might seem like a crush, but it doesn't mean that I'm serious,' you sing. And you make it rhyme. Not many singers can do that!

And you cover The Rolling Stones' (I Can't Get No) Satisfaction. That took nerve. Friends must have been, like, 'Oh Britney, maybe you should stay away from one of the greatest songs in rock history. People will laugh at you.' You're like, Whatever!

Your version is way better than the Stones' because you can dance to it, you know? And it doesn't have that annoying guitar riff that just keeps repeating, over and over. Instead, the beat is kind of like Michael Jackson's Billie Jean.

Britney Spears

Things get even better with Don't Let Me Be the Last to Know, co-written by Shania Twain. The country queen of bare midriff helps the teen queen of bare midriff—can you say 'genius'?

Omigod, there's so much more. On Lucky you sing about a miserable child star who's beloved by everyone but bawls her eyes out wondering 'If there's nothing missing in my life/Then why do these tears come at night?' Is it about you? Who knows? The key is that people will ask!

The whole album is so … edgy. Because you're 18 now, and singing lines like 'I'm not that innocent', and wearing all those skintight bustiers and stuff.

And then you're quoted in magazines saying how icky it is that men fantasise about you, how that sort of freaks you out and everything.

It's perfect. You come on all half-naked and barely legal, and the next moment you're like, 'Perverts!'

The virgin-hussy thing. It's awesome and nobody does it like you. Run with it. Don't change it. And when you record album No. 3, just do it again.

PS: The album made its debut at No. 2 this week in Australia and your single is in the same spot.

love, David Segal

Activities

1. What are the indications that the writer is being ironic here?
2. What criticisms is the article making of Britney Spears and her album while seeming to praise them?
3. In addition to making fun of Britney Spears, this article can also be read as making fun of her fans. What ideas about her fans are implied by the article?
4. What experiences, understandings and values does a reader need to share to find this article funny?

'Tips for Mum: how to rear real boys'

The following passage is an article which appeared in the Melbourne newspaper, *The Age*, in 1994.

The Age, 29 May 1994.

Tips for Mum: how to rear real boys

Michelle Marks points out the obvious pitfalls in parenting males

After months of urine samples and the formation of stretch marks, you have finally given birth to an angelic boy.

The most divine creature you have ever laid eyes on, he is more heavenly than any other child. Yes, your son is the paradigm of excellence.

However, raising a male can be difficult. With all the SNAG (Sensitive New Age Guy) pressure on today's male, it is easy for your son to lose his masterful superiority to modern peer pressure.

To save our desolate society from the menace of SNAGS, follow these simple, yet effective guidelines and you'll produce the best son possible:

As soon as you bring your son home from the hospital, surround him with the company of violent figure action heroes and toys, such as Teenage Mutant Ninja Turtles.

These toys will teach your child that violence is the only means of getting his own way, and also demonstrate the futility of communication and compromise.

Do not surround your child with any educational toys, or with anything coloured pink. However, if this situation is inescapable, the observation of Barbie Dolls will do no harm as it depicts a desirable image of women.

One necessary skill that is vital for your son to acquire is the art of burping. The humble burp is a bonding of male egos, and can be taught at an early age. To burp is human, but the true skill lies in the prolonged belch. Variation in tone and pitch are credible, but bonus points are scored for a deep bass sound.

Once one can burp after any digestion, he is ready for a public performance.

Linguistic skills and conversation will consume a major amount of your son's education. Not only does he have to learn social terminology, but also the ability to communicate with his male counterparts.

This is a totally foreign dialect, mainly comprising a series of grunts and colloquialisms (the interrogative grunt is an absolute necessity).

For example, when expressing to a fellow male his intimacy with a female, he will say something like: 'As long as the sheila cooks for me and holds me stubby while I change channels, I'll let her hang around me for a while.'

For your son to survive in the social mayhem of males, he must drink beer. If he drinks non-alcoholic beverages or cocktails, his masculinity will be questioned.

Therefore it is essential to start feeding your boy beer at an early age. Anecdotes of mothers feeding their sons beer via a bottle after birth do seem a bit extreme. I would, however, encourage the serving of breakfast cereals with beer from about the age of five.

Sport will also play a major role in your son's life. But it is necessary for you to control your son's sporting activities.

Ballet and chess do not count as sports, and any interest or curiosity directed towards these 'sports' should be terminated as soon as possible. Instead nourish your child with footy and 'piffing yonnies'.

Piffing yonnies is the custom of throwing

pebbles, stones, rocks and, in the more extreme cases, boulders, at anything that moves. Piffing yonnies is a great stress reliever which, in turn, will make your child extremely well adjusted.

Footy to your son will be his religion. It is every young boy's dream to make his pilgrimage to that Mecca of footy, the MCG.

Footy is a game of sweat, simple rules (therefore making it easy for males to comprehend) and violence. Teaching your son to adore football not only means educating him to the rules, but to that time-honoured tradition of hurling abuse at the umpire and the opposition.

Footy is an essential survival tactic in the primitive world of males as, without it, sparse communication between males would exist.

You'll find once your son hits puberty he will take an interest in the opposite sex. When teaching your son the correct ways of courting a young lady, begin with the basics.

Firstly, your son has to ignore his feelings and try to humiliate the young lady in question. For example, pulling her bra strap or, for the more eager suitor, attempting to actually undo the bra whilst sitting behind her in class.

This is a good introduction to the art of courtship, as it teaches the male to degrade his love interest in public and also shows the female that the male is always in control.

These guidelines are just the basics for your son to acquire. Once he has mastered all these skills he will be well on his way to asserting himself in the wonderful land of Oz!

Activities

1 Discuss how funny you found this article and the reasons for your response.
2 What ideas and attitudes about males does this article take as given? To what extent do you agree with these ideas and attitudes?
3 Write a response to this article, perhaps in the form of a letter to the author, either agreeing with or criticising the views put forward.
4 Write an equally satirical article entitled 'Tips for Mum: how to rear real girls'.

'Let's peep inside'

The following passage is a newspaper article by the Australian writer Lennie Lower published in 1928. The article was a response to the development of what was then called 'domestic journalism', articles describing the design, appearance and decoration of attractive houses. Not surprisingly, most of the houses featured were owned by fairly wealthy people. Lower was reacting to this form of journalism at a time when many people were living in poverty. Of course 'domestic journalism' has now become extremely common, especially in the homes supplements of weekend newspapers, and there are still many people living in poverty.

Let's peep inside

Lennie Lower

Imitation is the sincerest form of flattery, and in borrowing this idea from the *Sunday Sun* and *Sunday Telegraph*, we show our appreciation of the new domestic journalism.

The charming home of Mr and Mrs John Bowyang, tucked away in Pelican Street, Surry Hills, is a revelation in piquancy. From the backyard one has a view of every other backyard in the street, and the tall chimneystack of Tooth's Brewery looms majestically in the distance.

An antique casket, known to connoisseurs as a 'dirt-tin', stands by the back entrance. It is one of Mrs Bowyang's great sorrows that the lid has been pinched.

Mrs Bowyang has an artistic taste and an eye for effect. Two lines have been stretched between long poles at either end of the yard, and when these lines are full of clothes, the sight is bewitching in the extreme.

Empty salmon tins, kindly thrown over the fence by the next-door neighbours, and a worn-out bath and a coil of wire-netting on top of the washhouse roof, complete the picture.

Fascinating though the yard is, it is not until one enters the house itself that one gets a glimpse of the interior.

The motif throughout the whole house is one of antiquity. The wallpaper is mellow with age, and the ceilings have not been kalsomined* for forty-seven years.

Hardly any of the doors shut properly, and the windows are held open by bright clean lemonade bottles.

Mrs Bowyang points with pride to an old meat safe which hangs in the drawing-room, where the lodger sleeps.

There is a history attached to the old safe.

It was rescued from Mark Foy's** big fire many years ago, and for a long time the parrot lived in it; but as the family grew the parrot had to be given away and the infant Bowyang sleeps in it now.

The old clock is another interesting relic. It was given to Mrs Bowyang by her mother, who was one of the Maloneys—the Woolloomooloo Maloneys who were so prominent in society a few years ago when the younger set ran a two-up school*** down at the wharves.

Though it has been in the family for many years—excepting occasional visits to the pawnshop—the alarm still works.

The bedroom furnishings are symbolic of that affectionate family life which seems to be fading into oblivion in these modern times. There are two double beds and a stretcher in the room, cleverly arranged so that one may walk from one bed to the other without climbing over.

Mr and Mrs Bowyang and little Jacky sleep in one double bed, the three youngest girls in the other and Mr Bowyang's brother-in-law, who is out of work, sleeps in the stretcher.

Mrs Bowyang's hobbies are washing and mending, and some of the mending she does is nothing short of marvellous.

Business takes Mr Bowyang away every morning at 6.30, he being engaged in the sewer-digging profession; but he still finds time for his diversions, namely, washing up and placing tins where the rain comes in. The younger children have a magnificent playground in Pelican Street, where they have a jolly time daubing themselves with mud, eating stray apple-cores, and escaping being run over by passing lorries.

Viewed from the front, Mrs Bowyang's home is extremely attractive. It seems to attract all the dust in the streets, and although it has never been renovated since it was built, it is remarkably cheap for 25 shillings a week, and the brass door-knob takes an excellent polish.

The writer was intrigued by the quaint, old-world, worn-out, bashed-in atmosphere of the locality, and it was with great reluctance that he left. He lingered for a while, hoping to see the owner of Mrs Bowyang's residence, with the idea of strangling him when he saw him, but realising the futility of the idea he left.

* kalsomined—whitewashed
** Mark Foy's—a department store
*** two-up school—an illegal gambling ring

Cyril Pearl, *The Best of Lennie Lower*,
Angus and Robertson, Sydney 1983, pp. ix–x

Popcorn by Ben Elton

The following passage is an edited version of the opening of Ben Elton's novel *Popcorn*, published in 1996.

On the morning before, Bruce had been sitting in a television studio. Opposite him, across the sweeping curve of the presentation console, were two Ken-and-Barbie-style presenters of indeterminate age.

'His name' (pause) 'is Bruce Delamitri,' said Ken, employing the sincere, plonking tone he reserved for really big guests.

…

'He is probably the most celebrated artist working in the motion picture industry today. A great writer, a great director. Hollywood's golden boy.'

'I heard he makes great pasta sauce too,' interjected Barbie, by way of adding a little human interest.

…

'But career excellence takes its toll, and Hollywood was recently saddened by the news that Bruce's marriage to actress, model and rock singer Farrah Delamitri was in big trouble. We'll be talking about that also.'

The red light on top of the camera facing Bruce lit up. He adopted a suitably sardonic '**** happens' expression …

…

'You're watching *Coffee Time USA*. We'll be back after these messages,' said the male presenter, whose name was not Ken but Oliver Martin. The studio lights dimmed and the *Coffee Time* logo came up while Oliver and his female colleague, Dale, stacked their papers in an important manner. There was of course nothing on their papers, but maintaining the fiction that TV presenters are proper journalists, as opposed to people who read whatever comes up on the autocue, is one of the principal duties of current affairs broadcasting.

Bruce watched on the monitor in front of him as Oliver and Dale disappeared and were replaced on the screen by four bikini-clad babes clutching soda bottles and tumbling ecstatically out of an old VW Beetle.

'A girl, a beach, it's happening, it's real.
It's a boost, it's a buzz, it's the way you should feel!'

The studio controller killed the volume, and the bikini babes were left sucking on their bottles in muted delight.

'One and a half minutes on the break,' said the floor manager.

This was the signal for the make-up girls to rush in and pat gently away at all available faces. Oliver turned to Bruce, addressing him through a flurry of powder and pads.

'I think what we need to concentrate on here is the fact that our industry is not a dream factory any more. We deal in gritty realism. We show it like it is.'

The make-up lady applied another layer of slap to Oliver's already heavily caked features. The gritty reality was that anyone who had acquired such a deep and lustrous tan would long since have died of skin cancer. But Oliver was of the old school of TV presenting: he believed that sporting a thermo-nuclear tan was a mark of respect to the viewer, like wearing a nice shirt and tie. You had to show you'd made the effort.

'One minute to the break,' said the floor manager.

Across the vast pastel-coloured desk, Dale's voice could be heard from the midst of a cloud of hair-spray. 'I mean, surely the big issue, Bruce, has got to be this whole copycat killing thing, hasn't it? I mean that's what America is concerned about. As an American woman, it sure is what I'm concerned about. Are you concerned about that Bruce? As an American man?'

'America's population is not as young as it was, and soon the number one issue concerning the majority of Americans will be adult incontinence.'

This was not Bruce. It was the TV. The studio controller had pumped the volume back up preparatory to going back on air. It was after nine, and the network advertisers were beginning to switch their focus from workers and schoolkids to a 'coffee time' audience, which meant young mums and old lonelys. Soda-sucking babes were giving way to nipple pads, denture fixative and nappies both infant and adult.

'No, I am not concerned about copycat killings,' said Bruce, speaking with difficulty because a young woman was painting some kind of menthol-flavoured grease on to his lips. 'I don't believe that people get up from the movie theatre or the TV and do what they just saw. Otherwise, the people who watch this show would all have their hair set in concrete and their brains sucked out along with their cellulite.'

It was scarcely a comment calculated to endear him to his media colleagues, but that was Bruce. Tough, sarcastic and a bit of a stirrer. If you wore a leather jacket and shades on TV at nine in the morning, you were almost duty-bound to be abrasive.

'Good, good, you should make that point on air,' said Dale absently, checking her eye-liner.

Ben Elton, *Popcorn*, Simon & Schuster, London 1996, 1–5

Activities

1 Discuss the criticisms of television made in this passage.
2 What other subjects are being satirised, criticised or ridiculed?

Documentary

6

Documentary films are often treated as factual presentations of reality or as sources of neutral information. For instance, the *Pocket Macquarie Dictionary* defines a documentary as a 'factual presentation of a real event, person's life etc in a television or radio program, film, etc'.

In the study of English, you will take a different approach. You will treat documentaries as constructions that offer particular versions of reality. Rather than treating documentaries as neutral sources of information, you will keep in mind that documentaries, like all texts, often work to persuade an audience to accept the version of reality they offer.

To say that documentaries offer versions of reality rather than reality itself is not to criticise documentaries nor to suggest that they should present reality. It is simply to recognise the nature of textual construction. Textual construction by its very nature involves the selection, structuring and reshaping of information in particular ways. Thus the final product is not reality but a version of it. It is simply not possible to reproduce reality in all its complexity.

A good definition of documentary comes from the British film-maker John Grierson, often called the father of documentary, in 1934. He defined documentary as 'the creative interpretation of reality'. This is a useful definition because it reminds us that a documentary presents an interpretation of reality, not reality itself. It also reminds us that the construction of a documentary is a creative act in which the film-maker shapes the raw material. Further, it reminds us that, like all acts of creativity, documentaries can be looked at as works of art and sources of entertainment, something that tends too often to be overlooked.

Can't you get him to cry? This is a no-holds-barred, in-your-face, warts-and-all, true-to-life documentary!

Construction process

The construction process overview:
* ☆ choice of subject
* ☆ approach
* ☆ choice of shots
* ☆ shot construction ←
* ☆ sound track
* ☆ editing

* ● camera angle
* ● camera distance
* ● camera movement
* ● shot duration
* ● lighting
* ● special effects

The idea that documentary should be treated as a construction rather than a window onto reality becomes clear when you examine how a documentary is made. Every stage of the process involves the making of decisions, either consciously or subconsciously, and all these decisions involve value judgements. The fact that a decision is made subconsciously does not mean it is less important or irrelevant. Subconscious decisions are usually the result of unquestioned assumptions and values and thus may be the result of the values of a society or culture held by the film-makers. They can reveal the effect of the film-makers' context on the final product. Of course, when you view a documentary, you are not usually in a position to distinguish between those aspects of the film that are the result of conscious decisions and those that are the result of subconscious ones. In many ways the distinction is irrelevant. What matters is the effect those decisions have on the audience's response to the film.

Choice of subject

Perhaps the first decision made by the makers of a documentary is the choice of subject. Of all the possible subjects in the world, the documentary makers choose one subject; clearly this is a value decision reflecting certain views about what is important in the world. The value decision might reflect the documentary makers' view about what is important and what people should be told about. Alternatively, it might be a purely commercial decision reflecting the documentary makers' assumptions about what audiences would like to see. In this case, the values embedded in the choice of subject reflect the values of the audience.

Approach

Another level of decision-making lies in the approach the documentary makers take to the subject. There are myriad views on any subject; the documentary can only reflect some of these. For example, a documentary on a new highway may portray the highway as a benefit to the community and a sign of progress or it may portray the highway as a destructive force harming communities and the environment.

A documentary on a famous figure may present her as a hero, a villain, a well-intentioned person who has made some errors of judgement, the unwilling puppet of others, a naïve fool or in a range of other ways.

Highlighting the fact that a documentary always approaches its subject from a particular view is not meant as a criticism of documentary makers. The approach or 'angle' is actually what makes a documentary interesting; it is what enables it to tell a story and be entertaining, rather than be just a boring collection of information.

Usually the approach adopted by documentary makers is the result of their research and thought, not simply their unthought-out opinion. Documentary makers may not always begin shooting with a fully worked-out approach in mind. The actual treatment of the subject may emerge during filming and editing. But buried within the choice of subject and the decisions about what to film will be many unconscious assumptions and value judgements.

Choice of shots

The shots you see in a documentary do not usually just happen. They are there in the film because the documentary makers have made a decision to shoot certain scenes or to seek out particular footage from such places as film libraries. The selections involved in the choice of shots will reflect a host of value judgements and particular attitudes to the subject.

Some of the decisions about what to film and what not to film may be forced upon the makers. For instance, they may be prevented from filming certain things. Some people may refuse to be interviewed or may be unavailable. These factors will have an effect on the final shape of the documentary and the responses of the audience.

When considering the choice of shots in a documentary, you should also pay attention to the use of sub-titles and graphic material such as charts and diagrams.

Shot construction

There are a number of decisions involved in the construction of every shot in a documentary.

Camera angle

Camera angle refers to the vertical angle of the camera in relation to the subject.
- High camera angles look down upon the subject.
- Eye level shots are on the same plane as the subject.
- Low camera angles look up to the subject.

The important thing about camera angles is the impression they create of the subject and the relationship they create between viewer and subject.

When examining the use of camera angles in a particular film, look for patterns at work over the course of the film and read the use of camera angles along with other elements of the films. For example, are certain people or objects regularly shot from a particular angle? What is the likely effect of this on the viewers' response to the subject?

It has become a bit of a cliché to say that high camera angles construct the subject, especially if it is a person, as weak, powerless or vulnerable, whereas low camera angles construct the subject as strong, powerful or threatening. While this is not a bad starting point for analysis, you need to beware of being simplistic. Read an angle in conjunction with other elements of the shot, such as body language, framing and lighting. For instance in the documentary *Triumph of the Will* there are many high camera angles of Adolf Hitler. Rather than constructing Hitler as weak, however, it can be argued that they emphasise his power by placing him in the centre of the frame and by surrounding him with supporters.

Camera distance

The main terms used to describe camera distance are long shot, medium shot and close-up. Within these categories are sub-categories—extreme long shots, extreme close-ups, medium close-ups and so on. The main effect of camera distance is on framing—the creation of a frame that determines what appears in the image and what does not.

Long shots usually allow the viewer to take in a large scene and are sometimes used to create a sense of dramatic action. Close-ups, on the other hand, are usually used to focus the viewers' attention on facial expressions or details and to signal to the viewer that these facial expressions or details are significant or important. Close-ups are often used to establish empathy between the audience and a character.

Camera movement

The three main forms of camera movement are panning, tilting and tracking.
- Panning occurs when the camera swings on the horizontal axis to take in a scene.
- Tilting is much less common and occurs when the camera swings on the vertical access.
- A tracking shot is one where the camera actually moves through a scene. In the early days of film-making the camera was placed on tracks, resembling railway tracks, to allow this to occur. These days with lighter equipment most tracking shots in a documentary are created with hand-held cameras. An example of a tracking shot is when the camera follows a person down a corridor. Tracking shots are also sometimes taken from cars to create a form of filmic drive-by shooting.

The zoom shot is not strictly speaking an example of camera movement, but it does create a similar impression of moving towards or away from a subject.

Shot duration

Shot duration refers to the length in time of a shot. A series of brief shots in succession can convey a sense of pace, action or excitement. Sometimes a camera may linger on the subject for longer than is usually expected to allow the viewer to take in particular details. A technique seen in some documentaries is for the camera to remain running in silence after a person has answered a question, the effect often being to create a sense of disbelief or doubt about what the person has just said.

Alternatively, the effect may be to encourage the audience to feel the person's emotions more deeply.

Lighting

Lighting is important in the creation of mood. Low lighting is generally associated with mystery or sadness, but can also be evocative of romance. Bright lighting is often evocative of happiness.

Special effects

A variety of special effects may be used in documentaries. These can include:

- freeze frames
- accelerated action
- slow motion.

Soundtrack

The soundtrack includes:

- voice-overs
- music
- sound effects.

These elements are important in their interplay with the visuals. They may act to reinforce the ideas in the visual, to contradict them or to create a sense of irony.

Editing

The scenes in a documentary are rarely shot in the order in which you see them on screen. The various shots are put together into a coherent pattern through the process of editing. Editing is perhaps the most important stage of film-making. It is really in the editing suite that the film the audience finally sees is put together.

A series of shots cut together is referred to as a montage. The meaning of any shot in a film depends to a large extent on its relationship to other shots. The meaning of almost any shot can be changed by juxtaposing it with another, by adding a different soundtrack or by cutting it in particular ways. Juxtaposition is the most important editing technique at the micro level. This is placing two shots next to each other in such a way as to suggest a particular meaning beyond that of each of the individual shots. Effective use of juxtaposition can be seen towards the end of *Roger & Me*, where a scene of Roger Smith, CEO of General Motors, reading a Christmas message of goodwill is juxtaposed with a scene of the family of a former General Motors employee being evicted from their house. The effect is to undermine the sincerity of Roger Smith's message.

At the level of the film as a whole, it is largely the process of editing that gives a documentary its overall narrative structure.

CASE STUDY

10

Roger & Me

Roger & Me was a documentary made in the 1980s by Michael Moore, who has since gained some fame as the producer and host of the television shows *Television Nation* and *The Awful Truth*. It exposes the effects on the town of Flint, Michigan, of decisions by General Motors to close down their car manufacturing plants in Flint. *Roger & Me* is to date the most successful documentary in the history of the world in terms of box-office takings. It is both very funny and very serious. It is very cleverly constructed and has had a major impact on the style of subsequent documentaries. It is for these reasons that *Roger & Me* is often used as an example of various techniques in this chapter. *Roger & Me* was distributed by Warner Brothers.

Like to know more?

Visit the Longman website www.longman.com.au for some recommended sites on Michael Moore.

Narrative structure

To make documentaries entertaining and enhance audience involvement, documentary makers often use a range of narrative techniques similar to those found in other types of text.

> **Narrative structure overview:**
> ⋇ **focalisers**
> ⋇ **central problems or enigmas**
> ⋇ **conflict**
> ⋇ **archetypal narratives**

Focalisers

A focaliser is the person through whom you experience the events of narrative. A focaliser provides viewers with a point of identification and a point of entry into the film. Sharing the experiences portrayed with a real person humanises the film and helps hold the film together. The focaliser may be a character, an on-screen presenter or an unseen narrator.

In *Roger & Me*, the director Michael Moore constructs himself as the focaliser by highlighting his position as a member of the community of Flint and by presenting himself as the hero on a quest to track down Roger Smith. He also uses the deputy sheriff involved in the eviction of families as a focaliser.

Central problems or enigmas

Another narrative technique to involve the audience in a documentary is to build the narrative around a central problem or enigma. An enigma is a puzzle. This technique keeps the audience involved because they want to find the answer to the problem or puzzle. Most investigative documentaries use this technique. The narrative in the documentary *Kurt and Courtney* is built partly around the question, 'Was Kurt Cobain murdered and if so who murdered him?'

Conflict

Similar to the use of a central problem is the technique of building the narrative around a conflict. This involves the audience by creating interest in the outcome of the conflict. In *Painted Babies* produced by the BBC, for example, the film is structured around the rivalry of the parents of Brooke and Asia, two entrants in a child beauty pageant.

Often the use of a central conflict also involves the construction of heroes and villains. The construction of heroes and villains can humanise and make understandable a complex set of issues, and can enhance audience involvement by giving the audience someone to side with. In many modern documentaries, the conflict created is between the director or presenter of the documentary and another person. In these cases, it is the director or presenter who is invariably the hero. Both *Roger & Me* and *Kurt and Courtney* use this technique.

With many documentaries, the conflict is ready made because of the subject. In *Painted Babies*, the documentary makers draw on the rivalry between the mothers of Brooke and Asia and the suspense over which child will win the beauty pageant because that is what actually happened. Although the narrative was available within the subject matter, it is not hard to imagine the possibility of a very different documentary on child beauty pageants based around a different narrative structure. Like *Painted Babies*, *When We Were Kings* bases its narrative around the preparations and lead-up to the fight between Mohammed Ali and George Foreman in Zaire.

Archetypal narratives

Archetypal narratives are commonly repeated story patterns, such as those found in myths, fairy tales and elsewhere. Documentary makers often draw on archetypal narratives to give structure to a film in a way that audiences can relate to. *Roger & Me*, for example, appropriates the quest genre, using Michael Moore's attempts to track down General Motors chief Roger Smith and persuade him to come to Flint, to give the film a storyline. It's a bit of a gimmick because very early on the audience realises the quest is fruitless, but it holds the documentary together in an entertaining manner, and provides a sense of conflict and suspense.

One of the most common archetypal narratives in documentary is that of the underdog against the more powerful foe. Often it is the documentary maker who is constructed as the underdog. The more powerful foe may be an individual, but increasingly in modern documentaries it is a corporation or government organisation.

Other structures

In *Dear America*, the narrative is structured around the chronology of the Vietnam War. This film provides a useful example of the difference between the actual narrative of Vietnam and the film narrative. Troops arriving coincide with the beginning of the war. Scenes of homecoming coincide with America's withdrawal. In fact, troops were arriving and leaving throughout the war.

Key terms for discussing documentary

In order to talk about the construction of a documentary, it is useful to be familiar with a number of key terms. These are explained below.

Actuality footage

Actuality footage is footage of action as it actually occurred.

Constructed footage

Constructed footage is where the action has been performed for the purpose of being filmed. A maker of a war documentary, for example, may ask soldiers to perform certain actions for the camera.

Reconstructed footage

Reconstructed footage is where action that had occurred some time before is re-enacted for the purpose of being filmed.

Archival footage

Archival footage is footage taken from archives and inserted into a new documentary. Quite often archival footage shot for one purpose is used, or 'appropriated', for a quite different purpose.

Docudrama

A docudrama is similar to reconstructed footage, but docudramas take more liberties with what 'really occurred'. One of the most famous examples of docudrama is *Culloden*, a 'documentary' about an eighteenth-century battle between the Scots and English. There is often not much difference between docudrama and historical drama, although producers of docudramas usually make more effort to get the facts right. Makers of historical drama allow themselves much more creative licence and liberty with the facts, often inventing events and characters.

Fictional documentary

A fictional documentary is a fictional film presented as if it were a documentary. Famous examples are *The War Game*, a fictional documentary about Britain in the aftermath of a nuclear war, *Barba Kueria*, a fictional documentary in which the social roles of Aboriginal and white Australians are reversed and the hilarious *This is Spinal Tap*, about a fictional British heavy metal band.

Cinéma verité or direct documentary

Cinéma verité is a French term meaning film truth. It is a style of documentary making that tries to minimise the intervention of the film-maker. It attempts to give the impression of capturing reality as it is. It is often characterised by the lack of a narrator and 'rough' film work. Cinéma verité is discussed in more detail in the following section on the history of documentary.

History of the documentary

To understand the way in which any particular documentary is constructed, it is useful to have an overview of the development of various styles and genres of documentary. This can allow you to identify the various techniques that a documentary is drawing on and manipulating, and thus read the documentary intertextually. The diagram on the next page provides a simple outline of the history of documentary.

One of the important points illustrated in this diagram is that documentaries have always been influenced by the context in which they were produced. These influences have been both social and technological.

There are a number of patterns in the history of the documentary:

- a continuing belief in the use of the documentary as a tool to inform and educate
- a developing awareness and exploration of the potential of the documentary to entertain.

Two points need to be made. First, informing and entertaining are not necessarily separate. The history of the documentary shows a developing awareness of the power of the documentary to educate and inform in an entertaining way. Second, informing and entertaining are not innocent and ideology-free. Information and entertainment are influenced and shaped by particular attitudes. From the beginning, documentaries have been purveyors of attitudes, values and ways of thinking. Within this trend, there is a further pattern. This pattern takes the form of a conflict between:

- the use of documentaries to support the status quo, dominant ways of thinking and existing power relationships, on the one hand

and

- the use of documentaries to challenge the status quo, dominant ways of thinking and existing power relationships, on the other hand.

Early documentaries

The very earliest films of any type were documentaries. Most of these were simply brief films of everyday life, such as a train arriving at a station or workers leaving a factory. Such scenes allowed audiences to see the familiar in new ways, thus being both entertaining and educative at the same time.

As film developed, film-makers travelled the world in search of more interesting and entertaining footage and commercial public exhibitions of compilations of such footage were held. Some of the most popular subjects were:

- royal occasions such as coronations, marriages and royal visits
- wars or natural disasters
- scenes of famous places
- scenes of 'native' life in colonial nations.

Ideological issues infused the production of documentary making from the beginning. Coverage of royal occasions, for instance, was actively encouraged by the members of royal families as a form of public relations and a means of inspiring loyalty in their subjects. War reportage was often one-sided and intended to inspire patriotism in audiences. In America in the early 1900s, for example, audiences cheered scenes of

American troops preparing for battle in the Spanish–American war. In other documentaries of the same period, the portrayal of life in colonial nations was from a decidedly Eurocentric view of the world:

> The leading film-producing countries of this period were nations with colonial empires. Not surprisingly, their work reflected the attitudes that made up the colonial rationale. Coverage of 'natives' generally showed them to be charming, quaint, sometimes mysterious; generally loyal, grateful for the protection and guidance of Europeans. Europeans were benevolently interested in colourful native rituals, costumes, dance, processions. The native was encouraged to exhibit these quaint matters for the camera.

> Erik Barnouw, *Documentary: A History of the Non-fiction Film*, Oxford University Press, New York 1983, revised edition, p. 23.

Development of documentary genres and styles

Exploration documentaries
extolling the wonders and virtues of the primitive and the exotic

Early documentaries

Documentary as an instrument of state propaganda
- poetic and lyrical in style
- usually an abstract authoritative, unseen narrator
- famous examples include *Triumph of the Will* (Germany), *Night Mail* (UK)

Great events
such as coronations and royal visits

Art documentaries
- drew attention to their own construction as film
- extensive use of innovative editing and montage
- audience is encouraged to admire the artistry of the film-maker
- most famous example: *City Symphonies*

Documentaries of political advocacy
- made by small left wing groups or individuals
- critical of the status quo and exposing suffering

1920s
★ **Lack of sound**

1930s
★ **Invention of sound**
★ **Competition from feature film**
★ **Government financing of film**
★ **Totalitarianism**
★ **Socialism in the democracies (e.g. the New Deal)**

1940s
★ **Second World War**

Reconstruction and fakery were also part of the tradition of documentary making from the very beginning. In a documentary of the Boer War in South Africa, for example, the director had British soldiers dress up in the uniforms of their enemies, the Boers, in order to create the impression that he had filmed close shots of the Boers. During the Spanish–American war, the director added to his actual footage by reconstructing a naval battle using miniature ships in two-centimetre-deep water on a table top with cigar smoke to simulate explosions. Audiences were apparently prepared to accept the reconstruction as actual footage. A 1905 film, *Eruption of Mount Vesuvius*, was also faked. As Erik Barnouw put it: 'Film companies did not want to ignore catastrophes or other headline events merely because their cameraman could not get there' (p. 25).

Nature and science documentaries
famous example: Jacques Cousteau's *The Silent World*

Historical chronicles

Short film poems

Cinéma verité
● sometimes called observational documentaries
● challenged the dominant forms in terms of both subject matter and style
● subjects were often the marginalised of society (drunks, prostitutes, people with disabilities) or famous people seen in private
● subjects talking to camera
● lack of a narrator
● emphasis on actuality footage
● higher shooting-to-editing ratio

Documentaries of dissent
critical of the status quo and power figures and structures; or supportive of the marginalised

The crusading journalist and documentary maker as central figure in his or her own film

Post-modern blending of styles and genres

1950s
★ Availability of archival film
★ Lighter equipment
★ Miniaturised lenses
★ Magnification possibilities
★ Timelapse possibilities
★ Cameras capable of filming high speed action
★ Growth of television
★ Corporate promotion and sponsorship

1960s
★ Equipment more transportable
★ Wireless mikes

1980s and 1990s
★ Cheaper equipment allowing for independent and home-based film-making

The 1920s

From about 1907, documentaries were overtaken in popularity by film dramas, but in the 1920s, the documentary underwent a revival in popularity. Whereas early documentaries were little more than brief scenes, often no more than a couple of minutes in length, in the 1920s the documentary began to take the shape it has today, as a carefully created film of substantial length. In addition to this, documentary underwent a change in the nature of the subjects with which it dealt. The 1920s saw the development of two important types of documentary:

- ethnographic documentaries
- art documentaries.

Ethnographic documentaries in one way grew out of the earlier popularity of newsreels of colonial 'native' life. Whereas the earlier newsreels had provided scenes of quaint 'native' life, ethnographic documentaries attempted to explore in some detail the experience of 'primitive' peoples. This approach, rather than being one of condescending curiosity, tended to be a romanticisation of their lives. The most famous of these was *Nanook of the North*, a documentary made by the Canadian Robert Flaherty. *Nanook of the North* portrayed the lives of Inuit people before the impact of European culture. While the aim of the enterprise, to encourage an appreciation of Inuit way of life, was noble, the film involved a great deal of falsification. Much of the film, for example, centred on Inuit people hunting and killing a walrus with traditional harpoons. In reality, Nanook and his people had been using rifles to hunt for some years.

Art documentaries explored the use of film as an artistic medium. They treated a film rather like a painting, exploring the use of composition, lighting, special effects and editing to create something that was pleasing to the eye rather than informative. The most famous of these was *Berlin: Symphony of the City*. Art documentaries also performed an educative role by encouraging the audience to see the familiar in new ways. For example, in *Berlin: Symphony of a City*, the director intercut busy office scenes of frenzied telephone and typewriter activity with scenes of monkeys chattering and dogs lunging at each other. In *Only the Hours*, a film about Paris, there is a scene of a man eating a steak. The director superimposed a slaughterhouse scene on the steak.

The 1930s and 40s

In the 1930s, documentaries became tools in the hands of governments. Realising the potential of documentary to persuade, many governments established film units or financed the making of films that promoted them and their achievements. The most famous of these was *Triumph of the Will* made in Germany under the Nazis. In Britain, films were made promoting the fishing industry, the tea industry and even the work of the post office. The purpose of many of these films was to encourage people to support the work of the government and business but also to portray ordinary working people as heroes and thus encourage them to accept their role in society.

These films were not simplistic, brutal propaganda, however. Drawing on the techniques developed in the art documentaries, the films also offered audiences art and entertainment. *Night Mail*, a film about the British postal system, was accompanied by a voice-over reciting a poem by the famous poet W. H. Auden written specifically for the film. Governments realised that persuasion can be more effective if it is pleasing or entertaining to watch. The most famous example of an 'artistic' documentary serving the purposes of propaganda was *Triumph of the Will*.

At the same time as governments were using films to encourage support for the status quo, a number of film-makers were realising its potential for achieving the opposite: challenging the status quo. In America, a number of independent film-makers documented the effects of the Depression—evictions, poverty, strikes and protests.

The trend for documentaries to be used in the service of propaganda reached its height during the Second World War.

The 1950s

Three developments in the 1950s had an important impact on the nature of documentaries. First, the growth of television created a new market for documentaries and led to an upsurge in production. Television also had an important effect on the form of documentaries. Instead of being the length of feature films, they had to fit into the one hour allowed by television schedules.

Second, a range of technical innovations allowed documentary makers to film things never before possible. Some of these innovations were:

* lighter equipment
* miniaturised lenses
* magnification possibilities
* timelapse photography
* cameras capable of filming high-speed action.

These innovations led to an upsurge in nature and science documentaries, further fuelled by the growing demand from television. The development of nature documentaries as a genre also had an important ideological effect, contributing to the growth of people's awareness of environmental issues. One of the most famous nature documentaries was Jacques Cousteau's *The Silent World*, which brought the wonders of life beneath the oceans to audiences for the first time. Interestingly, *The Silent World* was only made possible by a technical innovation unconnected with film-making, the self-contained underwater breathing apparatus or scuba.

The third important development was the increase in the number of film libraries and the greater availability of archival film. This made possible the development of the compilation documentary.

The 1960s

The main development in the late 1950s and early 1960s was the development of a new style of documentary called cinéma verité or direct cinema. Tired of the style of existing documentaries, which appeared highly constructed and dependent on the film-makers interpreting the subject for the audience, some film-makers tried to develop a style of film-making that would allow the audience unmediated access to a subject. At its most extreme, this involved allowing the camera to run for hours and hours, an approach sometimes known as the fly-on-the wall technique. Cinéma verité was characterised by a lack of narration, shots that were not carefully framed and confusing soundtracks.

Of course the claim to present reality without the intervention of the film-maker was an illusion. To point to just one aspect of film-maker intervention, cinéma verité documentaries had to be edited—no-one was going to watch a ten-hour film—and as soon as the process of editing is involved, you are back in the world of construction rather than unmediated reality. The techniques of cinéma verité, however, created an air of authenticity that is still drawn on today in many documentaries in an attempt to create an aura of realism.

Since the 1960s

The main development since the 1960s has been the development of cheaper and more portable equipment which allows anyone to make a documentary. This has given rise to what is sometimes called guerrilla film-making, where documentaries are made by independent film-makers working on small budgets and supposedly representing the views of ordinary people in opposition to the views of the rich and powerful. This style of film-making is often very confrontational, involving a form of foot-in-the-door journalism where the film team intercepts a person unannounced to subject him or her to questioning. Films such as *Roger & Me* and *Kurt and Courtney* are examples of this style and would not have been not possible with the heavier and more expensive equipment of earlier eras.

Case studies

The following case studies were selected because they are very different in many ways and thus offer contrasting examples of the nature of documentaries. *Triumph of the Will* is old. *Kurt and Courtney* is relatively new. *Triumph of the Will* documents major political events. *Kurt and Courtney* is concerned with pop culture and personalities. *Triumph of the Will* is a traditional authoritative documentary in which there appears to be no film-maker. In *Kurt and Courtney*, the film-maker is a major character within the text. *Triumph of the Will* is deadly serious. *Kurt and Courtney* is very funny in places. These films have also been chosen for case studies because they are fairly easy to obtain.

The case studies are not intended primarily as texts for you to study. Rather they are intended as examples of how readings of documentaries can be constructed. You should take the ideas and ways of discussing documentaries provided in these case studies and apply them to other documentaries.

CASE STUDY

Triumph of the Will **directed by Leni Riefenstahl**

Triumph of the Will was produced in Germany in 1934 and portrays the 1934 Nuremberg Nazi Congress, a rally for members of the Nazi Party. It has been included as a case study for a number of reasons. First, it is one of the most famous documentaries ever made. It is also one of the most controversial films ever made. It has been both praised as an example of the film-maker's art and criticised as an extreme and offensive form of propaganda. Thus it raises a question for you to think about: to what extent can we admire the construction of a film while rejecting the ideologies it promotes?

Many students find *Triumph of the Will* difficult to view at first. This is because it was made over sixty years ago and uses filmic conventions very different to those you are used to. To overcome this difficulty and get the most from your study of the film, you need to approach the film in an appropriate way. If you approach it like the latest Hollywood film, expecting exciting action, a strong plot and characters you can identify with, you will be disappointed. You will learn more if you treat the film as a historical artefact, a text that reflects the context in which it was made. As part of your approach, you will also need to overcome any colour prejudice you might have, as *Triumph of the Will* is a black-and-white film.

Background and context

You will better understand *Triumph of the Will* and the way it is constructed if you have some knowledge of German society in 1934.

In the late nineteenth and early twentieth centuries, Germany was one of the most powerful nations in Europe. In 1918, however, Germany suffered a humiliating defeat in the First World War. The country was forced to disband most of its army and pay huge reparations to those who had defeated it. In the 1920s, Germany suffered horrendous inflation and then in 1929 it was hit by the Great Depression. There was widespread unemployment and poverty.

It was in this situation that Adolf Hitler came to power, promising to restore Germany's military might, create employment, rebuild the economy and restore the country's pride in itself. An essential element in Hitler's ideology was a belief in the superiority of the Aryan race to all others. Scapegoats—Jews, Gypsies, Slavs, homosexuals and communists, the mentally ill and people with disabilities, among others—were targeted for persecution and eventual extermination. *Triumph of the Will* is noticeably silent on this aspect of Nazi policy.

In 1934, when *Triumph of the Will* was made, Hitler's position was not as secure as it would later become. He had become leader of Germany as a member of a minority party and there was opposition to the Nazis, although much of this was quickly being eliminated through the use of violence and concentration camps. There were divisions within the Nazi Party itself. Some supporters wanted more radical change to society than Hitler was proposing. This was especially the case amongst the SA or

Nazi stormtroopers, a paramilitary force of thugs who had helped the Nazis gain power. Hitler knew that if he went too fast or too far with change he would lose the support of the conservative German middle classes, who were in any case nervous about the thuggish behaviour of the stormtroopers. The other group whose support Hitler wanted was the armed forces; they were nervous that they would be taken over by the stormtroopers. One of the aims of *Triumph of the Will* was to convey the idea of a Germany united behind the Nazi party and a Nazi party completely united behind Hitler.

Another important aspect of the context of the film is the nature of communications in the 1930s. We are now used to seeing our political leaders on the television set almost every night. They are familiar figures. In the 1930s, television did not exist. While most Germans were well aware of the Nazi party, they were less familiar with the individual, Adolf Hitler. Many would never have seen him and to most he was an unknown quantity. One of the other aims of *Triumph of the Will*, therefore, was to introduce Hitler, the man, to the German people.

Making of the film

The following passage describes the making of *Triumph of the Will*. It provides a useful insight into the complexity involved in the making of a documentary at this time, and illustrates the way in which images that seem natural to the audience are in fact highly constructed.

As soon as Hitler came to power in 1933, his thirty-six-year-old Minister of Popular Enlightenment and Propaganda, Joseph Goebbels, began steps to bring all media under his control. On political or racial grounds, countless workers were driven from their jobs; many went abroad. These were replaced by Nazi adherents. By October 1933 anyone with editorial duties had to be licensed by Goebbels. Proclaiming that censorship would be positive, not merely negative, he gradually took charge of all aspects of production, distribution, and exhibition.

In Germany, as in a number of countries, cine-clubs had operated outside regular rules of censorship. Goebbels abolished the distinction, decimating the cine-clubs. There would be no independent cine-club movement in the new Germany.

As a result of these sweeping moves, films in Nazi Germany began a rapid, catastrophic decline. But there was an exception: the work of one genius who—due to unusual circumstances—flourished outside the Goebbels dominion.

Leni Riefenstahl was a dancer before turning to acting, and a screen star and pin-up beauty before becoming a director. As fiction-film star and director she was especially associated with 'mountain films'—a German genre often compared to American westerns. The setting evoked heroism and virtue, and had mythic overtones. For a highly industrialized nation, the misty peaks and streams and crashing storms provided a sense of contact with primordial beginnings; the films sometimes reached back into Teutonic mythology. Among successes in which she appeared were *The Sacred Mountain* (*Die Heilige Berg*, 1926), *The White Hell of Piz Palu* (*Die Weisse Hölle von Piz Palu*, 1929), and *The Blue Light* (*Das Blaue Licht*, 1932), which she also directed.

A prominent Riefenstahl admirer was Adolf Hitler. In 1933 she received a call from him. It was a few months after he had achieved dictatorial power, and just two days before the annual rally of the National Socialist German Workers party—the Nazi party. According to her account he asked how she was getting on with the work. She asked, 'What work?' He said that months earlier, he had ordered his propaganda ministry to have her make a film about the rally. She had heard nothing of this, but he insisted she proceed, doing whatever she could. Without time to prepare, she gathered equipment and a few assistants and rushed to the rally. There a succession of bureaucratic harassments—emanating, she thought, from a Goebbels resentful at being bypassed—made the experience a nightmare, but she completed the short film *Victory of Faith (Sieg des Glaubens*, 1933), financed by the Nazi party.

Exhausted, she left for Spain for work on a new feature, but there she collapsed, spending two months in a Madrid hospital—an aftermath, she was sure, of the sufferings Goebbels had caused her. Their mutual resentment grew into a feud.

On her return to Germany, Hitler got in touch with her again. He wanted her to make a film of the 1934 party rally, which was to be the largest ever staged—announcement and demonstration, to all the world, of German rebirth. For this film she must have all necessary time to prepare, and all resources would be at her disposal.

She demurred. She suggested Walther Ruttman, creator of the famous *Berlin: Symphony of the City*, and even discussed it with Ruttman. Though he had been considered on the left politically, he was eager to do the project and drafted plans. But Hitler insisted it must be Leni Riefenstahl. According to her account, she then agreed on condition that neither Hitler nor Goebbels nor anyone else would interfere, nor even see the film until it was finished. The film appears to have been made under these terms. An ample budget was set up by the UFA studio—Universum Film Aktiengesellschaft—which also distributed the film.

She got to work. Never had there been such mobilization and deployment of resources—men and gear. Before long she had assembled a staff of 120 people, including sixteen leading cameramen, their assistants, and supporting technicians. Thirty cameras and four sound trucks would be in operation. Twenty-two automobiles and their drivers were assigned to her, along with uniformed field police. She felt they must all live together in Nuremberg, location of the rally, for constant coordination through the week of scheduled events—September 4–10, 1934. But all hotels were booked. More than a million people were expected in Nuremberg, tripling its population. Leading Nazi official Julius Streicher owned a large Nuremberg building and offered it. Making an advance inspection, she was dismayed to find scores of empty rooms without furniture, water, light, or telephone. But within forty-eight hours miracles had been performed for her—bedrooms for all her 120 people had been fully furnished; offices, conference rooms, dark rooms stood ready; a telephone switchboard had been installed; kitchen and dining hall were being equipped and staffed.

Meanwhile with relentless drive and sense of detail Leni Riefenstahl—then thirty-two years old—was plotting camera locations and movements with her staff, and the town of Nuremberg was constructing, to her specifications and on a scale without precedent, special bridges, towers, ramps. A 120-foot flagpole at the Luitpoldhain was being equipped with an electric elevator, which was to be able to take a cameraman to the top in seconds. Along Adolf Hitler Square a ramp was being built at second-floor level to allow a camera dolly to move with marching troops while photographing them from bird's eye vantage. She commandeered a fire department truck; atop its ninety-foot extension ladder, a cameraman would be able to soar over the gables and monuments of Nuremberg, high above marching troops and their banners. Other vehicles with extension ladders were put at her disposal by utility and streetcar companies.

Planning of rally events and of their film coverage went on together. On a field, huge parades of spade-carrying men—the Labor Service—were to march past Adolf Hitler, then line up in perfect order to hear his speech extolling labor. Wooden rails were laid out so that cameras would be able to photograph the men from within their ranks. A camera platform was built at the precise spot where they would give the Führer an 'eyes right' salute. Camera positions were staked out on city rooftops, on church towers, and in roadside ditches. In meeting halls cameras would peer down through skylights and up from orchestra pits. All cameramen were given elite-troop uniforms; the Chief of Staff had expressed the opinion that the presence of cameramen in civilian dress would 'mar the solemnity of the occasion.'

As crowds began to descend on Nuremberg, Riefenstahl's cameramen were rehearsing on their fantastic ladders, ramps, and towers.

....

According to her own accounts, of then and later, Riefenstahl was at this time dazzled by Hitler, though disliking many around him. And he had put her as film maker in a position unique in film history.

She did not invent the actions captured by her cameras. She saw it as her task to bring them to the screen with maximum impact.

During the week of photography she coordinated her forces with an almost maniacal drive and discipline, mirroring the atmosphere of the events themselves. Then she gave months to editing. A score in Wagnerian style was provided by Herbert Windt. The final result, *Triumph of the Will* (*Triumph des Willens*) was premiered in March 1935 and was at once hailed as a masterpiece—inspiring to some, sinister and terrifying to others. The Venice film festival gave it a top award; so did a Paris festival.

The opening credits stated:

Produced by Order of the Führer

Directed by Leni Riefenstahl

Triumph of the Will has no spoken commentary; she considered any commentator an 'enemy of film.' Verbalization of the message is left to speeches by Hitler and other Nazi leaders. But the almost physical impact of the film derives much from her choreography of images and sounds: marching men, cheers, banners, swastikas, eagles, crowds, ancient German streets and towers, folksongs, clouds, oratory, uniforms, women, children—and above all, in a series of apparitions, the Führer.

The film opens with an amazing sequence—one that makes Hitler a sort of deity descending to earth to save the German people. This sequence uses subtitles, which Riefenstahl credited to Walther Ruttman. They were, according to her account, the only part of Ruttman's proposals used in the final film. The sequence shows us a lone plane skimming over cloud tops; occasionally mists obscure it, but it re-emerges. Eventually the earth is seen: spires of Nuremberg, wrapped in mists. The shadow of the plane touches the city. Crowds are waiting, looking up. Finally the plane lands. A door opens. After a moment, Hitler appears. Deafening roars of vast crowds split the air.

The subtitles have set the stage:

On September 5
1934

20 years
after the outbreak
of the World War

16 years
after the start
of German suffering

19 months
after the beginning
of Germany's rebirth

Adolf Hitler flew
again to Nuremberg
to review the columns of his faithful followers

Triumph of the Will was considered an overwhelming propaganda success, rallying many to the Hitler cause. Some critics have felt that the role of Leni Riefenstahl in this success was unforgivable. But it is also pointed out that no film has been more widely used by opposition forces. Every nation ultimately arrayed against Hitler used huge segments of *Triumph of the Will* in its own propaganda films; nothing else depicted so vividly the demoniac nature of the Hitler leadership, and the scarcely human discipline supporting it. Riefenstahl's cameras did not lie; they told a story that has never lost its power to chill the marrow.

Erik Barnouw, *Documentary: A History of the Non-fiction Film*,
Oxford University Press, New York 1983, pp. 100–5.

Synopsis of *Triumph of the Will*

1. Scene 1: Arrival in Nuremberg (10:30 mins.)
   A. Main titles, in four separate shots, here in English translation
      1 *Triumph of the Will*
      2 The Documentary Film of the Reich's Party Congress 1934
      3 Produced by Orders of the Führer
      4 Created by Leni Riefenstahl
   B. Historical background, in four rolling titles, in four separate shots, here in English translation.
      1. On September 5, 1934, 20 years after the outbreak of the world war
      2. 16 years after the beginning of our suffering
      3. 16 months after the beginning of the German renaissance
      4. Adolf Hitler flew to Nuremberg again to review the columns of his faithful followers
   C. The *Führer's* flight to Nuremberg
   D. Motorcade from airport to city
   E. Arrival at hotel
2. Scene 2: Band Concert and Rally (2:54 mins.)
   A. Hitler reviews band concert and rally outside hotel
3. Scene 3: Nuremberg at Sleep, Play, Work (10:27 mins.)
   A. The sleeping city
   B. The tent city of soldiers and workers
   C. The folk parade
   D. Troop review
4. Scene 4: First Party Congress (9:30 mins.)
   A. Greeting of delegates by Rudolf Hess
   B. Remarks by 12 Nazi Party leaders
5. Scene 5: Labor Service Rally (7:03 mins.)
   A. Konstantin Hierl introduces Hitler
   B. Labor service ceremony of loyalty
   C. Hitler addresses workers
6. Scene 6: Storm Troopers Rally (3:36 mins.)
   A. Viktor Lutze addresses storm troopers
   B. Fireworks display
7. Scene 7: Youth Rally (10:04 mins.)
   A. Entrance of Hitler and party officials
   B. Address by Baldur von Schirach
   C. Address by Hitler
   D. Hitler's review of youth groups and departure
8. Scene 8: Military and Cavalry Review (1:28 mins.)
   A. Hitler and military officials review display of military, artillery, and cavalry
9. Scene 9: Twilight Rally (8:14 mins.)
   A. Twilight parade of flag bearers
   B. Hitler's address to assembled troops
   C. Parade of flags, banners, standard

10. Scene 10: Tribute to War Dead (11:17 mins.)
    A. Hitler, Lutze, and Himmler pay tribute at war memorial
    B. Hitler reviews parade of storm troopers
    C. Lutze and Hitler address the storm troopers
    D. Consecration of flags ceremony
11. Scene 11: Military Parade (18:04 mins.)
    A. Hitler and military and party officials review lengthy parade of troops leaving Nuremberg
12. Scene 12: Closing Party Congress (15:10 mins.)
    A. Entrance of party officials and standard bearers
    B. Hitler's address to congress
    C. Hess' closing remarks
    D. Marching soldiers
    E. Closing titles (here in English translation)
       1. *Triumph of the Will*
       2. The End

R. M. Barsam, *Filmguide to Triumph of the Will*. Indiana University Press, 1975, pp. 5–7.

Activity

Discuss how the opening titles position the audience.

Elements of construction
Characterisation–Adolf Hitler

The portrayal of Hitler in the film is carefully constructed. Although the opening shots of the aeroplane descending from the clouds portray Hitler as almost a deity, in the first shots the audience sees of him he appears rather shy and embarrassed about the fanfare of his arrival. The following shots of Hitler are almost in the form of glimpses. The film audience sees him only from the back or the side. These shots are accompanied by crowd shots of people straining to catch a glimpse of Hitler. There are also numerous shots of people gazing in awe at Hitler, but at this stage of the film, a Hitler whom the film audience has not yet seen in full.

The effect of this construction is to portray Hitler as both ordinary and extraordinary. In the actual shots of Hitler himself, fleeting as they are, Hitler comes across as a fairly ordinary person, almost surprised at the fanfare surrounding him. The shots of people straining to catch a glimpse of him or staring in awe at a figure the audience has not yet fully seen construct him as extraordinary because he is portrayed as an object of the gaze, an object of desire and a charismatic figure. Hitler is constructed as extraordinary not in himself as a person, but because of what he represents, a sense of hope for the German people.

As the film progresses, however, the portrayal of Hitler changes. From an apparently diffident, half-seen figure, he emerges in full and in close-up at the Hitler

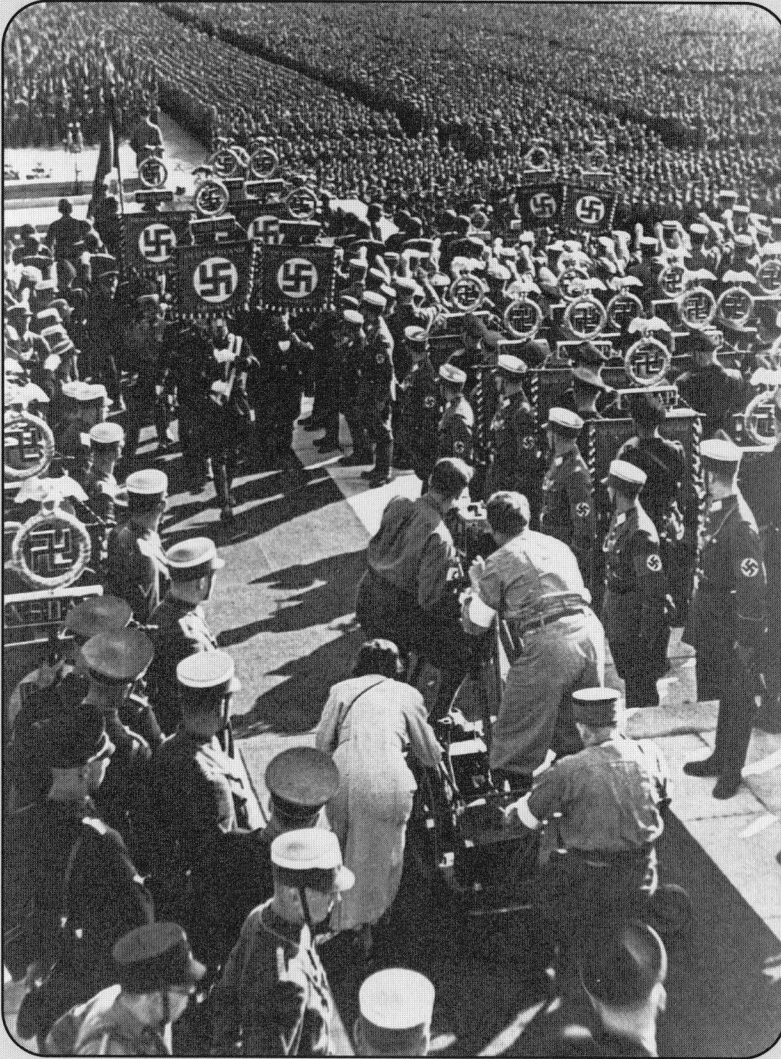

Filming *Triumph of the Will*

youth rally in scene 7. From this point on, there is much more emphasis on Hitler being seen in full. There are many low-angle shots that are designed to construct him as a figure of awe. There are also many high-angle shots of him as a fairly insignificant figure in a much larger crowd, emphasising his role as an embodiment of the people as a whole.

In summary, then, there are two construct-ions of Hitler at work:

- Hitler as a charismatic individual
- Hitler as an instrument or embodiment of a much larger force— the new spirit of the German people.

The concept of Hitler as embodiment of the German people is reinforced throughout the film in other ways. In scene 5, for example, the Labor Service rally, the audience sees the image of Hitler dissolve into an image of labor workers. This suggests a shared identity.

Film technique

Rather than examining the film technique in *Triumph of the Will* by listing the techniques themselves, it is more useful to examine it through the ideas all the various techniques work together to suggest.

Tradition

Although Nazism was actually a radically new ideology, *Triumph of the Will* associates Hitler and the Nazis with German history and tradition. This theme is established in the opening shot of the film, which presents a statue of the German imperial eagle, a traditional symbol used by German monarchs before 1918.

The emphasis on history and tradition is further accented in the scenes of Hitler's entry into Nuremberg by the use of cutaways to historic buildings and statues. As well, the folk parade presenting crowds of people in traditional national costume is strategically placed between the tent city scenes and the review of the troops. This juxtaposition tempers the modern militaristic overtones of the scenes with scenes that reach back into a more stable peaceful time.

The emphasis on tradition is further reinforced by a number of other cutaways throughout the film to people, especially women, dressed in traditional costume. In scene 11, the military parade, the idea that there is continuity between tradition and Nazism is emphasised by shots framed through the windows and arches of historic buildings.

Unity

The idea that Hitler and the Nazis are the embodiment and instruments of the German nation is portrayed by the use of techniques that emphasise unity and solidarity. One of the slogans of Nazism was 'Ein Volk, Ein Reich, Ein Führer' (one people, one empire, one leader). This idea of one people united together is most strongly emphasised by the domination of the film by crowd shots, particularly crowd shots of people all doing the same thing—standing in the same way, looking in the same direction, marching in step in the same direction, making the same gestures.

The scene of labour workers calling out which part of Germany they have come from plays an especially important role in communicating the idea that all parts of Germany are united together in a common cause. The later parts of the film are dominated by seemingly endless shots of soldiers marching. It is not just the actual appearance of the crowds, but the way the shots of the crowds are constructed that makes them seem endless.

Aspects of construction include:

* tracking shots, where the camera moves along the front of the crowd thus drawing attention to its size—this technique is especially noticeable in the tracking shot of the crowd in the stadium in scene 7D of the Hitler Youth rally
* pans, where the camera pans across a crowd, emphasising its size—a good example can be found in scene 7, the Hitler Youth rally
* wide-angle line shots, where the audience is presented with a line of individuals all performing the same action—examples are the soldiers in scene 1D, the motorcade, and the drummers in scene 7, the Youth Rally.

Another important way in which the idea of unity and oneness is communicated is through the film's extensive use of dissolves. Frequently images dissolve into each other, suggesting a connection and unity between the images. Examples include:

* the dissolve of the image of Hitler into the image of the labour workers
* the final dissolve where the swastika dissolves into an image of soldiers seeming to march on clouds into the future.

Adolf Hitler and
Leni Riefenstahl
on location

Productivity and abundance

A number of scenes are clearly designed to associate Nazism with abundance, plenty
and health. This is achieved through scenes of firewood-throwing, stoking fires,
eating and drinking, spooning pots of food and food preparation.

Youth

As well as the portrayal of young people in the tent city scenes and the youth rally,
the film makes frequent use of cutaways to children in crowds. There are almost no
shots of old people in this film. The emphasis on youth in the film is not only
obviously designed to appeal to the German people's desire for a better future for
their children, but also works on a more general level because young people are
traditional signifiers of the future. The Nazi party is thereby portrayed as the party of
the future.

Athleticism, physical strength and masculinity

The fetishisation of the male body was an ideology characteristic of many fascist
regimes of the 1930s and of the work of Leni Riefenstahl. The emphasis on
athleticism and physical strength is most evident in the tent city scenes where there
are scenes of:
* barechested males
* wrestling
* men throwing large pieces of timber
* men pulling a cart loaded with firewood.

Athleticism and physical strength are traditionally associated with masculinity. The traditional conception of masculinity is further emphasised in the number of shots constructed to draw attention to male profiles, chins and eyes gazing firmly into the distance.

Militarism

Athleticism and physical strength are often closely associated with militarism. The association of Nazism with militarism is reinforced by the frequent shots of the military or others in military-like attire, including Hitler himself.

Your response to the film

Many students find *Triumph of the Will* difficult to view at first. In considering your response to the film, you need to consider two important factors:

• your context
• the filmic conventions you are familiar with.

Your context

Quite clearly you are not a member of the audience this film was originally made for. You have not experienced the things that the members of that audience had. Therefore the aspects of the film that might have struck a chord with the German people of the 1930s quite possibly have no effect on you.

A second aspect of your context is that you have knowledge of things that the members of the German audience of the 1930s do not. You know something of the course of history since 1934—the subsequent actions of Hitler and the Nazis and the Second World War. This knowledge may colour your view of the film and encourage you to read the film resistantly, in complete contrast to the way in which Leni Riefenstahl intended it to be read.

Filmic conventions

Many students immediately assume that one of the reasons they find *Triumph of the Will* difficult to watch is because it is in black and white. This is too easy and too shallow a response. Modern audiences, including teenagers, do not really have a problem with a film that is not in colour. One of the most successful films of the late 1990s was *Schindler's List* which was made almost entirely in black and white.

The real problem modern audiences have with *Triumph of the Will* is its narrative structure. First, compared with most modern films, including documentaries, *Triumph of the Will* does not tell a story in the way that modern audiences are used to. There is no central problem or conflict to be resolved. There is no real focaliser, a character with whom modern audiences can identify with and accompany on the filmic journey, not even in the form of a voice-over narrator.

Second, because modern audiences have grown up in a film culture, they have learnt to read visual information very quickly. In contrast to this, many of the scenes in *Triumph of the Will* are too long for the taste of modern audiences.

11

Activities

Discuss the following questions.

1 In what ways did your context and your familiarity with certain film conventions influence your response to *Triumph of the Will*?

2 How might the narrative construction of *Triumph of the Will* have been different if it had been made in 2002?

CASE STUDY

12

Kurt and Courtney, 1998, directed by Nick Broomfield, distributed by Roadshow Entertainment

Kurt and Courtney is supposedly a tribute to rock star Kurt Cobain and an investigation into conspiracy theories surrounding his death. Cobain's death was officially attributed to suicide, but some people claim that Cobain was murdered, with some of the more outlandish theories implicating his wife Courtney Love.

Characterisation
Kurt Cobain

The first thing to note about the characterisation of Kurt Cobain in this film is how little footage there is of Cobain the rock star himself. Apart from two brief excerpts (one-and-a-half minutes out of a total film time of ninety-seven minutes) from an interview with him at the height of his fame, the characterisation of Cobain relies almost entirely on:

• comments by Broomfield
• recordings, photos and videos of Cobain as a child or teenager
• comments by other people.

Broomfield introduces Cobain with the words 'Kurt Cobain was an icon, an inspiration to millions'. He also describes him as a 'folk hero' and 'almost a god in his own right'. But Broomfield also says that despite his fame, Cobain 'remained true to his roots'. This is the key element in the portrayal of Cobain in this film.

This portrayal of Cobain as true to his roots is reinforced by the interview excerpt Broomfield has chosen for inclusion at this point in the film. Here Cobain states that money 'can't buy happiness' and speaks of the joy of finding a treasure in a second-hand store being far more important than the joys associated with fame and wealth. Thus the introductory scenes construct Cobain as an ordinary person, who, despite his celebrity, is uninterested in the trappings of success. This characterisation:

• sets up a contrast between Cobain and Courtney Love
• establishes Cobain as a sympathetic character, someone to whom the general public can relate: even though he was, according to the film, a gifted musician, he was at heart a simple, ordinary person just like them.

Remaining close to one's roots and rejecting the trappings of fame was an important part of the ideology associated with punk music, which grew out of a rejection of the glamour and hype associated with rock music in the 1970s and 1980s. It is also likely to appeal to the general public because it implies that the simple pleasures of our own lives are more desirable than the pleasures that come with fame and wealth.

The idea of Cobain as a simple, ordinary person is further reinforced by the inclusion of the recordings, photos and videos of him as a child or teenager. The images show him in ordinary surroundings, participating in the sorts of activities many 'ordinary' families participate in. The images of Cobain as a child or teenager are used to frame the film as a whole; they are among the first and last images with which the audience is presented. The home video used at the end, with its outdoor setting and the presence of children playing around Cobain, is especially important in reinforcing the impression of him as an innocent, unspoiled person, if somewhat isolated.

The comments by those interviewed also construct Cobain largely as a simple person, uninterested in the trappings of fame and success. His friend Alice Wheeler, for example, is shown saying 'he was embarrassed by fame and the trappings of fame' and talks about his embarrassment at travelling with her in a limousine. Amy, who claimed to know Kurt and Courtney, says that Kurt was 'very nice … really quiet … Happy not to be the centre of attention'.

Kurt Cobain

If you read the characterisation of Cobain intertextually, you notice that it is very similar to the way many other celebrities who have died at a relatively young age are often presented. There are similar discourses—ways of speaking and writing about a subject—in texts about rock stars such as Jimi Hendrix, Jim Morrison, Janis Joplin and Michael Hutchence; actors such as Marilyn Monroe, River Phoenix and Andy Kaufman; and, of course, the greatest celebrity of the late twentieth century, Princess Diana. There are a number of aspects to this discourse.

One aspect is a sense of loss. While this is similar to the personal sense of loss we all feel at the death of a loved one, with celebrities there is a stronger sense of the world as a whole having lost something special and precious, not just the celebrity as a person, but the contributions to society, music or entertainment the celebrity would have made had he or she lived. The opening of *Kurt and Courtney* participates very strongly in this discourse.

Accompanying this sense of loss is a desire to preserve the memory of the dead person. Surf the Internet and you'll find many shrines and memorials to dead celebrities, even one to the strange fringe rocker El Duce who appears in *Kurt and Courtney*. The beginning and ending of Broomfield's documentary present it as in part a tribute to the memory of Kurt Cobain.

A third feature of the discourse, one that seems to grow naturally out of the first two, is often described as hagiography or sanctification, both of which mean to make someone out to be a saint. While there is always a tendency when people die to emphasise their good qualities, with celebrities, especially young ones, this tendency is stronger, often to the point, some would argue, of distorting reality.

> Four years ago this month Kurt Cobain joined the elite crew of Dead Celebrities Who Can Do No Wrong. We Americans just love stars who die young enough to leave a good-looking corpse which might explain why all dead stars are immortalized on film sooner or later.
>
> Jacqui Kramer, 'Documentary Asks: Who Killed Kurt Cobain', *From Script to Screen*, 1998.

A common way of portraying artists, such as painters, writers and musicians, who have died young is as gifted but tortured souls unable to cope with the harshness of the world—'too good for this world', as the saying goes. It is this attitude, it can be argued, that the film finally takes to the death of Cobain: dead because he wished to escape the pressures associated with fame and success, pressures personified in the film in the figure of Courtney Love.

A fourth common feature of the discourse governing celebrities who have died young is curiosity, a desire to find out more about their lives, often as a means of understanding why they died. This aspect of the discourse seems to be a response to the fact that the early death of a celebrity touches a raw nerve within our culture. In a culture that teaches us to admire and aspire to success, fame and wealth, the death of someone who appears to 'have it all' seems inexplicable and threatens to expose these values as false. This apparent contradiction between the values we are taught and the reality we see in people's lives, often leads us to want to find answers: why would someone who is successful and has it all want to kill himself or be so careless with his own life as to allow himself to die?

One of the ways of answering these questions is to seek explanations in the form of conspiracy theories and scapegoats. Conspiracy theories have provided a profitable goldmine for writers and film-makers; the World Wide Web is full of conspiracy theories concerning the deaths of Marilyn Monroe, President Kennedy, Jimi Hendrix, Princess Diana, Elvis Presley—probably every celebrity who died young. Conspiracy theories and scapegoats can be quite useful ways of dealing with the death of celebrities because if someone else can be found responsible for the death, then it means that we don't have to revise our positive view of the celebrity, nor do we have to question the ideas taught by our culture that success, fame and wealth are the keys to the good life.

Broomfield draws on this discourse early in the documentary when, after presenting the news footage of Cobain's death, he says 'many people couldn't believe he took his own life' and that as a result 'I travelled up to Seattle to find out more'.

Skipping very quickly over the details of Cobain's early life, Broomfield quickly moves onto an exploration of the conspiracy theories surrounding Cobain's death which become the central focus of his film for the first hour. Broomfield eventually dismisses the conspiracy theories and the idea that Cobain was murdered, but he offers the audience a scapegoat for Cobain's death in the form of Love by creating the impression in some places that she actually drove him to suicide. This verdict allows Broomfield and the audience to preserve the saintly character of Cobain intact, rather than considering the alternative—that he was a weak, ill, disturbed or selfish person who showed no concern for his wife and daughter in taking his own life.

Pointing to the archetypal construction of Cobain by Broomfield is not meant to suggest that Broomfield has cynically copied existing ways of portraying dead celebrities. Rather it is meant to suggest that Broomfield has, probably subconsciously, simply slotted Cobain into certain existing ways of thinking made available to Broomfield by his culture. It is also meant to suggest that the characterisation of Cobain in this film reflects and promotes a set of attitudes not just about Cobain, but also about celebrities and artists in general.

The dominant image of Cobain conveyed by the film as an ordinary nice guy is contradicted by the tape recording of him threatening a journalist. Broomfield's response to this is interesting. He describes it as 'disturbing' and claims that Cobain sounded 'psychotic and crazed'. The recording is, not surprisingly, accompanied by a photo of Cobain looking psychotic and crazed. It can be argued that Broomfield glosses over this possible contradiction by presenting it as an out-of-character episode, rather than evidence that his portrayal of Cobain and his relationship with Love as dysfunctional may not be all that accurate. The recording can actually be read against the grain of Broomfield's film, as evidence of Cobain's closeness to Love and his desire to protect her, and that he too succumbed to the power mania accompanying wealth and fame.

Despite this contradiction within the film, the overall impression of Cobain as innocent and ordinary is important in setting up a contrast between him and Love who is portrayed as the very opposite.

Activities

1. Discuss to what extent you agree that the film presents a sanctified image of Cobain.
2. How convincing do you find the film's portrayal of Cobain? In answering this, discuss the factors affecting your response, such as pre-existing knowledge and values, as well as the material in the film itself.
3. Following is an article from the World Wide Web that criticises people's attitudes to the death of celebrities. Discuss the extent to which you agree with the views put forward.

On Dead Celebrities and their Fans

It just has to be said.

JFK Jr.* was not an important man. He was the son of an important man, but that doesn't make him someone innately worthy of reverence. Princess Diana just stood around looking good and being famous. True, sometimes she did it for charity, but for all her lip service, how many sandwiches did she make for the poor?

I have this small problem with dead celebrities, or more precisely, with their fans. Someone famous kicks the bucket and the media (and the gullible public) turns them into a saint. They moan about the loss to society now that this famous and attractive person is gone, how valuable they were to us all and all the good things they did …

Such as?

John F. Kennedy was very important to the U.S., and his death was a major tragedy. His son's death is not. It's a tragedy for the family, a very *personal* loss. Let's face the simple fact that JFK Jr. is not his father. We haven't lost an important political figure, a national leader. We've lost hours of news time devoted to nothing but family home movies mixed with sappy music. There was no 'death of potential'—he wasn't a young political ingenue ready to rebuild his father's dreams of Camelot, he was a middle aged playboy who'd turned away from the family business of politics and who was trying very hard to make a go at magazine publishing.

This is not to say he was worthless, but how was his life worth more than the unnamed young man shot in the street the same day? Because he was rich, attractive, and famous, his death is a loss we should all feel, says the media. When it's all added up though, why is his contribution to society—being the son of a famous man—worth more than anyone else?

'But Princess Diana did lots of charity work! She campaigned to get land mines outlawed, yeah!'

And for that, let's go tell Mother Theresa that her sainthood will have to be delayed. She got in there and worked with the poor face to face, got her hands dirty and got personal, but Princess Diana had to endure those long charity dinners and had to wear those trendy little ribbons.

I'm happy that the woman did something good for society, that she used her position to do some good. Everyday people who put in a holiday at a homeless shelter or send money to third world children do as much, however. Diana wasn't going to usher in a new era of peace on earth and land mine bans.

They were famous, now they're worm food. Let their deeds speak for themselves, and stop trying to make them something they're not—important.

Kristen Leigh 2000, 'On Dead Celebrities and Their Fans', *Paper Tigers*, www.paper-tigers.org/life/kv-celeb.html

* J. F. K. Jr was John F. Kennedy Junior, the son of President Kennedy who was assassinated in 1963. J. F. K. Jr died in a light aeroplane crash in 1999. His death received extensive publicity.

12

Courtney Love

The general impression of Love promoted by the film is of a violent, manipulative, ambitious figure who will stop at nothing, including using others, in pursuit of success, fame and wealth. As with Cobain, however, the characterisation of Courtney Love is achieved largely through the opinions of other people, in other words through what you are told about her, rather than what you see yourselves. Amy, for example, describes Love as 'a harpie' and 'a vampire of sorts'. Love's former boyfriend Rozz Rezabeck portrays her as attempting to control and manipulate him and his career for her own purposes. He states that she believed the 'only way to achieve stardom was through a man' and that if he and Love had stayed together he 'would have ended up like Kurt, shoving a ... gun down my throat'. The nanny employed by Cobain and Love states that 'she [Love] just totally controlled him' and that 'if he wasn't murdered he was driven to murdering himself'.

Courtney Love

The worst impression of Love is created in the extensive first interview with her father, Hank Harrison, who emphasises her violence and manipulative nature. In this interview, the fact that it is her father talking seems to add weight and credibility to this characterisation of Love. Harrison's credibility is undermined later in the film, but it is arguable that by this time considerable damage has been done to Love's reputation in the eyes of the audience.

The only times the audience sees Love herself is in an interview at the Academy Awards, an interview with her on the *Today* show and at the end, where she is briefly interviewed by Broomfield. In all of these interviews she is unwilling to discuss aspects of her past, but her behaviour in these segments hardly seems to support the impression created of her in the rest of the film.

The final thirty minutes of the film, after the conspiracy theory has run out of steam, is devoted to portraying Love as someone who seeks to influence and control media representations of her and Kurt and who threatens and attacks journalists. As evidence, Broomfield describes her attack on *Vanity Fair* writer Lynn Hirschberg, whom Broomfield describes as a 'respected and esteemed writer'. What Broomfield fails to mention is that Hirschberg's article was a vicious character assassination of Love (see Like to know more? on page 110) and that its claims that Love had been taking drugs while pregnant with their child Frances led to attempts to take the child away from its parents. He also provides an interview with writer Victoria Clarke, who describes Love physically attacking her.

12

As with Cobain, if you read the characterisation of Love intertextually, you will find it reflects a number of pre-existing discourses.

One is the discourse of iconoclasm. Iconoclasm literally means the smashing of idols. Alongside our culture's tendency to idolise celebrities lies a desire to bring them down, 'to cut down the tall poppies'. Some writers and film-makers, and some readers, like to expose the foibles and faults of celebrities. This may be because they want to reject the idolatry that seems to accompany the cult of celebrity and want to believe that celebrities are no better and perhaps worse than ordinary people. Interestingly, hagiography seems to be applied to dead celebrities and iconoclasm to live ones. Does our culture prefer its celebrities dead?

Broomfield can also be read as constructing Love within the archetypal role of the evil manipulative woman who bewitches a male and uses him as a means of rising to the top. At the very least, he constructs Love in a way that allows audiences to slot her into this pre-existing category. Female characters who fit within this category are quite common in soap operas and romance novels. Some fans and sections of the media often presented Beatle John Lennon's second wife Yoko Ono in this way.

This stereotype can be read as an extremely patriarchal, anti-female set of attitudes which seek to explain a woman's success in terms of trickery and guile, rather than accepting that it may be her own talent that gave her success. In relation to Love's attempts to stop production of the film, it is worth asking whether most people being accused of being complicit in the death of their spouse would not try to do the same thing.

Some reviewers have argued that the film's attempts to blacken the reputation of Love are so over-the-top and unconvincing that they have the reverse effect of encouraging sympathy for Love.

> [Broomfield's] film is so unprofessional and so lacking in proportion, though, that you can't help siding with Love—whatever her defects and excesses—and discounting her accusers.
>
> Edward Gurhmann, 'Cobain Film a Hatchet Job on Love', *San Francisco Chronicle*, 27 February 1998.

> Unfortunately for Broomfield, most viewers are likely to see it as more a one-sided rip job on Love. She may not be a saint, and may even be as manipulative as she is portrayed, but even Love deserves a little more objectivity than Broomfield brings to the film.
>
> Craig Marine, 'Kurt and Courtney', *San Francisco Examiner*, 27 February 1998.

Clearly it is possible to create a very different reading of Love to the one the film seems to be encouraging. It is possible to feel sympathy for her because of her troubled childhood and her apparently crazy father, to admire her for the success she has achieved and to see her as the victim of unsubstantiated accusations by a bunch of unreliable lowlifes and crazies whose views are given credence by a biased film-maker in search of a sensational celebrity-bashing story.

Activities

1. Discuss to what extent you think the above discussion of the portrayal of Love in the film is too kind to Love.
2. Discuss whether the desire of some people to find fault with celebrities is just nasty jealousy or a healthy scepticism.

The 'witnesses'

A key issue in determining your response to Cobain and Love in this film is your response to the witnesses. Broomfield has been accused by a number of reviewers of being very selective in his choice of interviewees.

> Broomfield sticks to interviewing people who knew Love years ago and have little good to say about her.
>
> Gina Arnold, 'Love Kurts', *Metro*, 5–11 March 1998.

> If people don't have something nice to say about Courtney Love, you can bet Broomfield found them.
>
> Richard Harrington, *Washington Post*, 17 July 1998.

> … what puzzles me is how he didn't even try to interview members of Nirvana and Hole—equally troubling is the omission of his interview with legit local scenesters Jack Endino and Dawn Anderson. Says Anderson, 'Neither one of us said anything inflammatory about Courtney, so I guess he wasn't interested'.
>
> Claire Dederer, 'Love, among the Ruins', *Seattle Weekly*, 2–8 April 1998.

Another issue is the credibility of the interviewees.

> The rest of the 'cast' of deranged druggies, star-mad groupies, self-promoting mythomaniacs and plain vindictive liars are wholly unreliable witnesses … Topping all of them is Courtney Love's avaricious old man, author of a bestseller accusing his own daughter. Asked if he used Dobermanns to discipline her as a child, he replies, 'No—it was pitbulls'.
>
> Alexander Walker, *Associated Newspapers Ltd*, 1 July 1998.

> Frankly the film's conspiracy supporters are not what you would call real believable. In fact, most of them could star in a 'Partnership For a Drug-Free America' campaign.
>
> Jacqui Kramer, 'Documentary Asks: Who Killed Kurt Cobain', *From Script to Screen*, 1998.

> Unfortunately for Broomfield, the people he talks to in the movie, including Love's father and a private eye who is obsessed with the murder angle, come across as paranoid conspiracy theorists at best and just plain weird at worst.
>
> Craig Marine, 'Kurt and Courtney', *San Francisco Examiner*, 27 February 1998.

Activities

1 Discus how fair it is to see many of the witnesses as unreliable.
2 Discuss to what extent this view simply represents prejudice against people who do not conform to our society's definition of normal?

Nick Broomfield

Perhaps the main character in this film is neither Kurt nor Courtney but Nick Broomfield himself. In fact some reviewers suggested that the film should be called *Nick and Courtney*. In many ways, *Kurt and Courtney* can be read as a film about Nick Broomfield, the hero on a quest to discover the truth. In this respect, *Kurt and Courtney* reflects the 1980s trend in documentaries to centre the crusading guerrilla journalist as hero of his own film, a trend also evident in Michael Moore's *Roger & Me*.

Broomfield's portrayal of himself in *Kurt and Courtney*, and indeed in most of his films, seems almost deliberately constructed to be as different as possible to the slick professional presenters from television current affairs. Broomfield presents himself as ordinary and somewhat naïve: his speech is often slow and hesitant as if he is thinking through things on the spot and making up his questions as he goes; it is characterised by the use of such phrases as 'So aaah ...', 'You know', 'You're kidding' and 'Reaallly'. His representation of himself as an ordinary person is especially emphasised at the ACLU dinner towards the end of the film where he portrays himself as overawed, stating that he was 'taken aback by the whole occasion'. In addition to this, his appearance is not particularly well-groomed and his clothing is casual. He is shown with his own sound equipment doing his own interviewing and recording.

Nick Broomfield

This manner of presentation has a number of effects.

- First, it constructs Broomfield as the representative of the viewer, an unsophisticated person trying to figure out a complex and bizarre set of events.
- Second, it enhances the contrast and therefore the conflict between Broomfield and Love: he is the poor film-maker under threat from powerful figures and powerful forces. Related to the construction of this persona is the fact that

Broomfield presents himself as commencing the film without any preconceptions or biases. At one point he says, 'I have no angle' and, 'I was just trying to find my way through'. This is a point Broomfield has also emphasised in a number of interviews about the film.

There are a number of questions about Broomfield's representation of himself. Rather than an ordinary naïve stranger in a strange land, Broomfield is in fact a highly experienced and sophisticated film-maker who has made a career of exploring the more bizarre aspects of American society and the lives of celebrities. In this light, his claim about being taken aback by the ACLU dinner is pretty hard to take.

Broomfield's naïve persona can be seen as a way of excusing or glossing over some of the questionable aspects of his film-making practices in *Kurt and Courtney*, and especially his choice of subjects and the people to whom, by placing them on film, he gives credibility. Many of his subjects were clearly under the influence of drugs, a fact Broomfield admitted in an interview. Especially questionable is his association with the stalkerazzis Al and Jack and the rock singer El Duce.

> There's also a burly, tattooed musician called 'El Duce' who appears drunk, flips the bird at the camera and claims with a psychotic leer that Love offered him '50 grand to whack Kurt Cobain'. Broomfield paid the man $100 for that interview—a fact he acknowledged in a recent interview but doesn't include in his film.
>
> Edward Gunthmann, 'Cobain Film a Hatchet Job on Courtney',
> *San Francisco Chronicle*, 27 February 1998.

Rather than seeing Broomfield as the little guy at the mercy of more powerful people, it is possible to read him as a participant in the media industry which seeks to make money out of exploiting the public's curiosity in the lives of the rich and famous and its gullibility towards conspiracy theories.

Activity

Discuss whether you think the above discussion is too critical of Nick Broomfield.

Narrative structure

Kurt and Courtney is held together by a number of narrative threads. The first is the investigation into the truth about the death of Cobain. The investigation as a journey to find the truth is portrayed metaphorically through the punctuation of the film, with shots looking through the windscreen of a travelling car carrying Broomfield and his camera operator. The central character in this narrative is Broomfield himself in the role of investigator. The central question driving this narrative is, of course, 'How did Kurt Cobain really die and who was responsible?'

This investigation narrative is essentially divided in two. In the first hour of the film, the 'evidence' supporting the conspiracy theories is presented in a way that creates the impression that there might be some truth to the theories. In the final thirty minutes of the film, evidence is presented that tends to undermine this view and encourage the audience to discount the possibility that Cobain was murdered.

The highly contrived nature of this structure can be seen in the film's treatment of evidence by Tom Grant, the private detective. Early in the documentary, Grant is shown making the claim that Cobain would not have been able to shoot himself given the amount of heroin he had injected. This claim is allowed to stand unchallenged for some time and is instrumental in giving weight to the conspiracy theories.

The turning point in the investigation narrative is some time later when Broomfield presents the opinion of a British doctor that it would indeed have been possible for Cobain to shoot himself with that amount of heroin. This effectively disposes of the credibility of Tom Grant's claims and the possibility of suspicion of murder recedes from here. Broomfield underscores this with his voice-over comment 'I no longer believed in the conspiracy theories'. What is important to note, however, is the structuring of these claims. At the time of editing the documentary, Broomfield would have been in possession of the doctor's opinion—but he does not let the audience in on this straight away, letting Grant's opinion stand for some time. Presenting the doctor's opinion immediately after Grant's claims would have destroyed the investigative journey narrative.

A similar strategy in Broomfield's technique is the way other witnesses are treated. Witnesses such as Hank Harrison, Courtney's father and Amy, the 'friend' of Kurt and Courtney, are treated with some credibility in the first hour, but in the last section have their credibility undermined. Amy, who claimed to be friends with Kurt and Courtney, is unable to produce the photos she said would verify her claim. Hank Harrison, who appears a reasonable man in the first part of the film, comes across as vindictive, aggressive, slightly off-balance and bent on pursuing publicity himself in the interview in the second part.

Closely connected with this investigation narrative is the narrative provided by the conflict between Broomfield's attempts to uncover the truth and the attempts by others, most noticeably Love, to stop the film being made. This can be called the film-making narrative, the central question being whether Broomfield will be prevented from making the film he wishes to make. To keep this film-making narrative in the forefront of the audience's mind, the film is punctuated by voice-overs of Broomfield describing the music he would like to have included at particular points but was prevented from doing so, and explanations of the attempts to stop the film and shots of Broomfield discussing these attempts on the telephone. The shots of Broomfield on the telephone are especially interesting because, although the audience is permitted to hear the voice on the other end of the line, the audience is never told to whom Broomfield is speaking, or their role. The effect is to create a sense of mysterious but powerful dark forces working against the innocent Broomfield.

The central conflict established through this storyline is between Broomfield as pursuer of the truth and Love as hider of the truth. This second, film-making, narrative thread comes to be the dominant one in the final thirty minutes of the film, after the credibility of the conspiracy theories and their supporters collapses. This narrative draws on the archetypal conflict between the small powerless person and the large powerful person, the audience naturally being drawn to the side of the underdog. It reaches its climax at the ACLU dinner with Love at centre stage and Broomfield portrayed as a marginalised outsider who attempts to grab some attention and is bustled off.

The other narrative conflict around which the film centres is that between Love and Cobain. Cobain is presented as the innocent genius true to his roots, as an ordinary person, and Love as a manipulative grasping pursuer of success, fame and wealth.

Another important feature to note about the narrative structure is the use of Kurt's Aunt Mari, perhaps one of the few 'normal' people in the whole film, as a framing device. The framing device constructs Kurt as a normal person caught up in a weird world.

Filmic technique

An important part of the film language at work in *Kurt and Courtney* is Broomfield constructing himself as the naïve, ordinary 'little' person. Related to this is the way in which Broomfield actually shows the processes of film-making at work. There are many shots in *Kurt and Courtney* that would normally have been left on the cutting room floor: Broomfield blundering into the wrong apartment at one point, Amy kissing him on their second meeting, the sound of him telling the camera person where to point the camera at their first meeting with Hank Harrison, a shot of Jack the stalkerazzi buying soda pop from a vending machine. The effect of this is to portray Broomfield as a bit of an amateur rather than a slick professional and to reinforce the notion that he is just simply blundering about trying to find the truth.

Readings

Having examined the construction of *Kurt and Courtney*, what readings of the film as a whole can be constructed? There are a number of possibilities.

Tribute

The film participates in the hagiography of Cobain and a number of reviewers focussed on this aspect of the film.

> In the end the film leaves one thinking less about Ms Love's exploits and more about Kurt and his pain. Perhaps we get a sense of how unfathomable his misery must have been when we realize that even the surface of it can hardly be scratched after ninety-five minutes.

> Estera Zarko 2000, 'Review of *Kurt and Courtney*', *Entertainment Asylum*, http://www.asylum.com

> As a tribute, however, it seems to be seriously lacking in information about Cobain's life.

> But there's nothing to indicate that Broomfield ever had any interest in the music—there's very little sense of what drew Cobain to music, what inspired him, what he actually created and the impact it would have on popular music.

> Richard Harrington, *Washington Post*, 17 July 1998.

…he skips entirely any mention of Kurt's move to Olympia, Washington, the formation of Nirvana, the rise of grunge, the success of *Nevermind* and what it all meant to the music industry.

Gina Arnold, 'Love Kurts', *Metro*, 5–11 March 1998.

The treatment of Cobain in the film is simply a reworking of the tortured genius myth, which pays little attention to the actual individual himself.

Investigation

On another level, *Kurt and Courtney* can be read as an investigation into the death of Cobain, which essentially fails to produce any credible evidence to support the theory that Cobain was murdered or that Courtney Love was in any way involved in his death. As a serious investigation, however, the film is hard to take seriously. Many of the 'witnesses' lack credibility and as one reviewer pointed out:

> Broomfield did not produce this film as a serious investigative documentary about a possible murder. The Seattle police were never questioned about the loopholes in their investigation. Courtney Love was never questioned about her activities during the time Kurt was missing. Michael Dewitt, the male nanny who was living at the Cobain house when Kurt was found dead, was not interviewed or even mentioned in this film. Most of the evidence was not discussed in detail or analyzed by Broomfield.

Tom Grant 2001, 'Nick Broomfield's *Kurt & Courtney*', http://www.cobaincase.com/k&c.html

To be fair to Broomfield, it should be pointed out that Love refused to be interviewed or co-operate in the making of the film.

> Broomfield doesn't discriminate enough among his sources—Love's father seems at least as screwy as he claims his daughter is, for instance, and some of Kurt and Courtney's friends are laughably stoned—and it's not clear at all that he cares to. It's finally more a film about groping for the story than a film about the story itself.

Shawn Levy, 'Kurt and Courtney: Nirvana Hell', *The Oregonian*, 10 April 1988.

A story about the making of a film

> Less a damning expose on the homicidal sins of an overweening pop diva than an account of an innocent with a video camera trying to get a grasp on the story he's decided to follow. *Kurt and Courtney* spends at least as much time detailing Broomfield's odyssey as it does investigating Cobain's death or detailing the intricacies of the relationship after which it's named.

Shawn Levy, 'Kurt and Courtney: Nirvana Hell', *The Oregonian*, 10 April 1988.

Ethnographic entertainment

Perhaps one of the most effective ways to read *Kurt and Courtney* is as an ethnographic entertainment—a study of a group of people, those involved on the fringes of the punk rock and entertainment industry.

Other readings

Kurt and Courtney can also be read as:

- a character assassination of Courtney Love
- a voyeuristic insight into lives very different to our own
- an ironic and unintentional self-criticism of Broomfield himself.

Broomfield on *Kurt and Courtney*

Megan Spencer: I know you've been asked this question a million times before, but I just wanted to get a feel for how you came to make *Kurt & Courtney*. I believe you're an admirer of Kurt Cobain's music yourself.

Nick Broomfield: Yeah—I remember the first time distinctly that I heard 'Nevermind'. And I guess like everyone else, I heard 'Smells Like Teen Spirit' first, and I thought it was an incredible and very distinctive piece of music. I've always wanted to make a music film and at one point I was going to do something on The Clash, which didn't actually work out. But I was also interested in him [Cobain] so much because I think he represented more than just a rock star; he was from a small town where he was obviously very much an outsider, and I think his music drew a lot of its strength from that. And obviously a lot of his fans and supporters often I think had the same kind of thing—they weren't kind of mainstream in their music tastes or in their position in society. So I thought he'd make a very very interesting film.

And originally I was going to make much more of a music film using a lot more of his music and talking to other musicians and other bands about him and his musical influences and stuff, but then I wasn't able to license any of the music or only a little of it [Courtney Love owns the rights], so I started to make a different kind of film at that point.

MS: Did you decide to make a film about Kurt Cobain before or after his death?

NB: I think I was always interested in Kurt Cobain before his death, but it was only really last year—obviously he'd been dead for a couple of years—that I decided to make the film. I've been doing a series of films really about contemporary icons… and I felt that Kurt Cobain fitted into that series of icons, because I think he was such an incredible figure to so many people… I was just sort of curious as a fan myself, just to learn more about him and where he came from and what inspired him and all that sort of thing.

MS: So really this is really a classic documentary that became something else. I suppose you had different ideas about what the film might have been.

NB: Yeah—I think that I set out to make a much more traditional documentary than I did. The first part of the film is really about Kurt and his life… and where he grew up and so on… And then the film goes obviously into his relationship with Courtney who he only really knew in the last two years of his life. But then I think you get a sense of his life changing, and obviously he became very successful and I think his life was to change because he got much more into drugs. And at that point I think the film becomes a lot darker. You learn more about him at that period of his life. And then the film looks more into the mystery I would say of his death.

MS: For the rollercoaster ride the film takes us on, amid the humour and some of the incredulous scenes and characters, ultimately it is a very dark film, and in the end I was left with a very deep feeling of sadness, particularly when Courtney's father Hank Harrison explains his "philosophy" on how to bring up kids…

NB: I agree with you–I think the film is very dark but I also think it's a very, very black comedy… I think a lot of the characters are very extreme… and I think although the film is very dark, its power is because it works on lots of different levels. It's also very funny and hopefully entertaining. Because I think that the world that Kurt Cobain inhabited was a very bizarre world towards the end especially. I think the Northwest, where he came from–Seattle and Aberdeen–it's very much like scenes from the David Lynch film *Twin Peaks*. It rains a lot, there are incredibly dark skies and it's a very strange part of America. And I think you really get a sense of that in the film as well. And the characters are very eccentric. So I don't think it's a straightforward [film]–it's the opposite of what an MTV film is really. It's all to do with… what it's like to talk to people, a lot of whom are obviously on drugs when I interviewed them. And I think you get an overall sense I hope at least of what that world is like and what those people are like in both humour and darkness.

MS: For the most part here in Australia, the reaction to *Kurt & Courtney* has been pretty favourable, but I feel compelled to ask you this question because I think it's fundamental to defining documentary. How do you see your film as differing to say a character assassination a show like *A Current Affair* might run, in the more tabloid journalistic sense, and what you actually documented in your film?

NB: Let me say that I don't ever go into a film with a thesis. I didn't go into this film thinking "I'm going to make a film that's negative about Courtney Love". I went into the film if anything expecting to like Courtney, very much as I had done on a previous film about Heidi Fleiss. If anything I expected Courtney to be the protagonist. And in a way it would have made my life a lot easier had it worked out that way. What I do is I film for like 12 or 14 weeks, and the film is really more like a diary. I go in and I interview people, and I build the story around my experiences of making the film. The film that you will see in the cinemas is an edited version of that. So in a way I think whatever happened with Courtney was very much defined by Courtney–had Courtney wanted to use the film as something positive, that she could use to put her point of view over with or to have shown a different side, I was completely open for her to do so. But I think what the film reflects is someone who is extremely controlling, and who will go to almost any lengths–as she did with this film–to stop something from happening or from coming out. And this is a long time before the film was even finished–I mean I'd only been filming for two weeks when I got a message from Showtime in America that they were thinking about pulling out of a deal we were about to make, for them to finance the film, because they'd had pressure from MTV, who is their sister company and who Courtney has a very close relationship with, saying that Courtney didn't want the film made and that they should pull out.

MS: How angry did that actually make you–the threat of being censored? You looked pretty furious in the film…

NB: Well I found the whole thing very interesting in a way. I mean I felt it made it a more interesting film, because I think celebrities today–and this is not just Courtney–but celebrities generally today have such enormous control, and I felt that this was an illustration of that. Especially in America, if a major showbiz personality doesn't want a particular article written or a particular film made, it will simply be buried.

I mean I know of writers and critics who work for magazines like *Rolling Stone*, who have had their reviews and articles handed back to them when they've written bad reviews about a famous rock star, and told to rewrite them, because no-one wants to be alienated. And I felt that what was happening with this film was an example of that, that here's in this case Courtney, who has enough power to actually get a major TV station to pull out of financing a film they had decided they wanted to finance. And I felt that that was an interesting situation, which the film explores in a way. I think today it's almost impossible to do an in depth study of a major show business personality. So most of the stuff that people read in magazines and see on television are little puff pieces that often I think have very little to do with the truth.

MS: Could it have been that the censoring reaction Courtney had, was because she found out you were investigating the conspiracy theories about Kurt's death?

NB: No, that just started right from the beginning. Courtney and other celebrities, when they do interviews, they often select which journalist they will be interviewed by, and they'll also determine what questions can and cannot be asked… it's just the way people operate today and it's a form of censorship which I think is obviously very dangerous.

MS: A lot of your early films were purely observational–you rarely were acknowledged on camera as being part of the film making process. Over time it seems your style has evolved into exposing the documentary making process as well as including yourself as a character in the movie. Was it a conscious decision to step in front of the camera and become a part of the films, or was it something that occurred by accident?

NB: A few years ago I did a film about Lily Tomlin the comedian, and I really felt that the film had very little to do with my experience in making the film or what it was like to actually do it… The very next film I was going to do, I thought there's no point in making a film and just having great stories about things that happen that aren't in the film… Often in documentaries, the process of making the film are the things that normally get left behind on the editing room floor… But those are often the most interesting things that if you can somehow put into the film, make it a more unusual and much more revealing film about the person or the situation. So that's really why I put myself in the film and started making more diaries than observational films. I felt I could get much closer to what was really going on and what the people were really like.

MS: In essence, what attracts you to making documentary film–given that they can be pretty tortuous projects to complete, what drives you to make them year in, year out?

NB: I mean it's what I do. I'm a professional film maker, and you only get any good at something by refining what you do. And also I think one's like a contemporary historian, because you just spend a year or nine months on one film. You can get very very close to people and situations and really find out a lot about things.

Which I think is an incredibly privileged position to be in. You have much more time to find out about things than most journalists–most journalists only get a few days to cover a story. But as a documentary film maker, you've got months and months and months, and so you can really find out about the world that you're a part of, or different aspects of whatever you're interested in. And you get paid for it so it's a wonderful thing to be able to do.

MS: One of the most interesting things for me about your films including *Kurt & Courtney*, is that they're incredibly revealing about people's subjective perceptions of truth and reality, as well as your own perceptions as the film maker. I guess in some ways you're our guide through the maze of "smoke and mirrors", but do you think your style gives an audience enough room to doubt your own interpretation of what's going on in the film?

NB: Hopefully the audience knows enough about me in the film to decide whether or not they want to accept my version of what's going on or not–I'm not some sort of hidden person. What's very different [about my style of film making] in those older documentaries, the traditional BBC ones, you had an objective voice telling the audience what a situation is, as though it's complete fact and an objective truth. My films are very subjective, and they're very much constructed around the way I get on with people or my interactions with situations and so on. And I think the audience can decide for themselves what they think. They might think I'm a complete prick in some of the scenes or that I'm completely wrong, or that I'm unfair to somebody. But at least I think this particular style involves an audience a lot more than just giving them the facts. It's more about trying to put the audience in the driver's seat, and the audience going on a journey and learning more what it would be like to be there or to meet these characters, than me telling them what to think.

MS: So the traumatic experiences involved in making *Kurt & Courtney* hopefully won't deter you from making more documentaries?

NB: Yeah–I'm sure I'll make other films. I don't know how soon or what yet–I'm always fascinated by other subjects and I always want to find out about them, and I basically love being on the road and making them... Maybe I'll come and do something in Australia at some point... It's such an amazing country ...

Megan Spencer, Triple J film critic, *Documenter*, volume 2, issue 1, 1999.

Like to know more?

Websites
There are many websites on the Internet dedicated to Kurt Cobain, the investigation into his death, and Nirvana. For links to a number of recommended sites visit the Longman website www.longman.com.au

Expository writing

7

An expository text is a form of non-fiction that explains, instructs or persuades. There is a distinction between narrative writing and expository writing:

- the aim of narrative writing is simply to recount a series of events
- the aim of expository writing is to explain an issue or topic or put forward a view.

The boundaries between the two forms of writing are not hard and fast, however; some texts do both at the same time. Note, too, that the explanation in expository writing is not neutral. An explanation is always just one explanation from among a number of possibilities. It will always reflect certain opinions, attitudes and values, usually those of the writer.

Many of the concepts and skills involved in the study of documentary also apply to the study of expository texts:

- Expository texts are often read as factual presentations of reality or as sources of neutral information.
  - Expository texts are actually constructions that offer particular versions of reality. Rather than being neutral sources of information, like all texts, they often work to persuade an audience to accept the version of reality they offer.
    - Saying that expository texts offer versions of reality rather than reality itself is not a criticism. It is simply a recognition of the nature of textual construction which involves the selection, structuring and reshaping of information in particular ways.
    - The construction of an expository text is a creative act in which the writer shapes the raw material for particular purposes and effects.
  - Expository texts can be looked at as works of art and sources of entertainment, as well as sources of information and persuasion.

Types of expository writing

Expository writing takes a wide variety of forms, from book-length texts to short articles. Many newspaper and magazine articles, those which explore topics in some detail as opposed to simply reporting events, are examples of expository writing. Here are some more examples:

- Scientific writing: In addition to textbooks, scientific expository writing encompasses discursive texts for the general reader, such as the often passionate, and for many people inspiring, works of the astronomer Carl Sagan and the evolutionist Stephen Jay Gould. It also includes books like *When Elephants Weep: The Emotional Lives of Animals* by Susan McCarthy and Jeffrey Moussaieff Masson, which argues that animals share many of the emotions of humans.

- Writing about mathematics: To people used to mathematics books being full of little more than formulas and exercises, it may come as a surprise to learn that there have been many interesting books written discussing the nature and importance of mathematics. A recent example is *Zero: The Biography of a Dangerous Idea* by Charles Seife, which looks at the history and social significance of the concept of zero.

- History: Most histories are not simply chronologies of dates and events. They are extended discussions and explanations of causes and results offering interpretations of people and events.

- Biographies: Like historical writing, most biographies are more than simple recounts of the life of their subjects. Rather, they offer an interpretation of the life and personality of the subject. There have been biographies of the Australian outlaw Ned Kelly, for example, which have portrayed him as a hero and a model of Australian individualism and others which have portrayed him as nothing more than a murderous villain.

- Self-help and motivational writing: The bookshops and libraries are full of books giving advice on topics as diverse as giving up smoking, raising children, making a marriage work, getting satisfaction out of work, how to become rich, living a healthier lifestyle and finding inner peace. Magazines are full of many articles dispensing advice on the same topics.

Other areas covered by expository writing include:

- sociology
- philosophy
- psychology
- current affairs
- travel.

Much of the material on the World Wide Web takes the form of expository writing. The essays you do as part of your school work are examples of expository writing. In fact, expository writing covers every conceivable topic.

CASE STUDY

Down Under

In addition to being a narrative of a writer's experiences, travel writing offers ideas about and attitudes towards the countries and people encountered along the way. The following passages are from Bill Bryson's book *Down Under*. Bryson is an American who has written many other travel books. While *Down Under* was a best seller in Australia, it was written with an American audience in mind, as you will soon notice. In the United States, the book was released with the title *In a Sunburned Country*.

Focus question

How are Australia and Australians represented in these passages?

Flying into Australia, I realized with a sigh that I had forgotten again who their Prime Minister is. I am forever doing this with the Australian PM—committing the name to memory, forgetting it (generally more or less instantly), then feeling terribly guilty. My thinking is that there ought to be one person outside Australia who knows.

But then Australia is such a difficult country to keep track of. On my first visit, some years ago, I passed the time on the long flight from London reading a history of Australian politics in the twentieth century, wherein I encountered the startling fact that in 1967 the Prime Minister, Harold Holt, was strolling along a beach in Victoria when he plunged into the surf and vanished. No trace of the poor man was ever seen again. This seemed doubly astounding to me—first that Australia could just *lose* a Prime Minister (I mean, come on) and second that news of this had never reached me.

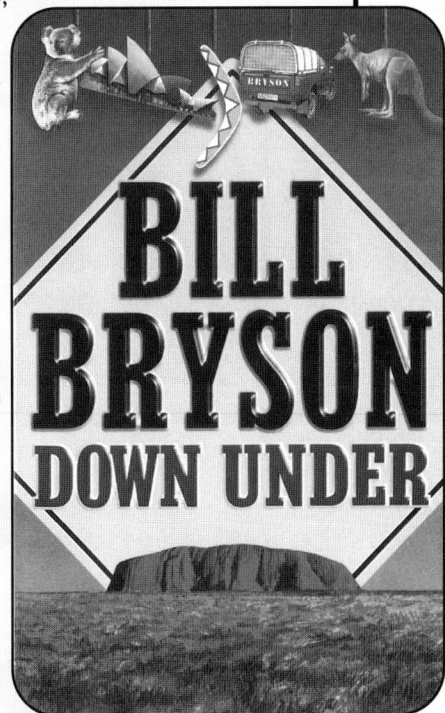

The fact is, of course, we pay shamefully scant attention to our dear cousins Down Under—though not entirely without reason, I suppose. Australia is, after all, mostly empty and a long way away. Its population, about 19 million, is small by world standards—China grows by a larger amount each year—and its place in the world economy is consequently peripheral; as an economic entity, it is about the same size as Illinois. From time to time it sends us useful things—opals, merino wool, Errol Flynn, the boomerang—but nothing we can't actually do without. Above all, Australia doesn't misbehave. It is stable and peaceful and good. It doesn't have coups, recklessly overfish, arm disagreeable despots, grow coca in provocative quantities or throw its weight around in a brash and unseemly manner.

But even allowing for all this, our neglect of Australian affairs is curious. As you might expect, this is particularly noticeable when you are resident in America. Just before I set off on this trip I went to my local library in New Hampshire and looked up Australia in the *New York Times Index* to see how much it had engaged attention in my own country in recent years. I began with the 1997 volume for no other reason than that it was open on the table. In that year, across the full range of possible interests—politics, sport, travel, the coming Olympics in Sydney, food and wine, the arts, obituaries and so on—the *New York Times* ran 20 articles that were predominantly on or about Australian affairs. In the same period, for purposes of comparison, it found space for 120 articles on Peru, 150 or so on Albania and a similar number on Cambodia, more than 300 on each of the Koreas, and well over 500 on Israel. As a place that attracted American interest Australia ranked about level with Belarus and Burundi. Among the general subjects that outstripped it were balloons and balloonists, the Church of Scientology, dogs (though not dog sledding), and Pamela Harriman, the former ambassador and socialite who died in February 1997, a calamity that evidently required recording twenty-two times in the *Times*. Put in the crudest terms, Australia was slightly more important to Americans in 1997 than bananas, but not nearly as important as ice cream.

As it turns out, 1997 was actually quite a good year for Australian news in the United States. In 1996 the country was the subject of just nine news reports and in 1998 a mere six. Elsewhere in the world the news coverage may be more attentive, but with the difference, of course, that no one actually reads it. (Hands up, all those who can name the current Australian Prime Minister or say in which state you will find Melbourne or answer pretty much any antipodean question at all not involving cricket, rugby, Mel Gibson or *Neighbours*.) Australians can't bear it that the outside world pays so little attention to them, and I don't blame them. This is a country where interesting things happen, and all the time.

Consider just one of those stories that did make it into the *New York Times* in 1997, though buried away in the odd-sock drawer of Section G. In January of that year, according to a report written in America by a *Times* reporter, scientists were seriously investigating the possibility that a mysterious seismic disturbance in the remote Australian outback almost four years earlier had been a nuclear explosion set off by members of the Japanese doomsday cult Aum Shinrikyo.

It happens that at 11.03 p.m. local time on the night of 28 May 1993 seismograph needles all over the Pacific region twitched and scribbled in response to a very large-scale disturbance near a place called Banjawarn Station in the Great Victoria Desert of Western Australia. Some long-distance lorry drivers and prospectors, virtually the only people out in that lonely expanse, reported seeing a sudden flash in the sky and hearing or feeling the boom of a mighty but far-off explosion. One reported that a can of beer had danced off the table in his tent.

The problem was that there was no obvious explanation. The seismograph traces didn't fit the profile for an earthquake or mining explosion, and anyway the blast was 170 times more powerful than the most powerful mining explosion ever recorded in Western Australia. The shock was consistent with a large meteorite strike, but the impact would have blown a crater hundreds of feet in circumference, and no such crater could be found. The upshot is that scientists puzzled over the incident for a day or two, then filed it away as an unexplained curiosity—the sort of thing that presumably happens from time to time.

Then in 1995 Aum Shinrikyo gained sudden notoriety when it released extravagant quantities of the nerve gas sarin into the Tokyo underground, killing twelve people. In the investigations that followed, it emerged that Aum's substantial holdings included a 500,000-acre desert property in Western Australia very near the site of the mystery event. There, authorities found a laboratory of unusual sophistication and focus, and evidence that cult members had been mining uranium. It separately emerged that Aum had recruited into its ranks two nuclear engineers from the former Soviet Union. The group's avowed aim was the destruction of the world, and it appears that the event in the desert may have been a dry run for blowing up Tokyo.

You take my point, of course. This is a country that loses a Prime Minister and that is so vast and empty that a band of amateur enthusiasts could conceivably set off the world's first non-governmental atomic bomb on its mainland and almost four years would pass before anyone noticed. Clearly this is a place worth getting to know.

* * *

… Sydneysiders, as they are rather quaintly known, have an evidently unquenchable desire to show their city off to visitors, and I had yet another kind offer of guidance before me, this time from a journalist on the *Sydney Morning Herald* named Deirdre Macken. An alert and cheerful lady of early middle years, Deirdre met me at my hotel with a young photographer named Glenn Hunt, and we set off on foot to the Museum of Sydney, a sleek and stylish new institution, which manages to look interesting and instructive without actually being either. You find yourself staring at artfully underlit displays—a caseful of immigrant artifacts, a room wallpapered with the pages of popular magazines from the 1950s—without being entirely certain what you are expected to conclude. But we did have a very nice latte in the attached café at which point Deirdre outlined her plans for our busy day.

In a moment we would stroll down to Circular Quay and catch a ferry across the harbour to the Taronga Zoo wharf. We wouldn't actually visit the zoo, but instead would hike around Little Sirius Cove and up through the steep and jungly hills of Cremorne Point to Deirdre's house, where we would gather up some towels and boogie boards, and go by car to Manly, a beach suburb overlooking the Pacific. At Manly we would grab a bite of lunch, then have an invigorating session of boogie boarding before towelling ourselves down and heading for—

'Excuse me for interrupting,' I interrupted, 'but what is boogie boarding exactly?'

'Oh, it's fun. You'll love it,' she said breezily but, I thought, just a touch evasively.

'Yes, but what is it?'

'It's an aquatic sport. It's heaps of fun. Isn't it heaps of fun, Glenn?'

'Heaps,' agreed Glenn, who was, in the manner of all people whose film stock is paid for, in the midst of taking an infinite number of photographs. *Bizeet, bizeet, bizeet,* his camera sang as he took three quick and ingeniously identical photographs of Deirdre and me in conversation.

'But what does it entail exactly?' I persisted.

'You take a kind of miniature surfboard and paddle out into the sea, where you catch a big wave and ride it back to shore. It's easy. You'll love it.'

'What about sharks?' I asked uneasily.

'Oh, there's hardly any sharks here. Glenn, how long has it been since someone was killed by a shark?'

'Oh, ages,' Glenn said, considering. 'Couple of months at least.'

'Couple of months?' I squeaked.

'At least. Sharks are way overrated as a danger,' Glenn added. 'Way overrated. It's the rips that'll most likely get yer.' He returned to taking pictures.

'Rips?'

'Underwater currents that run at an angle to the shore and sometimes carry people out to sea,' Deirdre explained. 'But don't worry. That won't happen to you.'

'Why?'

'Because we're here to look after you.' She smiled serenely, drained her cup and reminded us that we needed to keep moving.

Three hours later, our other activities completed, we stood on a remote-seeming strand at a place called Freshwater Beach, near Manly. It was a big U-shaped bay, edged by low scrub hills, with what seemed to me awfully big waves pounding in from a vast and moody sea. In the middle distance several foolhardy souls in wetsuits were surfing towards some foamy outbursts on the rocky headland; nearer in a scattering of paddlers were being continually and, it seemed, happily engulfed by explosive waves.

Urged on by Deirdre, who seemed keen as anything to get into the briny drink, we began to strip down—slowly and deliberately in my case, eagerly in hers—to the swimsuits she had instructed us to wear beneath our clothes.

'If you're caught in a rip,' Deirdre was saying, 'the trick is not to panic.'

I looked at her. 'You're telling me to drown calmly?'

'No, no. Just keep your wits. Don't try to swim against the current. Swim *across* it. And if you're still in trouble, just wave your arm like this'—she gave the kind of big, languorous wave that only an Australian could possibly consider an appropriate response to a death-at-sea situation—'and wait for the lifeguard to come.'

'What if the lifeguard doesn't see me?'

'He'll see you.'

'But what if he doesn't?' But Deirdre was already wading into the surf, a boogie board tucked under her arm. Bashfully I dropped my shirt onto the sand and stood naked but for my sagging trunks. Glenn, never having seen anything quite this grotesque and singular on an Australian beach, certainly nothing still alive, snatched up his camera and began excitedly taking close-up shots of my stomach. *Bizeet, bizeet, bizeet, bizeet,* his camera sang happily as he followed me into the surf.

Let me just pause here for a moment to interpose two small stories. In 1935, not far from where we stood now, some fishermen captured a fourteen-foot beige shark and took it to a public aquarium at Coogee, where it was put on display. The shark swam around for a day or two in its new home, then abruptly, and to the certain surprise of the viewing public, regurgitated a human arm. When last seen the arm had been attached to a young man named Jimmy Smith, who had, I've no doubt, signalled his predicament with a big, languorous wave.

Now my second story. Three years later, on a clear, bright, calm Sunday afternoon at Bondi Beach, also not far from where we now stood, from out of nowhere there came four freak waves, each up to twenty-five feet high. More than 200 people were carried out to sea in the undertow. Fortunately, fifty lifeguards were in attendance that day, and they managed to save all but six people. I am aware that we are talking about incidents that happened many years ago. I don't care. My point remains: the ocean is a treacherous place.

Sighing, I shuffled into the pale green and cream-flecked water. The bay was surprisingly shallow. We trudged perhaps 100 feet out and it was still only a little over our knees, though even here there was an extraordinarily powerful current—strong enough to pull you off your feet if you weren't real vigilant. Another fifty feet on, where the water rose over our waists, the waves were breaking. If you discount a few hours in the lagoon-like waters of the Costa del Sol in Spain and an icy, instantly regretted dip once in Maine, I have almost no experience of the sea, and I found it frankly disconcerting to be wading into a rollercoaster of water. Deirdre shrieked with pleasure. Then she showed me how the boogie board works. It was promisingly simple in principle. As a wave passed, she would leap aboard and skim along on its crest for many yards. Then Glenn had a turn and went even further. There is no question that it looked like fun. It didn't look too hard either. I was tentatively eager to have a try. I positioned myself for the first wave, then jumped aboard and sank like an anvil.

'How'd you do that?' asked Glenn in wonder.

'No idea.'

I repeated the exercise with the same result.

'Amazing,' he said.

There followed a half hour in which the two of them watched first with guarded amusement, then a kind of astonishment, and finally something not unlike pity, as I repeatedly vanished beneath the waves and was scraped over an area of ocean floor roughly the size of Polk County, Iowa. After a variable but lengthy period, I would surface, gasping and confused, at a point anywhere from four feet to a mile and a quarter distant, and be immediately carried under again by a following wave. Before long, people on the beach were on their feet and placing bets. It was commonly agreed that it was not physically possible to do what I was doing.

From my point of view, each underwater experience was essentially the same. I would diligently attempt to replicate the dainty kicking motions Deirdre had shown me and try to ignore the fact that I was going nowhere and mostly drowning. Not having anything to judge this against, I supposed I was doing rather well. I can't pretend I was having a good time, but then it is a mystery to me how anyone could wade into such a merciless environment and expect to have fun. But I was resigned to my fate and knew that eventually it would be over.

Perhaps it was the oxygen deprivation, but I was rather lost in my own little world when Deirdre grabbed my arm just before I was about to go under again and said in a husky tone: 'Look out! There's a bluey.'

Glenn took on an immediate expression of alarm. 'Where?'

'What's a bluey?' I asked, appalled to discover that there was some additional danger I hadn't been told about.

'A bluebottle,' she explained and pointed to a small jellyfish of the type (as I later learned from browsing through a fat book titled, if I recall, *Things That Will Kill You Horridly in Australia: Volume 19*) known elsewhere as a Portuguese man-of-war. I squinted at it as it drifted past. It looked unprepossessing, like a blue condom with strings attached.

'Is it dangerous?' I asked.

Now before we hear Deirdre's response to me as I stood there, vulnerable and abraded, shivering, nearly naked and half drowned, let me just quote from her subsequent article in the *Herald*:

> While the photographer shoots, Bryson and boogie board are dragged 40 metres down the beach in a rip. The shorerip runs south to north, unlike the rip further out which runs north to south. Bryson doesn't know this. He didn't read the warning sign on the beach.* Nor does he know about the bluebottle being blown in his direction—now less than a metre away—a swollen stinger that could give him 20 minutes of agony and, if he's unlucky, an unsightly allergic reaction to carry on his torso for life.

'Dangerous? No,' Deirdre replied now as we stood gawping at the bluebottle. 'But don't brush against it.'

'Why not?'

'Might be a bit uncomfortable.'

I looked at her with an expression of interest bordering on admiration. Long bus journeys are uncomfortable. Slatted wooden benches are uncomfortable. Lulls in conversations are uncomfortable. The sting of a Portuguese man-of-war—even people from Iowa know this—is agony. It occurred to me that Australians are so surrounded with danger that they have evolved an entirely new vocabulary to deal with it.

'Hey, there's another one,' said Glenn.

We watched another one drift by. Deirdre was scanning the water.

'Sometimes they come in waves,' she said. 'Might be an idea to get out of the water.'

I didn't have to be told twice.

* The statement is inarguable. However, the author would like the record to show that he did not have his glasses on; he trusted his hosts; he was scanning a large area of ocean for sharks; and he was endeavouring through-out not to excrete a large housebrick into his pants.

Bill Bryson, *Down Under*, Black Swan, Sydney 2001, 15–18, 28–34.

Activities

1. Write down or discuss your answers to the focus question, explaining which aspects of the passage support your reading.
2. Discuss what other possible representations of Australia and Australians there are in addition to those presented in these passages.

CASE STUDY

14

'At Sea with the America's Cup'

The following passage was written by another American P. J. O'Rourke. It is part of an account of his visit to Australia during the America's Cup yachting competition in 1983.

Focus question

How does the representation of Australia and Australians in this passage differ from the representation in the passages from Down Under?

Australia is not very exclusive. On the visa application they still ask if you've been convicted of a felony—although they are willing to give you a visa even if you haven't been. Australia *is* exotic, however. There are kangaroos and wallabies and wombats all over the place, and even the Australian horses and sheep and house cats hop around on their back legs and have little pouches in front. Well, maybe they don't. Actually I never saw a kangaroo. I saw kangaroo posters and kangaroo postcards and thousands of kangaroo T-shirts. Kangaroos appear on practically every advertising logo and trademark. You can buy kangaroo-brand oleo and kangaroo bath soap, and get welcome mats, shower curtains and beach towels with kangaroos on them and have kangaroos all over your underpants. But, as for real live kangaroos, I think they're all in the Bronx Zoo.

While I was visiting every bar in Fremantle, trying to recover from my *Sea Chunder* ordeal, I heard the Australians talking about how much they drink and punch each other. True, Australians do drink mug upon mug of beer. But these are dainty little mugs that hardly contain enough beer for one serving of fish-fry batter back where I come from. I could tell the Americans by the way they ordered four or six of these baby brewskis at a time. And the only fight I saw was between two US boat groupies because one threw the other into a swimming pool and ruined his favourite pair of purple boat socks with little pom-poms on the heels.

Australia was like 'Australia Nite' at the Michigan State Phi Delta house. The big excitement was driving on the wrong side of the road. Not that I drove on the wrong side. I was over on the right where I was supposed to be. But the Australians were on the left and coming straight at me. After ten or twelve of those lime juice G&Ts, this got very exciting.

I also went to the exciting Royal Perth Yacht Club Ball. The ticket prices were exciting anyway—$300 a pop. The invitation said black tie so I called South Perth Formal Hire and Live Bait and got a polyester quadruple-knit dinner suit with foot-wide lapels and bell bottoms in the Early Sonny Bono cut. When I arrived at the dance, I was too embarrassed to get out of the car, especially since it was 100 degrees and I was sweating like a hog and the polyester had made my whole body break out in prickly heat. But nobody else in Western Australia owns a tuxedo either. Every guy there was wearing a rented one exactly like mine. We all spent the evening itching and squirming and scratching ourselves like apes.

The RPYC buffet, booze-up and fox-trot exhibition had 2,500 guests. This was more than the Royal P's dinky clubhouse or even its parking lot could hold. So the ball was given in an old wool barn that had been decorated to look like, well, an old wool barn. And there was no air conditioning. Lanolin, ahoy.

At least the Australians weren't dressed the way they usually are, which is in kangaroo T-shirts, khaki short shorts, work boots and black mid-calf socks. You could tell this was genuine Perth and Fremantle high society because hardly anybody yelled, 'G'day, Mate!' They yelled, 'Ciao, Mate!' instead.

Australians are friendly, very friendly. I couldn't spend three seconds eating my dinner without one of them butting in at the top of his lungs, 'G'day, Mate! Eatin' are ya? Whatzit? Food? Good on ya!' Followed by an enormous backslap right in the middle of my mouthful of boiled lamb brisket (which is either the national dish or just what everything in Australia tastes like). The Australian language is easier to learn than boat talk. It has a vocabulary of about six words. There's *g'day*, which means 'hello'. There's *mate*, which is a folksy combination of 'excuse me, sir' and 'hey you'. There's *good on ya*, which means 'that's nice' and *fair dinkum*, which doesn't mean much of anything. Australian does have, however, more synonyms for vomit than any other non-Slavic language. For example: 'liquid laughter', 'technicolour yawn', 'growling in the grass' and 'planting beets'. These came in handy for the would-be boat reporter or the would-be Yacht Club Ball society columnist, for that matter.

P. J. O'Rourke, 'At Sea with the America's Cup', *Holidays in Hell*, Pan Macmillan, London 1989, 152–4.

Activities

1 Discuss or write down your answers to the focus question.

2 The meanings you construct of a passage depend on the approach or reading practices you adopt. Turn the previous exercise on its head and examine how the passages represent Americans by answering this question:

If you read the persona of each passage as a representative of Americans, what readings of Americans would you construct from each passage?

3 Find an example of a book-length expository text. Choose one that is discursive (that is, it has extended writing). Read it or skim it and present a talk to your class or group on the nature of the text and the views you believe it is putting forward on its topic.

Context, audience and purpose

Important considerations when constructing a reading of an expository text are context, audience and purpose. An understanding of context, audience and purpose makes it easier to understand the text because it helps you understand where a writer is coming from and who he or she is writing for. It can also help you to understand why the text is constructed in the way it is.

Sometimes you can use extratextual knowledge, knowledge from outside the text, to determine its context, audience and purpose. This might include your familiarity with the writer or the publication in which the text appears.

You might use the text itself in combination with intertextual knowledge gained from reading or viewing other texts on the same topic to slot the new text into a certain pattern of ideas. You might recognise, for example, that a particular use of vocabulary or phraseology indicates that the text is written for a specific audience. You might recognise that the ideas in the text seem to be supporting or challenging the views of other texts you have read or viewed on the topic.

Ideology

Relating a text to a particular context also enables you to determine its ideological function—the role it plays in the circulation of ideas, attitudes and values in a society. Like all texts, expository texts can be read as reflections of or interventions in particular ideological contexts.

Ideology is a way of thinking common to a social group that provides a framework within which members of the group operate even if they are not aware of it. Writers of expository texts, like all writers, are influenced by the ideologies of the social groups to which they belong.

The ideas, attitudes and values promoted by a text are often a function of the language available to and used by the writer. This can be described as the ideological purpose or function of the text. The 'purpose' of a text, in this sense, is the ideas, attitudes and values the text promotes through the way it is written. The difficulty with the word 'purpose' is that it may encourage you to think that the ideas, attitudes or values promoted by a text are deliberately promoted by the writer. Often this isn't the case.

The ideological function of a text often emerges, not from the overt ideas or attitudes expressed by the text, but from the underlying values, assumptions or implications of the text. The ideological function of a text also lies in the broader social purposes that a text serves. Ideology is closely connected with power relationships in society. This is because ideologies serve the interests of some groups more than they do others. Ideologies, and the texts that reflect them, are thus weapons certain groups use to maintain or enhance their power in society.

This can be seen in ideologies related to race. From about the 1600s to the latter part of the twentieth century, Western society attached particular importance to race and skin colour as major signifiers of difference. 'White' was constructed as the norm and non-white races as 'other', usually inferior.

The privileging of race and colour as signs of difference between people was actually quite a new idea. It would have seemed strange to the inhabitants of Europe before the sixteenth century. What mattered to them was whether one was a Christian or not, and Christians could be a range of skin colours. The idea that skin colour or race was important would also have seemed strange to the inhabitants of the Roman Empire. For them what mattered was whether one was a citizen of the Empire. Non-Roman citizens were seen as barbarians but this had nothing to do with skin colour. The Roman Empire included a wide variety of races as citizens, and many barbarian races were what we would call 'white', being the ancestors of many modern European nations, such as Germany.

> **Framework for exploring ideology in a text:**
> - What are the main ideas being overtly promoted?
> - What values, attitudes and ideologies underlie these ideas?
> - How do these relate to a particular context and audience?
> - What social purposes do they serve? Whose interests?

The whole idea of 'race' as a way of defining social groups is a relatively new invention and is entirely a social construction. The construction of the idea of race and of other 'races' as different was not a matter of lack of ignorance, which we have now improved on, nor was it an accident. It was intimately connected with the growth of European imperialism—the conquest of other nations by Europeans. The idea that other races were different and inferior provided a convenient justification for taking away their lands and exploiting them.

CASE STUDY

15

Novel reading

The following passage was published in 1902 in a book entitled *Ladies Guide in Health and Disease* by J.H. Kellogg M.D., who is described on the title page as Member of the British Association for the Advancement of Science. You may find the passage somewhat bizarre as it explains why teenage girls should be discouraged from novel reading.

15

*What ideas and assumptions about teenage girls are evident in the
passage?*

Novel-Reading

The reading of works of fiction is one of the most pernicious habits to which a
young lady can become devoted. When the habit is once thoroughly fixed, it
becomes as inveterate as the use of liquor or opium. The novel-devotee is as much
a slave as the opium-eater or the inebriate. The reading of fictitious literature
destroys the taste for sober, wholesome reading and imparts an unhealthy stimulus
to the mind, the effect of which is in the highest degree damaging.

When we add to this the fact that a large share of the popular novels of the
day contain more or less matter of a directly depraving character, presented in
such gilded form and specious guise that the work of contamination may be
completed before suspicion is aroused, it should become apparent to every careful
mother that her daughters should be vigilantly guarded against this dangerous
source of injury and possible ruin. We have dilated quite fully upon this subject in a
preceding section, and will not enlarge upon it here. Yet we particularly desire to
go on record as believing firmly that the practice of novel reading is one of the
greatest causes of uterine disease in young women. There is no doubt that the
influence of the mind upon the sexual organs and functions is such that disease
may be produced in this way. As remarked in the consideration of the physiology
of the reproductive organs, it is a common observation that the menstrual
function may be suspended suddenly as the result of grief or some other strong
emotion experienced by the individual. Haemorrhage or profuse menstruation
may result from a similar cause. These facts demonstrate beyond the possibility of
question that the circulation in the uterus and its appendages is greatly subject to
changes through the influence of the mind. Reading of a character to stimulate the
emotions and rouse the passions may produce or increase a tendency to uterine
congestion, which may in turn give rise to a great variety of maladies, including all
the different forms of displacement, the presence of which is indicated by weak
backs, painful menstruation, leucorrhoea, etc.

We do not insist that nothing should ever be read but history, biography, or
perfectly authentic accounts of experiences in real life. There are undoubtedly
novels, such as *Uncle Tom's Cabin*, and one or two others which we might mention,
which have been active agents in the accomplishment of great and good results.
Such novels are not likely to do any body any harm; but the number of harmless
works of fiction is very limited indeed. Many works which are considered among
the standards of literature are wholly unfit for the perusal of young ladies who
wish to retain their simplicity of mind and purity of thought. We have felt our
cheeks burn more than once when we have seen young school-girls intently
poring over the vulgar poems of Chaucer or the amorous ditties of Burns or

Byron. Still worse than any of these are the low witticisms of Rabelais and Boccaccio; and yet we have not infrequently seen these volumes in the book-cases of family libraries readily accessible to the young daughters or growing sons of the family. The growing influence of this kind of literature is far more extensive than can be readily demonstrated. Thousands of women whose natural love for purity leads them to shun and abhor everything of an immoral tendency, yet find themselves obliged to wage a painful warfare for years to banish from their minds the impure imagery generated by the perusal of books of this character. We have met cases of disease in which painful maladies could be traced directly to this source.

J. H. Kellogg M.D., *Ladies Guide in Health and Disease*,
Echo Publishing Company, North Fitzroy 1902, pp. 207–210.

Activities

1 Discuss your responses to the focus question with other students.
2 Compare your findings with the commentary that follows.

Commentary

The overt argument of this passage, that novel reading may lead to uterine disorder, can be dismissed as medical nonsense. But you need to look closely at the underlying assumptions and attitudes which the passage reveals. The passage constructs teenage girls as mentally weak and having poor self-control by comparing them to potential drug addicts. Teenage girls are also presented as easily swayed and subject to strong, almost uncontrollable, emotions. They are also constructed as physically weak and prone to sudden ailments. Significantly this physical weakness is located primarily in the sexual organs, the very thing that makes them female. For these reasons, teenage girls are portrayed as needing protection and constant supervision.

Strange as these ideas may seem to us in the twenty-first century, they were extremely common in the nineteenth and early twentieth centuries.

What were the social functions of these ideas? Basically they served to justify depriving teenage girls of power and independence. They also justified restricting the education of young women and thus restricting their access to life outside the domestic sphere.

Whose interests did this serve? Quite clearly, the interests of adults, because it gave them power over teenage girls. The other group that benefited was males because it meant that females would not have access to education and the benefits accruing from it, thus they would pose no threat to males' domination of these benefits.

While the idea that novel reading can lead to uterine disorder is no longer accepted in Western society, there are other ideas that are used in the same way to justify the power of one group over another. In other words, the ideas may be different but the ideological strategy of constructing a group as in some ways mentally or physically weaker and in need of supervision is the same. This was the way in which Aboriginal people were represented in Australian society for many years and led to the appointment of people who held the title of 'Protector of Aborigines'. The representation of teenagers as needing to be controlled and supervised is still extremely common in modern society. An example of this representation can be seen in *Anna's Story* by Bronwyn Donaghy, which sold many copies.

Construction of expository texts

This section describes some aspects of the construction of expository texts. These are not separate techniques which can be identified and discussed separately from each other. They are all related to and overlap with each other. They are not a checklist to be worked through when writing about an expository text but ideas to be kept in mind and drawn on if relevant when constructing a reading.

Persona

The term persona refers to the mask or role adopted by a writer. The term persona is more commonly used in relation to literature, poetry in particular, but you need to remember that the writer you encounter in an expository text is also a persona, a role adopted by the real writer. It is not a role adopted to hide the real writer, but a role used so that the writer can relate to the reader in particular ways.

Persona is revealed in the way the writer speaks to or addresses the reader. This is why some people prefer the term 'mode of address' to persona.

Some writers may deny that they adopt a persona, arguing that what you get in their writing is the real person. There are two points in relation to this. One is that writing as themselves is in itself a choice, a chosen role. The other point is that the adoption of a persona is not necessarily a result of a deliberate decision by a writer. It is often a function of the way language is used. Using language in certain ways conveys to the reader the impression of a certain sort of person addressing them and thus can affect the way they respond. A writer addressing a teenage audience, for example, may use popular teenage slang, inviting readers to see the writer as up-to-date and 'with it' and therefore to be trusted.

Writers may also create personas by bringing themselves into their writing with information about themselves or their experiences.

Types of persona that may be adopted by a writer include:
- an authoritative, knowledgeable, apparently superior person dispensing wisdom to a reader which it is the reader's obligation to accept
- a passionate advocate for a cause
- an apparently neutral observer
- an everyday person, trying to find a way through a confusing situation or topic

- a close friend or intimate of the reader
- an ordinary person in the same situation as the reader.

An important aspect of the persona is the tone adopted by the writer. Tone is a matter of the vocabulary and phraseology of the text. This shows how it is important to treat different aspects of construction as interrelated.

CASE STUDY

16

Men are from Mars, Women are from Venus
Remembering our Differences

Without the awareness that we are supposed to be different, men and women are at odds with each other. We usually become angry or frustrated with the opposite sex because we have forgotten this important truth. We expect the opposite sex to be more like ourselves. We desire them to 'want what we want' and 'feel the way we feel.'

We mistakenly assume that if our partners love us they will react and behave in certain ways—the ways we react and behave when we love someone. This attitude sets us up to be disappointed again and again and prevents us from taking the necessary time to communicate lovingly about our differences.

Men mistakenly expect women to think, communicate, and react the way men do; women mistakenly expect men to feel, communicate, and respond the way women do. We have forgotten that men and women are supposed to be different. As a result our relationships are filled with unnecessary friction and conflict.

Clearly recognizing and respecting these differences dramatically reduce confusion when dealing with the opposite sex. When you remember that men are from Mars and women are from Venus, everything can be explained.

J. Gray, *Men are from Mars, Women are from Venus*, HarperCollins, London 1993, p. 10.

'The Last American Hero'

The legend of Junior Johnson! In this legend, here is a country boy, Junior Johnson, who learns to drive by running whiskey for his father, Johnson, Senior, one of the biggest copper-still operators of all time, up in Ingle Hollow, near North Wilkesboro, in northwestern North Carolina, and grows up to be a famous stock car racing driver, rich, grossing $100,000 in 1963, for example, respected, solid, idolized in his hometown and throughout the rural South. There is all this about how good old boys would wake up in the middle of the night in the apple shacks and hear a supercharged Oldsmobile engine roaring over Brushy Mountain and say, "Listen at him—there he goes!" although that part is doubtful, since some nights there were so many good old boys taking off down the road in supercharged automobiles out of Wilkes County, and running loads to Charlotte, Salisbury, Greensboro, Winston-Salem, High Point, or wherever, it would be pretty hard to pick out one. It was Junior Johnson specifically, however, who was famous for the "bootleg turn" or "about-face," in which, if the Alcohol Tax agents had a roadblock up for you or were too close behind, you threw the car up into second gear, cocked the wheel, stepped on the accelerator and made the car's rear end skid around in a complete 180-degree arc, a complete about-face, and tore on back up the road exactly the way you came from. God! The Alcohol Tax agents used to burn over Junior Johnson. Practically every good old boy in town in Wilkesboro, the county seat, got to know the agents by sight in a very short time. They would rag them practically to their faces on the subject of Junior Johnson, so that it got to be an obsession. Finally, one night they had Junior trapped on the road up toward the bridge around Millersville, there's no way out of there, they had the barricades up and they could hear this souped-up car roaring around the bend, and here it comes—but suddenly they can hear a siren and see a red light flashing in the grille, so they think it's another agent, and boy, they run out like ants and pull those barrels and boards and sawhorses out of the way, and then—Ggghhzzzzzzzzhhhhhhggggggzzzzzzzeeeeong!—gawdam! there he goes again, it was him, Junior Johnson! with a gawdam agent's si-reen and a red light in his grille!

Tom Wolfe, 'The Last American Hero', *The Purple Decades*, Berkley, New York 1982, pp. 28–9.

Activity

Discuss or write about the different personas used by the writers in each of the above passages.

Supporting evidence and rhetorical devices

Expository writers use a range of different types of evidence to illustrate or support the views they offer. From a critical literary perspective, however, it is more useful to think of these forms of evidence or illustration as rhetorical devices. Rhetorical devices are persuasive techniques used to encourage the audience to accept the view offered.

Authorities

Authorities are people, organisations or texts that the reader is expected to accept as reliable because of their supposed expertise in their fields. For every authority that can be found to support a particular case, however, there is usually another one out there who could be used to support a different view. There is sometimes a high degree of selectivity involved in the use of authorities.

Personal touch

While authorities may add an air of credibility to an explanation or argument, many writers also attempt to involve readers at a more personal level as a way of encouraging them to accept the views being promoted. This personal touch can be achieved by drawing not on experts but on people like the readers themselves or representatives of ordinary people. This might involve anecdotes about ordinary people or comments by ordinary people that support or illustrate the view offered. The personal touch includes case stories, narratives, anecdotes, interviews, quotations and personal experience.

CASE STUDY

17

Manhood

The following passage is from *Manhood* by Australian family therapist Steve Biddulph. It was published in Australia in 1994. *Manhood* is subtitled 'An action plan for changing men's lives'.

The Problem

Most men today don't have a life. What we have instead is a big act. The act comes in two parts, both put there for protection. Firstly we pretend that we are happy and everything is okay. We plug away with this for years, hoping it will one day come true. On top of this, starting as young as our early teens, we choose from one of several standard roles, and pretend this is us. Hard working provider. Shrewd businessman. Caring professional. Cool dude. Good sport. Sensitive man. But of course it's not us, and pretending it is gets to be a pain in the neck. Having an act is not the same as having a life.

Most women are not like this. They live from inner feeling and spirit. Women have their problems, but most women at least act from a clear sense of self, with some spirit and confidence. Women generally know **who they are** and **what they want**.

How did this difference come about? Little children of both sexes start out well enough. A child's nature is to be self-aware, expecting to be happy, expecting life to be an adventure. That's why little children are so delightful to be around. But early on, a boy's spirit begins to shrivel, until gradually he loses touch with it altogether. By the time he is a man, he is like a tiger raised in a zoo—confused and numb, with huge energies untapped. He feels that there must be more, **but he does not know what that 'more' is**. So he spends his life pretending—to his friends, his family, and himself—that everything is okay.

Round-the-clock pretending is hard work, and so it's not surprising that sometimes a few cracks start to appear in a man's façade. Perhaps you have felt this yourself. Sometimes it comes through getting a taste of what real freedom could be like—a fleeting glimpse of being fully alive. Finding yourself alone on a beach, and suddenly dissolved in the waves, trees and sky. Or having a certain kind of moment with a woman—of intense passion, or the sudden sweetness of compassionate understanding. Or playing with your children and all at once feeling like a child again yourself, tingling with life. It could be as simple as listening to music, or a moment in a movie. You glimpse something, unsettling but beautiful … and then it passes. You almost feel worse off; you don't know how to get that moment back. So you shut the memory away, and go back to business as usual.

The cracks in a man's act may occur in more painful ways—pressure, failure, accident. Or more often, in the middle years of life, a deep despair combined with exhaustion settles on him as he realises that not only is he not loved by those around him, but he is not even **known** by them. His connection to his own life suddenly appears to be the thinnest of threads, ready to break at any moment. We hear such stories every day:

- A school teacher, rejected by his wife, walks into the sea late at night. He wears a diver's weight belt, the quick-release weights wired up so that he will have no chance to scrabble free. In seconds he is submerged in the dark water. His body, blue and swollen, washes in on the morning tide.

- A seventeen-year-old boy, top of his school, gains distinctions in only five of his six final-year subjects. (He has studied so hard that he makes small errors in the exams through sheer fatigue.) He borrows his father's shotgun, and that night on the riverbank by his home, puts the barrel into his mouth and tilts back his head.

- A young man watches a celebrity 'lingerie parade' in a department store. There is high-energy music playing and orchestrated hysteria. As he watches, he cannot resolve the conflicting feelings of shame and arousal that swirl through his body. What does it mean—these erotic posturings from women who will certainly offer him no love? Agitated, he climbs onto the stage, shouts abuse and is dragged away by security guards. Half an hour later he jumps to his death from a nearby building.

There is clear evidence (see table one) that all through the twentieth century men have been suffering uniquely and severely. Suicide, premature death, accidents and addiction—the statistics are all dominated by men. And hurt men also tend to hurt others. Physical violence against spouses, child sexual abuse, divorce, moral bankruptcy in business and politics, all point to something badly wrong with large numbers of men. Schoolyard shootings, serial killings.

Steve Biddulph, *Manhood: An action plan for changing men's lives*, 3rd edition,
Finch Publishing, Lane Cove 2002, pp. 1–2.

Commentary

The three case stories are clearly offered as random examples of the problems men are suffering from. Part of the force of the case stories comes from the use of graphic and dramatic details, such as the description of the 'blue and swollen' body and the detailed description of the boy putting the barrel in his mouth and tilting back his head. Case stories like these work to persuade the reader emotively by encouraging identification with people they know. The apparent ordinariness of the people suggests the widespread nature of the problem.

The context of the case stories in the passage is also important. The preceding text encourages readers to interpret the case stories in a particular way, as examples of the problems men are facing. If the case stories were surrounded by different text, you might interpret them in different ways unconnected with problems of masculinity.

The difficulty with case stories like these is that appropriately chosen case stories could be used to illustrate or support almost any argument. This does not mean that the author's argument is necessarily wrong. It may be true that there are widespread problems in men's lives. The case stories do not prove this, but they do encourage the reader to more readily accept the argument.

Activity

Write a case story in the same style as those above but which could be used to illustrate the view that men's lives are fine and which might encourage males to feel positive about their lives. Draw on your own experience or that of people you know or have come across in the news.

Statistics

Statistics should be more reliable than case stories or individual comments in that they do not just present random individual examples. But statistics are like authorities in that you can nearly always find some statistics to support different sides of an argument. The problem with statistics is that in themselves they do not tell us anything. It all depends on how they are interpreted.

CASE STUDY

18

Statistics in *Manhood*

In *Manhood*, the following statistics are used to illustrate the thesis that men are 'hurting', unhappy, unfulfilled and subject to 'pressure, loneliness and stress', that 'life is just not working' for most men and that 'we have a problem with men'.

Facing the facts

We are told it's a man's world, but the statistics on men's health, happiness and survival show this is a lie. Here are some of the *facts* about being a man in the late 20th century ...

- Men on average live for six years less than women do.
- Men routinely fail at close relationships. (Just two indicators: forty percent of marriages break down, and divorces are initiated by women in four out of five cases.)
- Over ninety percent of convicted acts of violence will be carried out by men, and seventy percent of the victims will be men.
- In school around ninety percent of children with behaviour problems are boys and over eighty percent of children with learning problems are also boys.
- One in seven boys will experience sexual assault by an adult or older child before the age of eighteen.
- Men comprise over ninety percent of inmates of gaols.
- Men are seventy-four percent of the unemployed.
- *The leading cause of death amongst men between twelve and sixty is self-inflicted death. In the 2000 ABS statistics, suicide accounted for one in every thirty-six male deaths overall.*

Surely it is the last point which most clearly shows we have a problem with men. Men and boys commit suicide four times more frequently than women.

Steve Biddulph, *Manhood: An action plan for changing men's lives*, 3rd edition, Finch Publishing, Lane Cove 2002, p. 6.

Commentary

These statistics are presented as illustrating that the world is not a 'man's world', implying that they show that men are not better off than women or at the very least that things are not good for men generally. Presented together in this manner, the statistics seem to provide pretty overwhelming evidence; but let's take each of these statistics in turn and examine them more closely.

'Men on average live for six years less than women do.'

It is always dangerous to extrapolate a cause from a statistic. The text here seems to be implying that men die earlier than women because of stress and unhappiness. In a study of life expectancy, the Victorian Department of Human Services states that the differences in life expectancy between males and females 'can largely be attributed to the greater health risks men take, resulting in more premature deaths from cardiovascular disease and injuries. There may also be a small "true" biological difference between men and women, attributed to the protective effect conferred by female hormones on cardiovascular disease' (Victorian Burden of Disease Study: Mortality, 1997). It could be argued that men take greater health risks than women because of stress and unhappiness, but there might be other explanations. Note that the Victorian study also points out that there may be an inbuilt biological cause for some of the difference.

The other dangerous thing to do is to interpret a statistic in isolation from other statistics. For example, *Manhood* does not mention that the life expectancy of men has actually been increasing and the gap between men and women has been decreasing since 1980. Another set of statistics not mentioned is that life expectancy figures for males in rural areas are lower than for those in urban areas. Does this mean males in rural areas are more stressed and unhappy than those in urban areas? In addition, life expectancy for Victorian males is higher than the Australian average, while that for Tasmanian males is lower. What does this say about Tasmanian males? (Australian Bureau of Statistics Press Releases 1999, 2000, 2001). In short it is very dangerous to extrapolate a simple cause from something as complex as life expectancy figures.

'Men routinely fail at close relationships. (Just two indicators: forty percent of marriages break down, and divorces are initiated by the woman in four out of five cases.)'

The fact that forty per cent of marriages break down does not necessarily prove that men routinely fail at close relationships. This is to attribute the breakdown of a marriage to one member of the partnership alone. The fact that it is mainly women who initiate divorces could in fact be interpreted to suggest that it is women who routinely fail.

'Over ninety percent of convicted acts of violence will be carried out by men, and seventy percent of the victims will be men.'

This appears to be suggesting that men are more violent than women because they are 'hurting' or under stress and that this stress is connected with their being male. Another statistic not mentioned, which could be used to undermine the impression of the extent of the 'problem' with men, however, is that the vast majority of men do not commit acts of violence. This statistic also neglects the high correlation between low socio-economic status, race, drug use and disrupted family life with violent crime. In other words, violence is not simply associated with maleness.

'In school around ninety percent of children with behaviour problems are boys and over eighty percent of children with learning problems are also boys.'

To know whether this provides evidence of a widespread problem among males, you would need to know the actual percentage of the school population with behaviour and learning problems. General observation and experience would suggest that the vast majority of boys are successful at school. This might mean that the problem may be with only some males.

'One in seven boys will experience sexual assault by an adult or older child before the age of eighteen.'

To know whether this proves that it is not a man's world, you would need to know the figures for sexual assault on women. Statistics from the Crime Prevention Branch of the Commonwealth Attorney General's Department show that the rate of sexual abuse of boys under 19 between 1989 and 1999 was 0.19 per cent or close to one in 500, which is a lot less than one in seven. In comparison, the rate for females was 0.91 per cent, or close to one in a hundred, five times the rate for men (*Crime in Australia*, Attorney General's Department, 2000).

'Men comprise over ninety percent of inmates of gaols.'

Given the figures for violent crime, this figure is hardly surprising. This presents the statistic for violent crime as if it is a separate additional piece of information which gives added weight to the argument that we have a problem with men, rather than being a related statistic.

'Men are seventy-four percent of the unemployed.'

As with the other statistics, *Manhood* does not give the source of this figure, but government figures for 2000 show that males made up 57 per cent of the unemployed and females 43 per cent. So the employment rate for males is higher, but not as high as suggested in *Manhood*. Why is this? Officially an unemployed person is someone who is not currently in employment but is seeking employment. A person who is not seeking employment is not considered unemployed. One of the reasons why unemployment is higher for males is that more males want to be employed. Government figures show that while 72 per cent of males are employed or seeking employment only 56 per cent of females are. This is because many females are engaged in home and family duties. Here's another statistic which casts a different light on the issue: of those who were employed in 2001, average weekly earnings for males was $821 compared with $550 for females (Australian Bureau of Statistics, *2001 Labour Statistics in Brief*).

'The leading cause of death amongst men between twelve and sixty is self-inflicted death. In the 2000 ABS statistics, suicide accounted for one in every thirty-six male deaths overall.'

This statistic can be misleading if not examined carefully. At first glance it appears quite shocking, but we need to realise that as medical progress has removed many diseases as leading causes of death and road safety campaigns have lowered the road toll, so these have been eliminated as major causes of death. It was almost inevitable therefore that suicide would become, in relative terms, a major cause of death.

A statistic that should cause concern is that showing that men and boys commit suicide four times more frequently than women, a figure supported by a number of studies. Note, though, that statistics also show that suicide attempts by females are 40 per cent higher than for males (Commonwealth Department of Human Services and Health, *Youth Suicide in Australia: a background monograph*, Canberra: AGPS, 1995).

In interpreting the higher rate of suicide among males, you also need to take into account the correlation between suicide and access to weapons, substance abuse, family dysfunction and socioeconomic status. Here's another important statistic: imprisonment increases by thirteen the risk of suicide among young males (Australian Bureau of Statistics, *Social Trends 1994*). In other words, the high suicide rate of males is related to their higher rate of imprisonment.

In conclusion then, the statistics in *Manhood* do not by themselves provide evidence that it is not a man's world. While there may be many men who are hurting, unhappy or stressed, the statistics themselves do not suggest this is widespread or that men in general do not have it better than women. They do suggest that there may be a small group of males who are prone to violence and thus imprisonment for a variety of complex factors, rather than simply being male, who are certainly worse off and more at risk than the rest of society.

Language

Language is not neutral but is imbued with connotations and values and capable of evoking response at an emotive level.

Framework for examining language in an expository text:

1 Highlight or note down words or phrases that seem to be highly emotive and any uses of figurative language.

2 Tease out the connotations of these words or phrases: what ideas and emotions are they likely to evoke?

3 See if you can discern any patterns to the use of emotive or figurative language: does the text draw extensively on one or more specific areas of discourse, such as the discourses of war, sport or masculinity? The case study on *The Beauty Myth* later in this chapter, for example, draws heavily on the discourse of conflict and violence to make its point about the effects of body image on females.

CASE STUDY

19

English is more than a power tool

The following passage is an editorial from *The Australian* of 9 March 2002. It discusses the New South Wales HSC (High School Certificate) examination of the previous year.

The Australian, 9–10 March 2002, p. 18.

English is more than a power tool

ONLY education bureaucrats could have the arrogance to demand school students "rewrite" George Orwell's classic essay Politics and the English Language —and miss the irony. But the ideologues who dreamed up this and other baffling NSW HSC English exam questions are the same people who think the ATSIC* website, the movie *Clueless*, and Natasha Stott Despoja's ** first parliamentary speech are as worthy of close study as the plays of William Shakespeare, Abraham Lincoln's oratory, Henry Lawson's poetry or Jane Austen's novels.

It's not that students shouldn't be equipped to critically evaluate all manner of "texts". In contemporary society young people are bombarded with information and entertainment from television, film, advertisements and the internet. English, if it is grounded in the written word, can help students learn how to think and critically evaluate their world. However, an insidious form of political bullying is impinging on the intellectual freedom, and enjoyment, of Australia's teenagers as they complete their secondary school studies in English. Frustration among students, teachers and parents has sparked an official inquiry in NSW. Yet NSW is one of the last states to fall into line with the post-modern orthodoxy— everything is a text and *Star Wars* and Socrates are of equal value—that has colonised university English departments and

secondary school curriculums across Australia. Cultural relativism swept Victorian education from the late 1980s under Cain and Kirner's VCE revolution***. In Queensland there are no prescribed English texts at all, and the new draft English syllabus looks more like that of its southern cousins.

The study of English at school level has been turned into a trendy version of film studies, as well as a vehicle for the latest thinking on political power, gender and race relations. Texts can only be discussed in their social context and in relation to one another. The author and reader have been replaced by "composers of texts" and "responders". Exam questions no longer require multiple essays with well-structured arguments. Now students are asked to "imagine" they are a bureaucrat/employee of the tourist commission/department of consumer affairs/actor, and write a letter/report/speech/ conversation about their texts and how they shape a particular response.

The most sinister aspect of this "reform" is the political agenda underpinning it. The public servants who devised the changes have signed up to the cultural nihilism at the heart of post-modern or deconstructionist theory, where truth is relative and greatness (as in Great Books or the Western canon of literature) a social construct. Students are in the intellectually restrictive position where they are delivering up politically expected answers, say about the "vision" expressed in Ms Stott Despoja's first speech. We doubt whether the speech Aboriginal leader John Ah Kit delivered this week, decrying the victim mentality in indigenous Australia, would be deemed an acceptable "text".

A bit of intellectual rigour is in order. The study of English lies at the heart of a liberal education. It is central to our understanding of language and our literary heritage. As the core humanities subject, English can help students know themselves, society and history. It can give a young person the communication tools needed to cope in a globalised and technologically advancing world. And it can spark a lifelong adventure with books. Students have their lives, and university courses, to analyse films and websites. Can't they appreciate a great essay, poem or novel on its own merits, rather than rewrite it for an English exam? But as Nobel laureate V.S. Naipaul said recently, even his alma mater, Oxford University, has turned English into a "political romp through a few simple texts". It's time for some retro fashion in English education circles.

*Aboriginal and Torres Strait Islander Commission
** An Australian Democrat senator
*** This refers to curriculum changes which occurred in Victoria under the Labor government in the 1980s.

Commentary

Notice the use of terms such as 'bureaucrats' and 'ideologues' to characterise those responsible for preparing the examination and deciding the syllabus. These terms have developed negative connotations in Australian society, connoting faceless people who are out of touch with the real world. Unfortunately even the term 'public servant' has this connotation for some people.

'Ideologue' also connotes someone with a hidden political agenda and often evokes associations with totalitarianism and Marxism. This impression of a hidden political agenda is reinforced by highly charged terms such as 'insidious' and 'sinister', which can be read as functioning to evoke readers' fears and the suggestion that public servants have 'signed up' in the manner a person might sign up to a political party.

Terms such as 'bullying' and 'colonised' suggest a degree of violence and oppression in the implementation of the English curriculum.

In contrast to the negative portrayal of the English curriculum, the passage makes extensive use of terms that appeal to strongly held values in Australian society: 'intellectual freedom', 'intellectual rigour', 'liberal education' and 'literary heritage'.

You might be interested in the following responses to the editorial.

NEWSPAPER ARTICLE

The Australian, 11 March 2002, p. 12.

Shakespeare no stranger to the popular culture bear pit

YOUR editorial on teaching English (9–10/3) raises important questions but protests too much. Arguably, it misses the point of its own examples.

The movie *Clueless* is well worth studying. It speaks to the experience of modern teenagers, and is also a witty re-telling of Jane Austen's *Emma*.

In some schools, they are studied together. They make similar points about class, morality, self-knowledge, and the wisdom of meddling in other people's lives. The movie even anticipates the present debate by showing that there are many paths to cultural literacy. Our schoolgirl heroine corrects her uni-student rival, remarking that it was Polonius, not Hamlet, who said "to thine own self be true". The student retorts that she "knows her Shakespeare". Our heroine counters that she "knows her Mel Gibson"—and thus knows Shakespeare too, only better.

As a former teacher in Melbourne's western suburbs, I have no doubt that modern films can engage students with literary works that for many are not so accessible.

We forget too easily that Austen and Shakespeare contributed to the popular culture of their own time, in the media available to them.

Geoff Sharrock
Northcote, Vic

YOUR editorial has made me compare my schooling with that of my son in Year 12. I remember answering interminable questions beginning, "What does the author mean when he writes …". As a schoolboy, I had no idea what the author meant but could produce some mangled account of what the teacher said he meant.

I also remember how I was distanced from the study of English literature by having the classics rammed down my throat like some medicinal substance that was declared good for me. Yet despite my education, I, possibly too slowly, learned to love the classics.

Today I watch with great pleasure as my son and his fellow HSC students discuss, analyse and challenge the meaning of the classics, speeches, advertisements, films, indeed any text that impinges on their lives.

And isn't this the point? The new syllabus puts these classics into contexts that are relevant for these young people. They are not some distant authority to which students must submit, but the great works are woven into their experience.

Alan Gold
St Ives, NSW

Structure

The structure of a text is the way in which the arguments or information is organised. Examining the structure of a text allows you to see how a reader may be drawn into accepting the views offered in that text.

Every text has its own particular structure. It is not possible to present a list of frameworks into which every text you encounter can be slotted. But it is possible to present a list of structural devices that are often used to organise information and arguments in a text. These devices can help you to follow the structure of an argument,, observe how it is developed and distinguish between main ideas, supporting ideas and examples. A text may use examples of some of these devices at different points in the text. They may occur at the level of the sentence or the paragraph. Not every text will use every structural device.

Recursion, repetition, re-emphasis

Recursion, repetition and re-emphasis all involve returning to an earlier point to re-emphasise it, illustrate it in a different manner or show how it is true in different ways.

Development

Development involves taking a point just made and developing it further or teasing out the implications.

Illustration, exemplification

Some parts of an expository text are not part of the argument but serve to illustrate or provide examples of a point being made.

Narrative incursion

Narrative incursion is a form of illustration that uses narratives to illustrate or support a point.

Transition

A transition is a movement from one point to another.

Cause and effect

A text or part of a text can be based around movement from a cause to an effect.

Problem–solution

Many texts or parts of a text begin by setting up a problem, often in the form of a question, and then showing the reader the solution to the problem.

Question–answer

Texts can pose a question which is then answered. This is similar to the problem–solution technique. The case studies later in this chapter, from *Inventing the Future* and *The Beauty Myth*, both use this technique.

Comparison, contrast

Texts can develop a case or seek reader assent by making use of comparison or contrasts. The passage from *The Beauty Myth* later in this chapter uses this device where the writer compares what has been achieved by women with the problems which they still, in her view, face.

CASE STUDY

Inventing the Future

The following passage was written by David Suzuki, a Canadian academic, writer and broadcaster on environmental issues. It was published in 1990. The annotations on the right are intended to 'walk' you through the passage and help you identify main ideas, supporting ideas and examples as well as understand the structure and rhetorical devices used in the passage so that you can apply the understandings you gain to other passages.

The Spiritual Value of Land

Can those of us who live with the attitudes of Western societies recognize anything of native values in ourselves? I believe that there are intimations of noneconomic, intangible factors that matter deeply to us.

I received a form letter the other day from a real estate agent. It seems that Vancouver real estate is "hot" right now and I can make a lot of money by putting my house on the market. It is said that there is a lot of "offshore money" flooding into Canada for investment in property and that drives land values up. People are buying houses as a hedge against inflation. And it is precisely this way of treating land as mere property for economic transactions that is leading us into a deep ecological crisis.

I will never willingly sell my house because the things that make it home have no economic "value," yet for me are beyond price. You see, in the fifteen years that I've owned my place, it has accumulated a history that is very real for me. My best friend, Jim Murray, helped me build the backyard fence and carved a gate handle. They remind me of him every time I enter the yard. Inside the house we still use a kitchen cabinet that my father made for Tara and me when we were just married. We salvaged it from our apartment because it represents a bit of Dad and our early years together. One of our prized possessions is an old table that recalls the friends who gave it to us when they left

Notice how Suzuki opens with a question as a means of engaging the reader. The following sentence answers the question in general terms, thus providing the central argument or thesis of the passage.

Note the use of 'us' in the second sentence, which establishes a sense of common identity between writer and reader.

Suzuki then makes use of a narrative of a personal experience to personalise the argument and to begin illustrating his thesis.

Here Suzuki moves away from the personal narrative to a more generalised statement about ecological issues. This provides a transition to the next paragraph, which will explain the importance of the spiritual value of land.

This is the topic sentence of this paragraph—the general idea that the rest of the paragraph will illustrate. It also develops the central thesis put forward in the first paragraph.

Here Suzuki begins a series of personal narratives that illustrate the importance of the spiritual value of his land to him, which continue into the following paragraph. He is using himself as an example to illustrate his thesis that we are beginning to realise the spiritual value of land.
Notice how the personal narratives encompass a wide range of personal relationships and experiences. Most readers could be expected to identify with one or more of these. Relationships include friendship, parents, spouse, parents-in-law, pets and children. Experiences include co-operating with friends, early marriage, losing friends, shared meals, death and watching children grow. Thus Suzuki has appealed to many commonly held values and common experiences.

Vancouver to return to Winnipeg. Each year I pick asparagus and raspberries that my father-in-law (who lives upstairs) planted for me because he knew how much I enjoy them. Our English flower garden is his pride and joy, and every time I admire it, I can picture him standing there, leaning on a shovel and puffing his pipe. Every Christmas brings memories of glorious feasts prepared effortlessly by Tara's mother.

We buried the family dog, Pasha, under the dogwood tree in his favourite digging hole. My daughters have turned that area into a cemetery for a hamster, a salamander and several other dead animals that they've found around the neighbourhood. In the branches of that tree is one of the girls' favourite play areas, a treehouse that I spent many happy hours building and many more just watching children playing in. And everywhere in the house and yard, my home is alive with reminders of my wife. A clematis plant has climbed along the back gate. Four years ago after my mother died, we scattered her ashes on the ground around it. Last year we added the ashes of my sister's daughter. Now when the purple flowers bloom, the pain of the loss of my mother and niece is softened because somehow I feel they are nearby.

In the real estate market, none of these things adds a cent to the "value" of the property, yet for me they are what make my house a home and represent value beyond price. In less than two decades, family and friends have become a palpable presence everywhere. What I'm talking about are things that exist only in my mind, memories and experiences that are an expression of my personal values and history. These are essentially spiritual values. I have accumulated memory and history in only fifteen years of occupation; native people have lived on their land for thousands of years.

Years ago I visited the Dome of the Rock in Jerusalem. That beautiful Muslim temple covers one of the most sacred places in all of Islam—a rock! A visitor from outer space would find completely incomprehensible the fuss made by a group of people over what is a rather ordinary geological formation. What makes it such an important site is the fact that the prophet, Mohammed, is said to have ascended to heaven from that rock. Human beings assign worth to objects, places or people on the basis of factors that have no physical or material reality—they are really in the mind.

This sentence re-emphasises the first sentence of the third paragraph. Thus Suzuki has started with a general statement—that the things which give his land value have no economic price but are nevertheless important—then given a series of examples to illustrate this and then reiterated the general statement after the examples. The sentences that follow are developing sentences—they develop and explain his point in more detail.

Here Suzuki moves from his personal experiences of the spiritual value of land to, for his readers, a more distant example. This has the effect of universalising his feelings, showing that they are not just personal but widespread and shared by older societies.

This is a concluding or summing-up sentence. It summarises the points Suzuki has made using his own experience and the example of the Dome of the Rock.

Our species has a great capacity for seeing value in intangible things. But as people in the highly industrialized countries have become increasingly mobile, our sense of permanence and connection with our surroundings is weakened. High-rise apartments, department stores, supermarkets and airports take on a global uniformity and interchangeability. We merely use them for their goods or services so property becomes another commodity to be used in the service of profit.

This sentence re-emphasises the point made in the previous sentence in different words. It acts as a transition to the next part where Suzuki compares an awareness of the spiritual value of land to what is happening in the Western world. Having been exposed to an awareness of the spiritual value of land, readers can be expected to look at their familiar world in new ways and disapprove of it. Note how Suzuki has gradually led the reader into this position. By this point in the passage he has established the Western world's approach to land as a problem. Now comes the solution.

The solutions to the biodiversity crisis—decreasing consumption and numbers of our species, reducing the inequities between nations, protecting wildlife habitat, eliminating pollution—demand a radical change of attitude to our relationship with the land and other species. Stanford University ecologist Paul Ehrlich believes that "A quasi-religious transformation leading to the appreciation of diversity for its own sake may be required to save other organisms and ourselves."

Here Suzuki uses an authority to move his essay away from being merely a personal reflection to being an essay that deals with an issue of importance because it is recognised as such by an authority.

The seeds of that "quasi-religious" change can be found in the spiritual connection that native people have with their home. There are faint echoes of that attachment in non-native society. It's there in the Saskatchewan farmer who refuses to follow the bank's advice and sell his farm because his father and grandfather farmed that land and he intends to pass it on to his children. This makes no economic sense, but the spiritual meaning of the farm transcends money.

Here Suzuki provides further examples of people who feel as he does, thus further universalising his arguments.

This is another example of the main thesis being reiterated.

In Newfoundland, the tiny clusters of people who continue to remain in the isolated coastal outports where their ancestors lived and fished for centuries inform us of the reality and power of other values. This is not foolish nostalgia but a hint of a new spiritual relationship with our homes that is of far greater value than anything economic.

Here Suzuki concludes by again reiterating his central thesis that the spiritual value of land is vitally important.

David Suzuki, 'The Spiritual Value of Land', *Inventing the Future*, Allen & Unwin, St Leonards 1990, pp. 245–7.

Values and the audience

So far this chapter has looked at the various ways in which expository texts encourage readers to accept the views offered. At the heart of this process is the appeal to values of importance to the reader. If the reader does not hold the values appealed to by the writer, however, the reader is unlikely to accept the view put forward. Similarly, if a text challenges a reader's usual view of the world, he or she may respond negatively towards the text.

Activity

Choose one of the case studies in this chapter and discuss what values might lead a reader to reject the views offered.

CASE STUDY

21

This and the following two case studies deal with the topic of female body image, but in very different ways. They illustrate different forms of expository writing that reflect differences in audience and purpose.

The Beauty Myth

The Beauty Myth was published in 1990 and was one of the first major texts to deal with the topic of female body image. In fact *The New York Times* called *The Beauty Myth* one of the seventy most significant books of the century. The following passage is taken from the opening three pages.

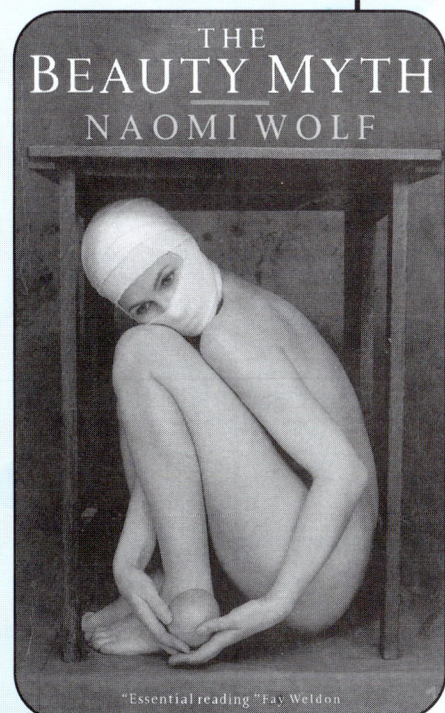

This passage argues that despite the gains of feminism since the early 1970s, which involved women achieving many freedoms and equalities, women are still oppressed by what Wolf calls the beauty myth: the idea that there is an absolute ideal of beauty to which every woman should aspire. Wolf sees this as part of a backlash against feminism and a means of controlling women by undermining their sense of self-worth.

One of the most useful ways to begin examining the structure and rhetorical techniques employed in a passage is to identify the paragraph or sentences that contain the central idea or argument. In the case of the passage below, the central argument is put forward in the fifth paragraph and especially in the sentence 'We are in the midst of a violent backlash against feminism that uses images of female beauty as a political weapon against women's advancement: the beauty myth'. Note how far into the passage the central argument appears.

If you compare this passage with the passage from *Manhood* in an earlier case study, you will see that they take very different approaches to developing their respective arguments. In the passage from *Manhood*, Biddulph puts his argument up front, in the very first sentence in fact, and then proceeds to develop and illustrate it. In the passage from *The Beauty Myth*, in contrast, Wolf gradually builds towards her central argument, gently bringing the reader along with her to an acceptance of her thesis. Wolf could have started by stating straight out that women have achieved a lot and they still do not feel free because of the pressure on them to conform to particular ideas of beauty. Instead of this, she gradually leads the reader towards an acceptance of this idea.

The technique used in this passage is similar to that used in 'The Spiritual Value of Land' by David Suzuki in Case study 20.

Here are some other points to note about the passage while reading.

Language and tone

Notice how the language and tone of the passage change in line with the development of the argument. Initially the passage is relatively unemotive and has a rather thoughtful, almost puzzled tone. As it develops, the sentences become more directly assertive and the language becomes increasingly emotive.

Persona

In this passage, Wolf presents herself as an authority by employing questions to which she then provides answers and strongly assertive generalisations. While the generalisations are unsupported here, this is because this passage is the introduction to the book. What Wolf is doing is setting up an argument in the form of a generalisation that the rest of the book will support with evidence and more detailed argument. In a way she is doing exactly what you do when you write an introduction to an essay.

At the same time as establishing herself as an authoritative persona, Wolf also establishes herself as one with her female audience. In particular, note the movement from paragraph two to paragraph three which involves a movement from talking about 'women' to talking about 'us'.

The annotations to the passage below explain the development of the argument, the structure of the passage and some of the rhetorical techniques employed. Read the passage straight through first, ignoring the annotations, to get a sense of the argument. Then re-read the passage paying attention to the annotations.

At last, after a long silence, women took to the streets. In the two decades of radical action that followed the rebirth of feminism in the early 1970s, Western women gained legal and reproductive rights, pursued higher education, entered the trades and the professions, and overturned ancient and revered beliefs about their social role. A generation on, do women feel free?

The affluent, educated, liberated women of the First World, who can enjoy freedoms unavailable to any women ever before, do not feel as free as they want to. And they can no longer restrict to the subconscious their sense that this lack of freedom has something to do with—with apparently frivolous issues, things that really should not matter. Many are ashamed to admit that such trivial concerns—to do with physical appearance, bodies, faces, hair, clothes—matter so much. But in spite of shame, guilt, and denial, more and more women are wondering if it isn't that they are entirely neurotic and alone but rather that something important is indeed at stake that has to do with the relationship between female liberation and female beauty.

The more legal and material hindrances women have broken through, the more strictly and heavily and cruelly images of female beauty have come to weigh upon us. Many women sense that women's collective progress has stalled; compared with the heady momentum of earlier days, there is a dispiriting climate of confusion, division, cynicism, and above all, exhaustion. After years of much struggle and little recognition, many older women feel burned out; after years of taking its light for granted, many younger women show little interest in touching new fire to the torch.

During the past decade, women breached the power structure; meanwhile, eating disorders rose exponentially and cosmetic surgery became the fastest-growing medical specialty. During the past five years, consumer spending doubled, pornography became the main media category, ahead of legitimate films and records combined, and thirty-three thousand American women told researchers that they would rather lose ten to fifteen pounds than achieve any other goal. More women have more money and

Notice how different the tone of the first paragraph is to that of the fifth, which contains the central argument. At first it is positive, celebrating the achievements of the feminist movement of the early 1970s. Then in the last sentence it undercuts this sense of achievement and celebration by raising the question, 'A generation on, do women feel free?' thus attempting to create a sense of doubt in the reader's mind.

The second paragraph answers the question posed in the first: women 'do not feel as free as they want to'. It develops this idea further, suggesting why women do not feel free: it is to do with physical appearance. But notice how mildly and hesitantly this idea is put forward: 'it has something to do with—with apparently frivolous things'. The pause and the repetition of 'with' almost suggest an unwillingness to state something. The next rhetorical movement in this paragraph is to suggest that these matters may not be trivial at all but may be connected with issues important to female liberation. Again the tone is hesitant and speculative rather than assertive. It is as though Wolf is gradually coaxing the readers to bring to the surface something that they, perhaps subconsciously, already realise.

The first sentence of the third paragraph is essentially a summary of the ideas suggested in the first two paragraphs. As with the movement from the first to the second paragraph, the movement from the second to the third is essentially a question–answer movement. Notice how different the tone of this paragraph is from the first two. It is much more forceful. The language is more highly charged with the use of emotive terms such as 'strictly, heavily and cruelly', 'weigh' , 'exhaustion' and 'burned out'.

The fourth paragraph is essentially an extension of the third, giving specific examples of how images of female beauty are weighing heavily on women. Notice how the first and third sentences work by contrasting achievements of the feminist movement with the negative effects of the obsession with appearance. Notice also how the language becomes increasingly emotive and graphic, culminating in the use of words such as 'poisoning', 'dark vein', 'terror' and 'dread'. By the end of this paragraph, Wolf has set up a conundrum or puzzle: women have achieved a lot but they feel bad about themselves. Why is this so?

power and scope and legal recognition than we have ever had before; but in terms of how we feel about ourselves *physically,* we may actually be worse off than our unliberated grandmothers. Recent research consistently shows that inside the majority of the West's controlled, attractive, successful working women, there is a secret 'underlife' poisoning our freedom; infused with notions of beauty, it is a dark vein of self-hatred, physical obsessions, terror of aging, and dread of lost control.

It is no accident that so many potentially powerful women feel this way. We are in the midst of a violent backlash against feminism that uses images of female beauty as a political weapon against women's advancement: the beauty myth. It is the modern version of a social reflex that has been in force since the Industrial Revolution. As women released themselves from the feminine mystique of domesticity, the beauty myth took over its lost ground, expanding as it waned to carry on its work of social control.

The contemporary backlash is so violent because the ideology of beauty is the last one remaining of the old feminine ideologies that still has the power to control those women whom second wave feminism would have otherwise made relatively uncontrollable: It has grown stronger to take over the work of social coercion that myths about motherhood, domesticity, chastity, and passivity, no longer can manage. It is seeking right now to undo psychologically and covertly all the good things that feminism did for women materially and overtly.

This counterforce is operating to checkmate the inheritance of feminism on every level in the lives of Western women. Feminism gave us laws against job discrimination based on gender; immediately case law evolved in Britain and the United States that institutionalized job discrimination based on women's appearances. Patriarchal religion declined; new religious dogma, using some of the mind-altering techniques of older cults and sects, arose around age and weight to functionally supplant traditional ritual. Feminists, inspired by Friedan, broke the stranglehold on the women's popular press of advertisers for household products, who were promoting the feminine mystique; at once, the diet and skin care

The answer is given in the second sentence of the fifth paragraph, which is the main argument of the text: because there is a backlash against feminism and the beauty myth is the weapon of this backlash. This is the point to which the passage has gradually been building.

The rest of this paragraph develops the idea of the beauty myth as a political weapon, explaining that it has replaced forms of control which have disappeared.

The sixth and seventh paragraphs are a development of the fifth. They contain no new ideas. Rather they explain in more detail how the beauty myth works to replace previous methods of control.

The final paragraph works, much like the fourth, through the use of contrast. It contrasts the forms of control over women which have been defeated with the new forms of control associated with the beauty myth. Notice how the language in the seventh paragraph makes use of terms with connotations of conflict and violence—'checkmate', 'stranglehold', 'invaded', 'strip'.

industries became the new cultural censors of women's intellectual space, and because of their pressure, the gaunt, youthful model supplanted the happy housewife as the arbiter of successful womanhood. The sexual revolution promoted the discovery of female sexuality; 'beauty pornography'—which for the first time in women's history artificially links a commodified "beauty" directly and explicitly to sexuality—invaded the mainstream to undermine women's new and vulnerable sense of sexual self-worth. Reproductive rights gave Western women control over our own bodies; the weight of fashion models plummeted to 23 percent below that of ordinary women, eating disorders rose exponentially, and a mass neurosis was promoted that used food and weight to strip women of that sense of control. Women insisted on politicizing health; new technologies of invasive, potentially dangerous 'cosmetic' surgeries developed apace to re-exert old forms of medical control of women.

Naomi Wolf, *The Beauty Myth*, Vintage, London 1990, pp. 9–11.

22

CASE STUDY

Real Gorgeous

This case study presents some passages from *Real Gorgeous: The Truth about Body and Beauty*, published in Australia in 1994 and written by Kaz Cooke, an Australian writer and cartoonist. This case study has been chosen to contrast with *The Beauty Myth* and to show how two texts on essentially the same topic can be written in very different ways. *Real Gorgeous* is aimed at a more general audience than *The Beauty Myth*. It seems to be targeted at younger women, especially teenagers.

Focus question

What differences are there between these passages and the passage from The Beauty Myth? Note them.

THE BESTSELLER IS BACK!

real Gorgeous

The truth about
body and beauty

KAZ COOKE

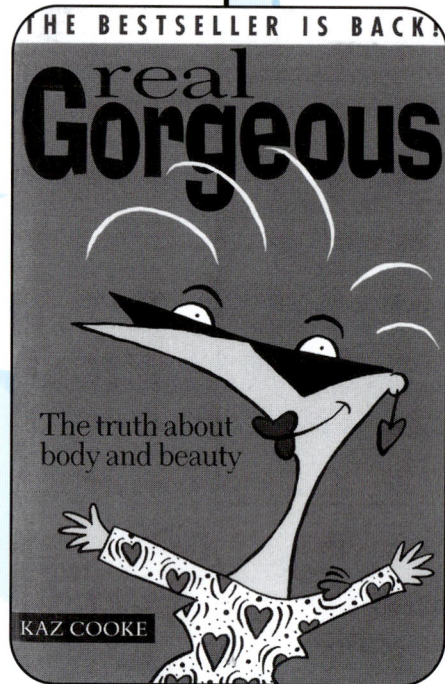

Introduction

We need something that will cheer up anybody who has 'the uglies'. Something to reassure all certifiably gorgeous girls and women that they are not Space Porkers from Hell.

We need the facts which will make us RELAX, not the overwrought opinions that send us fleeing to stupid diets, insane over-exercising and mirror-misery. We want to find out how to stop seeing our bodies as the enemy. And hey, let's face it, we wouldn't mind a laugh while we're at it.

We need some help with self-esteem which cuts through the mixed messages of magazine articles called 'Love your own body' illustrated only by professionally-lit, re-touched photos of a size-8, six-foot-tall, 13-year-old aerobics instructor-model wearing a frilly baby-doll dress, platform thigh-boots and a terminally bored expression.

We need to get away from too many dry statistics, relentless academic essays, incomprehensible diagrams and scientific formulas that don't seem to relate to real life. We need stuff which frees us to make up our own minds. And maybe cartoons would be a lot more fun than endless pictures of models.

We need a book that isn't just about theory but about action: *how* to break out of the useless dieting cycle, *how* to deal with dorks who make comments about our appearance, *how* to accept a natural womanly shape, whether tall, small, thin or rounded.

We'd like to know how to avoid and deal with eating disorders, and what we can eat without panicking. We want the truth about skincare products: which cheap ones work and which ones advertise using pretend science, fancy French and straight-out lies. We want to have fun with clothes and make-up, not feel that we have to spend a fortune on stuff to blindly follow fashion.

We need to know why cosmetic surgery is not about simple 'nips and tucks', but pain, and gouging, and self-hatred and desperation that has other answers than the knife. We'd like to be able to laugh off the *Allure* magazine suggestion that face-lift bandages might become 'a fashion trend'.

We need some information that, unlike magazines, isn't influenced by advertising. A book that isn't trying to sell you anything except more self-confidence and the truth. Something that we can always open to remind ourselves that it's okay that we have different shapes, different sizes and different skin. (Not to mention the odd tuft of body hair.) A book that we can run to any time we feel like screaming at the very sight of a cakie thing.

In short, we need a book that gathers all this stuff together, combines the facts and the fun and gives us some options about where to look for more help if we need it.

I couldn't find such a book, so I had to write one. Here it is.

Kaz Cooke

Pressure to have bad body image Where do we start? The censored image of women in TV and film shows only the thin; magazines suggest that body 'flaws' should be disguised, dieted against or exercised away. A Clarins ad (after writing this book I am beginning rather to despise the Clarins corporation) has the headline 'No body is perfect' next to a very thin, tall model with flawless (or airbrushed) skin. 'Get closer to the perfection you desire with Clarins plant extract-based treatments … You can concentrate on specific concerns like the bust or maybe you want a firmer derrière … Stubborn thighs, hips and bottoms … Lift and tighten … with the ultimate body control Clarins Body Shaping Gel'. Thighs, hips and bums are not 'stubborn' any more than they are 'confused' or 'happy'. Body parts do not have personalities or feelings.

> – How do you get a boyfriend?
> – Be yourself
>
> My boyfriend was attracted to me because of my size. He loves huge buttocks and breasts and the confident way in which I walk … I hope you're as happy as I am.
>
> Graffiti, Melbourne University woman's toilets

The woman on the billboard in the lingerie ads is nearly one quarter thinner again than the average woman, and much taller as well. Even if the model were of average height she could put on eight or ten more kilos without causing any health problems. But she is touted as having 'the perfect body'.

The definition of 'the perfect body', indeed, the idea that there might be only one, has been announced by media commentators who have no right to do so. There is more than one definition of a 'good body' or a 'fabulous body'. A 'perfect body' is a myth.

Body hatred is fashionable. Young girls watch adult women, and they know that one of the ways to be a big girl, a grown-up is that we have to grab hold of a part of ourselves with disgust and say, 'Look at this, I'm too fat.' Everyone else says, 'No you're not, I am. Look at this! Feel this!' grasping bits of themselves. Part of being a woman is projected as specific self-loathing in the face of evidence to the contrary. Anybody observing can see that the flesh being grabbed is not too fat. And still the self-definition insists: the distortion is lore, and law.

At only 42 kilos, 1960s model icon Twiggy said she 'hated what I looked like … I ate like a horse and just burned off everything. Like most skinny people, I desperately wanted to put on weight.' When very thin singer Margaret Urlich appeared on the Australian sports program *Live and Sweaty*, envious host Elle McFeast jokingly abused her for being thin, in the 'You're so thin, you bitch' tradition. Urlich stood up and twirled in mock triumph. Women who are thin are constantly referred to as 'lucky'. The rest of us, it is assumed, must work to become more like them.

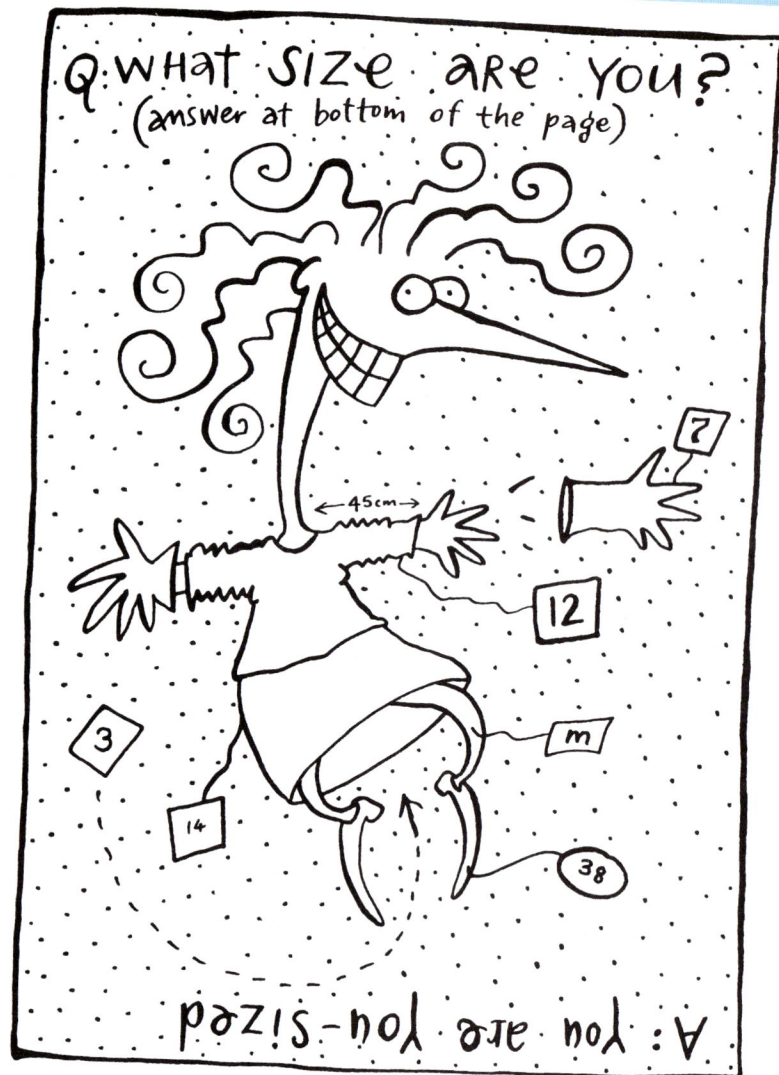

Q: WHAT SIZE ARE YOU?
(answer at bottom of the page)

A: You are you-sized.

The body police

Hassled by the body police Families, relatives and friends feel they have a right to comment on a girl's body when it begins to change at puberty. Girls are taught to expect exposure and commentary and judgement from others, often based on unrealistic ideals. The girls are shamed and turn to dieting and exercise. Penelope Goward, head of Victoria's VicHealth Body Image project, also notes this. 'If you have received negative feedback about your body as a child and adolescent, you will have low self-esteem about your body when you grow up.'

How to deal with the body police So many of the girls and women who wrote to me about this book, responding to a request printed by *Cleo* and *Dolly* magazines, could remember the comment that first started them dieting, and often spurred them on to an eating disorder, especially bulimia.

I loathed mirrors and shopping for clothes. When I was 16 something changed. I discovered the world of performing arts … I left my school to go to a performing arts course in Year12. My folks were horrified. They said I could not succeed because I was 'fat', but I wasn't doing it as a career move, I was doing it to gain confidence in myself. And I did gain confidence, slowly. According to conventional tables I am 40 kilos overweight. I've always had plenty of boyfriends and offers for as long as I have felt confident about myself. I have recently started working as a photographic model and a life-drawing model: confident women of my shape and size are in short supply so I'm getting plenty of work. I still have my 'fat days', my 'ugly days' and my 'bad hair days' but I am generally satisfied with the way I look.

Willa, 24, suburban Melbourne

Perhaps if you show this book to members of your family they will realise the damage their 'joking' or judgement may have. Explain to them they might have forgotten that the natural changes at puberty don't match the pictures of girls and women seen in magazines and on TV. Let them know that their comments—about something you cannot and should not try to control—are training you for food obsessions, eating disorders and a lifetime of self-loathing. Ask them to accept you they [sic] way you are.

If they don't, try to remember that so many parents, especially mothers, have been subjected to the same nasty pressure about bodies and the fear of fat. They can project their fears on to you through comments such as, 'You're getting fat', even when you are a perfect shape and size for your self. (Remember that you may have different genes than your mother or sisters.)

I hate being skinny. When I get sick I have no reserves and feel so weak and skinny: it's a really scary feeling. I believe there is too much pressure on females to look great. What is inside is much more important. I am finally learning this. Someone who is only average-looking can appear so beautiful—if they are happy and kind on the inside it will make them glow with beauty on the outside.

Mandy, 21, Perth

I hate my face because it's too fat. I would much rather be anorexic than obese or overweight. When I look in magazines I think how I'd love to be skinny. Everywhere I look there are skinny people, which makes me hate myself even more. I have tried to commit suicide about four times. I wish magazines would stop portraying 'fat' as being bad.

Amy, 16, Tasmania

Three years ago I put on a little bit of weight and went up to 66 kilos, which is okay. I was informed by grandparents, sister and parents that I was 'getting fat'. I then changed to a gluten-and dairy product-free diet and exercised like mad. I lost 12 kilos. I was then told I'd lost too much weight. I've been called ugly, beautiful and pretty, hassled due to my big breasts and hips, called fat, skinny and a rake. What am I supposed to think? The main influence on me in these areas is my family. I am doing nursing and we are educated about positive self-esteem, eating disorders, weight ranges. But somehow, I don't know why, the experts and print media, although (probably) they give more truthful information, do not have the same amount of influence as the visual media.

Kathleen, Newcastle

You can use this book to show your family that dieting does not work, and that if you eat healthy foods and exercise three times a week for more than half an hour, you are the right size and shape for you. Many people will be surprised at this information because of the diets and propaganda they see in television and magazines and their own history of struggle with body image. They may not believe you because it is too confronting for them.

Things to say to the body police

Sometimes ignoring them will help, sometimes it encourages further abuse. Try not to fall into the trap of always returning an insult, as you can just get into a slanging match that teaches them nothing and drives you crazy. Sometimes, however, it might be the only way to drive home your point. Enlist your friends so you can help each other go on the offensive.

Ask yourself not, 'What can I do to make myself more acceptable?' but, 'What is the matter with that person that they need to judge me by their own insecurities and standards?' People who are truly happy with themselves never bother to slag off other people. There is always a reason why you are being targeted, and it has nothing to do with you.

Some of these suggested retorts (below) can be used as all-purpose responses to any body commentary from someone else, such as, 'Are you feeling insecure?', 'You wouldn't say that without all your mates around you', and 'Grow up!'

If you just don't feel safe saying any of these things out loud, make sure you say them to yourself. This can be most satisfying. Laughing or smiling after people insult you can drive them crazy. It's a great way to show you don't take their uninformed judgment seriously.

THEY say:
'You're getting a bit fat' (or disapprovingly, 'You're putting on weight').

YOU say:
'No, I'm not, I'm just growing.'
'No I'm not. What did you say that for?'
'Who asked you?'
'Why are you trying to upset me?'
'What is it you are feeling insecure about?'
'I am not fat, I'm me-shaped.'
'I'm growing. Any objections?'
'Anything else? Perhaps you could write it down for me so I don't forget?'
'How kind of you to say so.'
'I have no intention of going on a stupid, impossible diet just so you feel that your outdated prejudices are validated by pressuring me

into action which would be counter-productive and unhealthy, thereby reinforcing the self-loathing recommended by you and your own fears. So, hey, get a life, …'

'And you're a real heart-throb.'

'A bit fat for you, or a bit fat for me?'

'Why don't you grab your bottom lip and pull it over your head?'

'You have no right to comment on my body.'

'Yes, thank you, I have put on weight, and I feel great.'

'Thank you.'

'I'm not worried about it, so relax.'

'I'm sorry, but I don't care what you think.'

'Nobody was ever thrown out of bed for being cuddly.'

'When I need your opinion to make me feel crappy, I'll let you know.'

'You're right. I guess I should become anorexic immediately. Would that be all right?'

'Are you trying to give me an eating disorder?'

'You can get a book from the library to explain what shape women are.'

'What makes you so interested in my shape?'

'I'm not getting fat, I'm growing. It's this inevitable thing that happens when you're a teenager, like people hassling you.'

'You are quite right. I do not have the body of a 12-year-old boy. Do you have one you're not using?'

'What is this? Body insult hour?'

Kaz Cooke, *Real Gorgeous: The Truth about Body and Beauty*, Allen & Unwin, St Leonards 1997, pp. ix–x, 237–8, 251–4, 260–2.

Activities

1. Share your responses to the focus question with other students and discuss the reasons for these differences.

2. Compare your findings and that of other students with the points made in the commentary.

Commentary

Although these passages are like the second half of the passage from *The Beauty Myth*, in that both employ a confident, assertive tone, they are clearly operating within a different discourse to the passage from *The Beauty Myth*. This discourse is characterised by:

- a lighthearted, chatty style
- the immediate identification of the writer with the reader: 'we need something that will cheer us up'

- the use of colloquial language such as 'uglies', 'dorks', and neologisms such as 'mirror-misery', 'cakie thing'
- the inclusion of specific dramatic incidents
- greater use of quotations, specific facts and figures
- humour
- the dispersal through the text of boxes with quotations from ordinary people
- directly addressing the reader
- the inclusion of practical advice and specific strategies to employ.

CASE STUDY

23

The following passage is from *Business as Unusual* by Anita Roddick, published in 2000. Anita Roddick is the founder and owner of The Body Shop.

THE TYRANNY OF THE BEAUTY BUSINESS

Ruby, the generously proportioned doll who first appeared in *Full Voice* in 1998, also filled the windows of the branches of The Body Shop that year. She has since appeared in magazines, newspapers and television all over Europe and gone on to take Australia, Asia and the US by storm.

Ruby was a fun idea, but she had a serious message. She was created by The Body Shop to challenge stereotypes of beauty and counter the pervasive influence of the cosmetics industry, and in doing so she kick-started a world-wide debate about self-esteem and body image. Ruby was here to say, 'If you *feel* gorgeous you'll *look* gorgeous.'

Looking at Ruby was supposed to remind people that beauty is about confidence, rather than the circumference of your thighs.

Ruby was not without her detractors. In the US, the toy company Mattel threatened to sue us because they claimed Ruby was

There are 3 billion
women who don't
look like supermodels
and only 8 who do.

THE
BODY
SHOP
®

ACTIVATE
SELF
ESTEEM

denigrating the image of Barbie, their twig-like bestseller. I was thrilled by the idea that Ruby was insulting to Barbie—the notion of one inanimate doll insulting another was absolutely mind-blowing. Then in Hong Kong, posters of Ruby were banned on the Mass Transit Railway because the authorities said she would 'offend' passengers. Of course, the much more seriously offensive pictures of pneumatically-breasted blondes remained on the railway for all to see.

And there is my relationship with the beauty industry in a nutshell. It makes me angry—not just because it's an industry dominated by men trying to create needs that don't exist, but for what it does at its worst. At its most extreme, the beauty industry seems to have decided it needs to make women unhappy with what they look like. It plays on insecurities and self-doubt about image and ageing by projecting impossible ideals of youth and beauty. It blinds us with science without giving us the kind of practical information we could use. And it has rarely celebrated women outside Caucasian culture. But then I don't believe an industry which so many women find so unsettling could really claim to celebrate or cherish women of *any* culture.

Leonard Lauder, son of Estée, once refused to advertise in *Ms* magazine because, he said, his products were for 'the kept woman mentality'. What a bizarre signal to send his female customers. I'm sure he lived to regret his declaration, but the bad taste still lingers. To this day, it crystallizes my suspicions about the business of beauty.

MAGNIFICENT BODIES ...

One of the beauty industry's biggest lies has always been that you can turn back the clock with a face cream. Even if this defies common sense, millions of women—and men too—have been suckered by it. After all, who wouldn't want to believe in something as easy as hope in a jar? There is no cream in the world that will restore youth to a 50-year-old woman. But for some reason, we let the beauty industry sell us that hope. For some reason, we let it portray female flesh as gross and in need of repair. For some reason, we allow it to portray youth as the ideal. We accept that the industry will spend millions of pounds concocting dubious potions to 'cure' conditions like cellulite and ageing–natural processes that occur in all women—and yet fail to broadcast the real messages about health. **Why do beauty magazines devote thousands of column inches to cellulite rather than exposing the tobacco industry's efforts to seduce a female audience?**

... BEAUTIFUL FLESH

The fact that so many women are unhappy with their bodies these days is evidence that the strategy of the beauty industry has worked. Something is badly awry in our world when half of all 11-year-old girls are dissatisfied with their bodies, when symptoms of anorexia have been detected in eight and nine year olds and when you have idiots in the media like the Manhattan doctor who joked: 'It's much more important to be thin than alive.' The point isn't so much that the beauty business is directly responsible for the eating disorder epidemic—it's not as straightforward as that—but it doesn't seem to recognize its responsibilities to its customers.

Statistics tell a disturbing tale. The US diet industry is worth $77 billion a year. Over half the female population of the US buy into it and a survey of 10-year-old girls found that 80 per cent were already on diets. Yet as many as 98 per cent of all those using the products and services supplied by this industry fail to achieve their objectives. In other words, the products and services don't work. The diet industry, America's fifth largest, is probably one of the most successful marketing achievements in history. What it sells is self-doubt, and it has relentlessly and successfully extended its grip on the minds and bodies of millions of women all over the world.

... BEAUTIFUL WRINKLES

The universal preoccupation with youth and conventional glamour creates a callous society in which women diminish in status as they age. Between them, the media and the beauty industry have successfully alienated us from our own bodies—and our own lives. Stretch marks and wrinkles show how we've worked hard, in and out of the home, raised kids, enjoyed good meals, tossed back a drink or two, laughed, cried and struggled. They are just symptoms of what gives our lives value. And yet the *wisdom* we have acquired is of no value compared to our appearance.

I think it is my job, and the job of all women my age, to redefine the notion of beauty and to legitimize the ageing process. We have to spread a new message.

Anita Roddick, *Business as Unusual*, Thorsons, London 2000, pp. 95–8.

Activity

Choose one of the two previous case studies, *The Beauty Myth* or *Real Gorgeous*, and write a comparison between this passage from *Business as Unusual* and that one. In your comparison discuss the similarities and differences in structure and rhetorical techniques relating these to context, audience and purpose.

Prose fiction

8

While this chapter focuses on prose fiction, many of the concepts apply to narrative in general, including feature film and stage drama. The chapter refers mainly to novels, but many of the concepts also apply to short stories. As Graham Little says,

> The principles of short story writing are, in general, the same as those for novel writing, with the vital difference of the overriding need for economy of effect and unity of impression in the short story.'

> Graham Little, *Approach to Literature*, Science Press, Marrickville 1981, p. 110.

Four novels are used as examples in the chapter:
- *Cloudstreet* by Tim Winton, first published in 1991
- *The Handmaid's Tale* by Margaret Atwood, first published in 1986—for a taste of *The Handmaid's Tale* see page 185
- *The Wife of Martin Guerre* by Janet Lewis, first published in 1941
- *Popcorn* by Ben Elton, first published in 1996—for a taste of *Popcorn* see page 67.

Because of their differences, these novels illustrate some of the diversity of prose fiction. The first two examples are commonly studied in English and references to them are likely to be widely understood. The latter two are less commonly studied and thus offer possible choices for teachers or students looking for something different in the area of prose fiction. Note though, that the violence, sexual references and language in *Popcorn* may be offensive to some people.

While you will be in a better position to appreciate the discussion in this chapter if you have read one or more of these novels, sufficient information has been provided so that the chapter will make sense to you if you have not read them. This chapter is not intended to help you learn information about these novels, rather it is intended to help you apply the understandings it describes to other novels you are studying or novels of your own choosing.

'The answers you get from literature depend upon the questions you pose', Margaret Atwood

157

History and nature of the novel

The novel is closely associated with the development of the modern age, roughly the period from the 1600s to the present day. In the history of humanity this is a very brief period, but in terms of development it has been momentous. More change to the nature of people's lives has occurred throughout this period than in the whole of previous history. At the heart of this change has been scientific, technological and industrial development through which humans have learnt to understand, control and influence the natural world in ways unimaginable to our ancestors.

Accompanying scientific, technological and industrial development have been massive social changes, the most important of which has been the development of democracy. The eighteenth, nineteenth and twentieth centuries were characterised by political conflict and turmoil driven by people's attempts to have more control over their own lives and the nature of the societies in which they lived.

Driving all these changes has been something deeper and far more fundamental: a belief in the importance of the individual and the power of the individual mind. Before the modern age, most people were not expected to think things out for themselves. They were expected to simply accept the explanations and decisions given by religious or political authorities. The scientific revolution was made possible by a rejection of received explanations and the development of the belief that people could understand the world in which they lived through the power of reason, thinking things through themselves.

We take this attitude so much for granted today that it is difficult to imagine how much of a revolution it was. Before the modern age, the world was conceived of as ordered and explicable, usually in terms of religion or superstition. To the modern mind, the world is conceived as an object of inquiry, something that needs to be worked out and understood by the reasoning of individuals.

The development of the novel as an art form reflects the development of the modern age and the ways of thinking associated with it. This is no accident. Ideas that permeate science and politics also permeate literature. The novel has been another way in which the modern age has represented and explored the power of individuals struggling to understand their place in the world in which they live. The difference between science and the novel, however, is that the focus of science is on the natural world and the focus of the novel is on the social world. The exploration of the individual's relationship with his or her social world naturally leads to and encompasses an individual's understanding of him- or herself. In this respect, the novel has foreshadowed and paralleled the relatively recent science of psychology.

This background may seem fairly abstract and far removed from the novels which you are studying but it is useful because it provides a framework for approaching most novels. It can give some order or system to your reading of a novel.

Framework for approaching novels

In summary, most novels are about an individual, sometimes more than one, who is placed in a situation where he or she has to learn how to cope with some problem or difficulty. In doing so, the character has to change or develop, which usually involves coming to a better understanding of the world and a better understanding of him- or herself.

Activity

Apply this framework to one or more novels you have read:
- Who is the central character?
- What is the problem or difficulty he or she has to respond to?
- How does the character overcome this problem?
- How does the character change as a result of his or her experiences?

This framework goes nowhere near explaining the richness and complexity of any individual novel. But it can be used as a starting point for analysis, interpretation and the construction of readings. It gives you some specific aspects to focus on to construct readings. These are:
- the problem
- the resolution
- the development of the character.

The framework also provides a way of relating a novel to the context in which it was produced and a way of examining its role in the circulation of ideas and feelings in a particular society. In doing this, you are treating the novel as a cultural artefact, rather than the creation of a lone individual. Treating a novel in this way recognises that texts are produced and read by societies, not just individuals.

You can see how novels are products of society by considering the production process. For a start, authors are members of a society and are influenced by that society. Second, an author writes for an audience which is made up of members of that society. This sense of audience will shape what is written and how it is written. Third, for a novel to be published, a publisher has to believe that there are enough people out there who will be interested in reading the novel to make it worthwhile spending money on publishing it. The publisher has to believe that the novel will tap into something that members of society are interested in or concerned about. It is especially this third point that highlights the way in which novels are products of society. If a novel is not of interest to a significantly large section of society then it is unlikely that it will even enter the public realm.

The framework also provides a way of relating your response to the novel to the context of your own life. What most novels present are ordinary people struggling to cope with and make sense of the world they inhabit. The extent to which you relate to a novel depends partly on the extent to which you relate to the problems the characters face and the extent to which you find their responses to these problems believable.

Central problem

The central problem arises from the initial situation on which the novel is based. The problem often takes the form of a conflict between the desires of the individual and constraints imposed by his or her situation. The desire of the individual may be to attain a goal, such as a new social position, a marriage partner, a material possession, justice, truth, revenge or freedom. In many novels, the desire of the central character is simply to regain the normality that existed before the problem arose.

In *Cloudstreet*, the problem the members of the Pickles and Lamb families face is their sense of displacement and their alienation from each other. In both families, their sense of normality has been disrupted by a horrific accident that leads them to leave their existing homes and move to a new house where they do not feel they belong and where members of the families are frequently in conflict with each other. The novel traces their attempts to come to terms with their new environment and each other as a family and their attempts to deal with the spirits of the past that inhabit the house, most notably the ghost of an Aboriginal girl. The central problem of this novel thus has a number of aspects to it.

In *The Handmaid's Tale*, which is set in the United States in the future, the main character, Offred, desires the return of the freedom and individuality that existed before her society was taken over by an extremist group of religious fundamentalists. This group has forced her into the role of a handmaid, a professional childbearer for the rulers of society, a role required because environmental devastation has rendered many people infertile.

Popcorn portrays Hollywood director Bruce Delamitri, who specialises in making films about serial killers. The problem Bruce faces is the accusation that he is contributing to a culture of violence in society and may even be responsible for copycat killings inspired by his films. This accusation is made by television interviewers, academics and members of the general public. Bruce's problem reaches crisis point when he is taken prisoner by real serial killers who try to force him to admit that he is indeed responsible for their actions. In addition to the problem that he may be murdered, Bruce has to seriously confront the extent of his own responsibility for contributing to a culture of violence in society.

Janet Lewis' novel *The Wife of Martin Guerre*, set in sixteenth-century France and based on an actual historical incident, portrays the character of Bertrande de Rols. After ten years of marriage, Bertrande's husband Martin Guerre leaves home promising to return in eight days. When a man claiming to be Martin does return eight years later he is welcomed by his townsfolk and he and Bertrande resume their marriage and have another child. Gradually, however, Bertrande comes to the conclusion that the man claiming to be Martin is not her husband, but an impostor. The problem Bertrande faces is this: her society has taught her to believe that to commit adultery is a mortal sin for which she will go to hell, but the man claiming to be Martin is a much better husband to her than the real Martin was. As well, in Bertrande and Martin's society the penalty for imposture, pretending to be someone else, is death. The problem is complicated by the fact that her family and neighbours believe that the man is her real husband. In accusing him of imposture she will be setting herself against all of them. What should she do?

Reading in terms of context

Examining the problem on which the novel is based can reveal the issues of concern to people at the time the novel was produced and thus provides insight into issues of concern to that society or at least some sections of it.

In reading the central problem of a novel contextually, you might read it in terms of its narrow historical and social context, which is its relevance at its time of publication. You might also read it in terms of a broader historical and social context, which is its relevance to society across a much wider timespan. You might focus on the relationship between the novel and its country of origin or on its relevance across national boundaries.

Reading a novel contextually involves a degree of speculation. You cannot know for certain what social and other forces contributed to the appearance and construction of a novel, but you can make educated assumptions and attempt to mount convincing arguments. There is often more than one way of reading a novel contextually and disagreements and debates about the social forces at work in a novel's construction are common. Sometimes these debates occur because novels can be read contextually on a number of levels.

Of the four novels used in this chapter, the easiest to read contextually is *Popcorn*, possibly because it deals with a topic undergoing considerable public debate in contemporary society. Quite clearly *Popcorn* can be read as a reflection of the growing concern of Western societies in the 1990s about violence in the media and in society and whether there is any link between the two.

Cloudstreet is an example of the way in which a number of social and cultural factors, rather than just one, can be read as influencing the nature of a novel. It also illustrates the way in which a variety of readings are possible. In its concern with the struggles of ordinary working class Australian people, *Cloudstreet* can be read as reflecting Australian society's desire to see such struggles valued through literary representation.

> I think the ordinary … things of life are worthy of celebration. They tend to be forgotten, particularly in this day and age when people

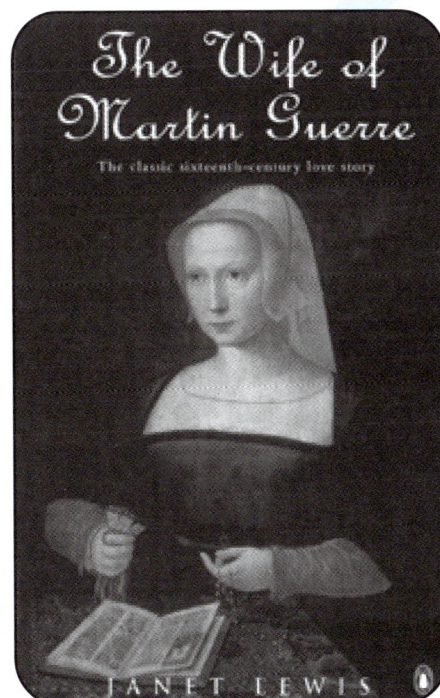

The Wife of Martin Guerre

The classic sixteenth-century love story

JANET LEWIS

seem most lured by the lifestyles of the rich and famous and people who are more talented and more this and that. In my stories I'm trying to render the commonplace worthy of attention. And then to have it looked at anew—and hopefully bring from that some kind of search for meaning.

Tim Winton quoted in Owen Salter, 'Suspicions of Hope in a Chaotic World', *On Being*, June 1987, pp. 7–10.

Cloudstreet portrays a society that no longer exists for its readers. This has led some people to see the novel as appealing to a sense of nostalgia, or a desire to relive the past, on the part of many Australians, occasioned by a sense of loss for a supposedly simpler world. This reading of *Cloudstreet* is reflected in and encouraged by the cover of the 1998 Penguin paperback edition which uses a sepia photograph —sepia often being used to connote memory and the past.

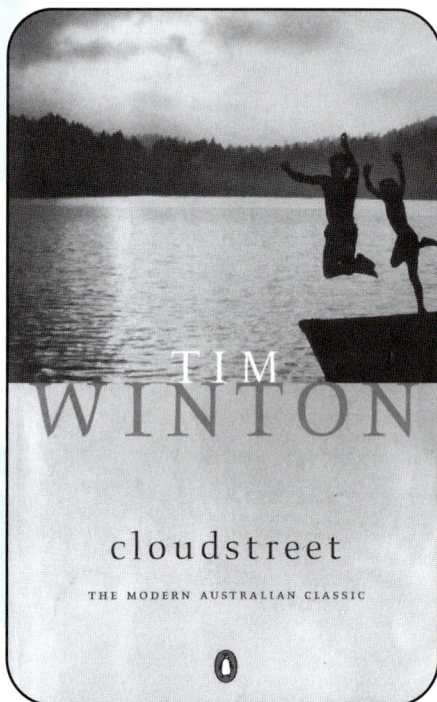

Some people see the book as reflecting the desire for Aboriginal reconciliation that emerged in Australia during the 1970s and 1980s . One critic has argued, 'The story is finally about reconciliation and resolving the pain from the past.'

At a deeper level, *Cloudstreet* deals with the search for meaning and the desire for satisfaction in life, issues of concern to all societies. In the past that search was conducted through religion; in contemporary society it is often conducted through literature. It is this deeper level of concern that may explain the novel's success outside Australia.

Sometimes novels do not reflect social problems directly, like a mirror, as *Popcorn* and *Cloudstreet* do. This is particularly the case with fantasies, satires or dystopic fiction like *The Handmaid's Tale*. Novels like this often extrapolate, or project, certain aspects of the author's society on to a fictional future society. *The Handmaid's Tale* was written at a time when concern about the effects of environmental devastation was growing, various forms of religious fundamentalism seemed to be on the rise in north America and a backlash against feminism was occurring. It was also written at a time when theocracies, societies ruled by religious leaders, were being established in some Middle Eastern countries. Atwood can be read as performing a 'what if?' exercise and showing the consequences of these trends continuing and strengthening. These issues may still resonate with many contemporary readers, as *The Handmaid's Tale* is still a very popular novel. Perhaps its continuing popularity can also be explained by the fact that on a deeper level it can be read as portraying the struggle against oppression and ascribed subjectivity, which means having roles forced on to us rather than being able to choose them ourselves. This is a common theme in much literature of the modern age, which suggests it is an ongoing concern.

Be wary of making simplistic connections between the central problem in a novel and the society that produced the novel. Sometimes the novel will need to be read on a deeper level. In the case of *The Wife of Martin Guerre*, for example, it would be silly to assume that American society of the 1940s was worried about men deceiving women into believing that they were their real husbands when they were not, although it is interesting to note that the story of a woman separated from her husband wondering whether he would return was written during the Second World War when many women were facing this problem. But the popularity of *The Wife of Martin Guerre* has lasted well beyond the Second World War. This suggests that it is dealing with something fundamental in human affairs, the conflict between doing what is of benefit to ourselves and what our consciences tell us is the right thing to do. This is another archetypal theme of the modern age—it appears in many narratives and we confront it regularly in our everyday lives.

Novels may also need to be read metaphorically in order to relate them to their context. Ken Kesey's *One Flew over the Cuckoo's Nest*, published in 1962, portrays the struggle between patients in a mental asylum and those in authority over them. You could conclude from this that the treatment of mental patients was an issue in American society in the early 1960s when the novel was written, but this would be a rather limited reading. On a deeper level, the novel can be read as portraying the struggle between the desire for individual freedom on the one hand and the pressure for social conformity on the other, an issue which developed in importance as American society became more homogenous and conformist during the 1950s. The revolt against this conformism is evident in the beat movement of the 1950s, of which Ken Kesey was a member, and also in its descendant, the hippie movement of the late 1960s. Reading the mental asylum in *One Flew over the Cuckoo's Nest* as a metaphor for American society as a whole is invited by the novel itself through the frequent references to 'the machine' which the Big Chief, the narrator, believes controls everything inside and outside the asylum.

On another level, *One Flew over the Cuckoo's Nest* is very much like *The Handmaid's Tale*. They both portray the struggle of individuals against a society that would oppress them and make them conform to its expectations of appropriate behaviour.

Novels are most likely to be successful and stay in print for a long time when they reflect problems both of contemporary interest and of longer lasting concern to modern societies.

As well as being read as a reflection of a particular social context, a novel can be read as an intervention in this context. In portraying a topic as a social problem the novel is privileging, drawing attention to or reinforcing the belief that the topic is indeed a problem within society. We can read *Popcorn* not just as reflecting concern about the link between the media and violence but as reinforcing this concern. Some people reject the idea that media violence is connected to violence in real life and thus reject the very existence of the problem. We can read *The Handmaid's Tale* as not just reflecting the existence of certain trends in society but as a warning against them. *Cloudstreet* can be read as reinforcing the idea of the family as a problem in society, a view that has emerged in some quarters over the past forty or so years as the traditional nuclear family has lost its position as the norm in Western societies.

Resolution

Another way in which a novel can be read as an intervention in a particular social context is through the resolution of the problem with which it deals. Here the term resolution does not mean the specific incident near the end where a problem or conflict is resolved, but the way in which the problem is overcome over the course of the novel. This resolution can be read as the novel's way of suggesting how the social problem it deals with can or should be solved, or its way of commenting on the way such a problem is likely to be solved. As with other aspects of novels, it is often possible to read resolutions in a number of different ways.

The resolution of *Cloudstreet* is the simplest of the four examples. It can be read as suggesting that alienation and displacement can be overcome by accepting life with all its ups and downs and accepting other people with all their faults.

Most readers expect a novel to portray, like *Cloudstreet*, a clear solution to the problems it portrays and to thus end happily. This is partly because such endings are ideologically reassuring; they reassure readers that the problems they face as individuals and as a society can be overcome. Not all novels do this. Novels that don't can be read as portraying life as more complex and containing some problems that are not always capable of resolution.

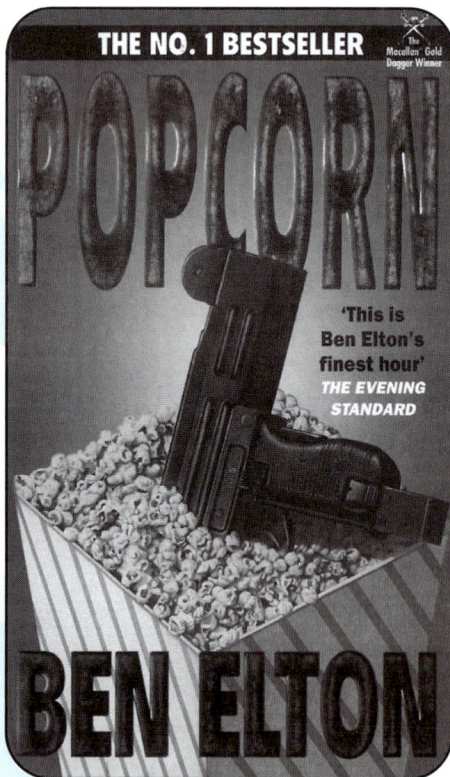

Popcorn ends with nothing solved. Bruce survives his ordeal and the killers are apprehended by the police—a satisfying narrative ending—but it is not clear that Bruce has learnt anything from his ordeal as he has been unwilling to accept even the possibility of his responsibility for contributing to a culture of violence. The central question of who is responsible for violence in society is never resolved, as nobody is willing to take responsibility for what has happened. This allows the novel to be read as offering a pessimistic view about whether the issue is capable of resolution and as suggesting that in real life people are increasingly unwilling to accept responsibility for their actions. It might also be read as the author not being certain about the issue of whether there is a link between media violence and real violence.

The resolution of *The Handmaid's Tale* is quite complex and also open to different interpretations. For most of the novel, Offred is able to maintain her identity and individuality and not succumb to the psychological pressure to acquiesce in her oppressive situation. She finds ways of resisting and subverting the powers that oppress her and uses the 'cracks' in the power structure to exert power of her own. To this point, the novel can be read as suggesting that it is possible to defy repression and totalitarianism. Then, near the very end, when her friend Ofglen has committed suicide and Offred believes she will be killed, she finally cracks.

Dear God, I think, I will do anything you like. Now that you've let me off, I'll obliterate myself, if that's what you really want; I'll empty myself, truly, become a chalice. I'll give up Nick, I'll forget about the others, I'll stop complaining. I'll accept my lot. I'll sacrifice. I'll repent. I'll abdicate. I'll renounce.

I know this can't be right but I think it anyway. Everything they taught at the Red Centre, everything I've resisted, comes flooding in. I don't want pain. I don't want to be a dancer, my feet in the air, my head a faceless oblong of white cloth. I don't want to be a doll hung up on the Wall, I don't want to be a wingless angel. I want to keep on living, in any form. I resign my body freely, to the uses of others. They can do what they like with me. I am abject.

I feel, for the first time, their true power.

Margaret Atwood, The Handmaid's Tale, Vintage, London 1986, p. 298.

Here it seems the novel is portraying the power of the totalitarian society as absolute and able to ultimately enforce obedience from all. This might be read as intensifying the nature of the novel's warning about the social trends it criticises. Offred only escapes either execution or submitting to the power of the state by her sudden rescue by unknown sympathisers.

How is this to be read? Can the rescue be read as providing a final message of hope by suggesting that it is possible to defy the forces of repression because Offred's attempts to establish networks with others opposed to the state have been rewarded? Or should it be read as suggesting that it is only by chance that the odd individual is able to escape the power of totalitarianism?

In *The Wife of Martin Guerre*, Bertrande resolves her dilemma by accusing the man claiming to be her husband of imposture. During the ensuing court case, the real Martin appears, the impostor is unmasked and Bertrande is vindicated. Rather than concluding with the real Martin being grateful and reconciled with Bertrande, however, the novel concludes with him accusing her of dishonouring him and his family by accepting the impostor in the first place. What are we to make of this? One way is to read the novel as implying that Bertrande was foolish to follow her conscience and that the world does not necessarily reward honourable behaviour. Another is to read it as implying that although we should follow our consciences, the results may not always be pleasant. Alternatively, if we read the novel from a feminist perspective, we might see the resolution as a criticism of Martin, and the patriarchal society he represents.

Character development

Character development is closely connected with resolution in that it is through his or her manner of resolving the problems faced that a character develops. Examining character development highlights the way in which reading is an active process on the part of the reader because a novel rarely articulates directly the ways in which a character develops. Character development emerges from changes in the way a character behaves and thinks over the course of the novel. As a reader, you construct a reading of character development by observing these changes and drawing conclusions from them. Sometimes a novel may emphasise certain actions and thoughts as a way of indicating or drawing attention to character development, but most of the work has to be done by you, the reader.

Character development is a matter of what characters learn about themselves and about the world as a result of their experiences. This knowledge can be read as part of the novel's values or ideologies—the beliefs about people and the world that are reflected in the novel. A useful starting point for examining character development is to compare what characters are like at the end of the novel to what they were like at the beginning, and what learning this implies.

In *Cloudstreet*, the obvious difference at the end is that the characters are at peace with each other and their home. Of the four examples, *Cloudstreet* is the one that most clearly deliberately articulates and draws attention to character development. This is especially so in the case of Quick and Rose, who can be read as the main vehicles for the ideas and values reflected in the novel. What they have learnt by the end of the novel is to accept their place in the world and to accept other people with all their faults. They learn this by discovering that basically most people are alike and that there is usually a reason for people's behaviour. This is articulated most clearly when Quick says,

> 'But it's not us and them anymore. It's us and us and us. It's always us. That's what they never tell you. Geez, Rose, I just want to do right. But there's no monsters, only people like us.' (p. 402)

In the case of *The Handmaid's Tale*, Offred's development as a character needs to be inferred by the reader. On the one hand, you could argue that through her experiences she has learnt a great deal about patriarchy and authority. Through her experience with the wives, the Aunts and the Marthas, for example, she has learnt how women can be complicit in their own oppression and in the oppression of other women. Through experiences with the commander, for example, she has learnt how women can exploit the weaknesses of males as a way of exercising power of their own. On the other hand, you could argue that Offred has not developed a great deal at all but managed to survive because of her pre-existing strength.

In *The Wife of Martin Guerre*, Bertrande is clearly a different character by the end of the novel in that she has defied her society and her supposed husband in her pursuit of the truth. What she has learnt from this depends on how you interpret the ending.

Sometimes characters do not develop at all. This lack of development can be read as part of the social commentary of the novel. In *Popcorn*, Bruce Delamitri does not develop as a result of his experiences. He 'now makes tired, cynical movies in France' and 'has written a book about the night Wayne and Scout entered his life called *Who is responsible?* [in which] he divides the blame equally between Wayne and Scout, the media, the police and the million of people who did not turn off their TVs', thus showing his refusal to admit the possibility of his own responsibility.

Theme

Most novelists do not write with a theme in mind, to put across a message or discuss an issue. What they start with usually are characters and situations. But by constructing a reading of the novel in terms of your own experience or your knowledge of society, which is what this chapter has been doing, you are also constructing a reading in terms of themes.

A Note to the Reader from Margaret Atwood

Dear Reader,

Every book is a sort of mushroom cloud thrown up by a large substance of material that has been accumulating for a lifetime. I had long been interested in the histories of totalitarian regimes and the different forms they have taken in various societies; while the initial idea for *The Handmaid's Tale* came to me in 1981, I avoided writing it for several years because I was apprehensive about the results—whether I would be able to carry it off as a literary form.

In form, the book is a dystopia (negative utopia). A cognate of *A Clockwork Orange*, *Brave New World*, and *Nineteen Eighty-Four*, it is the story of one woman's altered circumstances, presented as a first-person narrative novel.

The roots of the book go back to my study of the American Puritans. The society they founded in America was not a democracy as we know it, but a theocracy. In addition, I found myself increasingly alarmed by statements made frequently by religious leaders in the United States; and then a variety of events from around the world could not be ignored, particularly the rising fanaticism of the Iranian monotheocracy. The thing to remember is that there is nothing new about the society depicted in *The Handmaid's Tale* except the time and place. All of the things I have written about have—as noted in the 'Historical Notes' at the end—been done before, more than once.

Margaret Atwood

It is an imagined account of what happens when not uncommon pronouncements about women are taken to their logical conclusions. History proves that what we have been in the past we could be again.

An Interview with Margaret Atwood on Her Novel The Handmaid's Tale

Q: Was there any special research involved in writing *The Handmaid's Tale*?

A: I clipped articles out of newspapers. I now have a large clippings file of stories supporting the contentions in the book. In other words, there isn't anything in the book not based on something that has already happened in history or in another country, or for which actual supporting documentation is not already available.

Q: It's hard to pin down a genre for this novel. Is it science fiction?

A: No, it certainly isn't science fiction. Science fiction is filled with Martians and space travel to other planets, and things like that. That isn't this book at all. *The Handmaid's Tale* is speculative fiction in the genre of *Brave New World* and *Nineteen Eighty-Four*. *Nineteen Eighty-Four* was written not as science fiction but as an extrapolation of life in 1948. So, too, *The Handmaid's Tale* is a slight twist on the society we have now.

Q: You seem to see a role for the novel beyond entertainment.

A: I was once a graduate student in Victorian literature and I believe as the Victorian novelists did, that a novel isn't simply a vehicle for private expression, but that it also exists for social examination. I firmly believe this.

Q: What are we to learn from *The Handmaid's Tale*?

A: This is a book about what happens when certain casually held attitudes about women are taken to their logical conclusions. For example, I explore a number of conservative opinions still held by many—such as a woman's place is in the home. And also certain feminist pronouncements—women prefer the company of other women, for example. Take these beliefs to their logical ends and see what happens. As a writer, you can choose to create a mainstream novel in which these issues appear only as the characters discuss them sitting around the kitchen table. But I decided to take these positions and dramatize them, carry them to their furthest logical conclusions.

Q: How would the creation of your imagined republic of Gilead be possible?

A: First of all, ask yourself the following question: If you were going to take over the United States, how would you do it? Would you say, "I'm a socialist and we're all going to be equal"? No, you would not, because it wouldn't work. Would you say, "I'm a liberal and we are going to have a society of multiple toleration"? You probably wouldn't say that if you wanted mass support. You would be much more likely to say, "I have the word from God and this is the way we should run things." That probably would have more of a chance of working, and in fact there are a number of movements in the States saying just that, and getting lots of dollars and influence. The society in *The Handmaid's Tale* is a throwback to the early Puritans whom I studied extensively at Harvard under Perry Miller, to whom the book is dedicated. The early Puritans came to America not for religious freedom, as we were taught in grade school, but to set up a society that would be a theocracy (like Iran) ruled by religious leaders, and monolithic, that is, a society that would not tolerate dissent within itself. They were being persecuted in England for being Puritans, but then they went to the United States and promptly began persecuting anyone who wasn't a Puritan. My book reflects the form and style of the early Puritan society and addresses the dynamics that bring about such a situation.

Q: Why the intense focus on fertility in Gilead?

A: In a society in which the birthrate plummets below replacement, that body of people will be forced to determine whether or not it will simply slide gently into oblivion and vanish from the face of the earth. (One theory is there that will be no Germans by the year 2020 because their birthrate is so low;

Germany is going to be Turkish.) Scandinavian countries are now below replacement, as is Romania. What does a society do at this point? Either it accepts the situation or it puts into existence conditions that will increase the number of births.

Q: So in Gilead this process is taken to what you see as a logical conclusion?

A: Yes. It is a society in which you have a sort of "farming" of women. Parallel to that, you have to realize that male sterility is on the increase and so are spontaneous miscarriages and birth defects. How could this be? It's because we are pouring about 300,000 different chemicals into our water and drinking it. Plus, of course, there's a great deal of radiation. They've found PCBs in polar bears and they are worried about the future of the polar bear species because PCBs build up in their systems and produce male sterility. So fertility in Gilead is at a premium. Fertile women, women who can reproduce, are prize objects for those in power. And as is the case in which prize objects are Cadillacs and you want to have as many Cadillacs as you possibly can, so too when the prize objects are fertile women, then you want to have as many fertile women as possible. Thus in Gilead we return to biblical polygamy.

Q: Are there some good things about Gilead?

A: Yes, women aren't whistled at on the street, men don't come climbing in the window in the middle of the night. Women are "protected." Sardonically speaking, in totalitarian countries the streets are much safer, for the most part.

Q: It seems that within this frightening world, certain parts of the feminist revolution have survived. Is that true?

A: No power structure can institute total serfdom (unless they kill off most of the people) without giving a few "perks." If you were to go back and study what the Germans did during World War II, you would see that what they did was move into another country and find a group of people willing to help them out. They would develop a little army of Ukrainians in Ukraine, Poles in Poland, etc. Any imperial power does the same thing; the British in India developed terrific regiments made up of Indians. And so, in Gilead, we have troops of women.

Q: But wouldn't there be violent resistance against a system such as Gilead?

A: Yes, of course we would have resistance. After all, this is United States and it is North America and it is a pluralistic society and we have many people with differing points of view. A number of people would not take this lying down.

Q: The way the reader comes into *The Handmaid's Tale* is through a diary or a journal, memories rescued and viewed from a time in the future. The curtain is drawn back slowly. Why did you choose to write it that way?

A: What I've written is only the view of one woman who lives in that society. I reveal Gilead through the eyes of that one woman. It would be cheating to show the reader more than the character has access to. Her information is limited. In fact, her lack of information is part of the nightmare.

Doubleday 1998, 'Reader's Companion to *The Handmaid's Tale*', http://www.randomhouse.com/resources/bookgroup/handmaidstale_bgc.html

Other aspects of construction

Representation

So far this chapter has concentrated on constructing a reading of a novel by focussing on the central problem, its resolution and character development. It is also possible to construct readings of other aspects of the novel. Being the rich, complex texts they are, novels often deal with many aspects of the world and their construction may reflect particular ideas about social groups and institutions.

In *Cloudstreet* you could examine the representation of:

- the working class
- the middle classes, as represented by Toby Raven
- life in Perth from the 1940s to the early 1960s

- males
- children
- the past
- females
- Aboriginal people.

In *The Handmaid's Tale* you could examine the representation of:

- religion
- political power
- males

- females
- patriarchy
- relationships between women.

In *Popcorn* you could examine the representation of:

- criminals
- the Hollywood film industry
- males
- females

- the media
- the police
- the American judicial system
- American society.

In *The Wife of Martin Guerre* you could examine the representation of:

- religion
- the judicial system
- family life

- males
- females
- sixteenth-century France.

A novel may also be read as intervening in a social context by portraying a problem of concern to society but challenging established ways of thinking about it or by representing the lives of social groups which have been traditionally marginalised in literature. Chapter 3 contains a more detailed discussion of representation.

Like other aspects of texts, representations can be read in more than one way. This can be seen in the following essay on the representation of Aboriginality in *Cloudstreet* by a Year 12 student. *Cloudstreet* is widely read as representing Aboriginal people in a positive manner and one that supports the need for reconciliation between Aboriginal and non-Aboriginal Australians. This is the preferred or dominant reading. The term preferred reading is usually used to describe the reading that a text seems to be designed to encourage. The term dominant reading is usually used to refer to the reading that is most widely shared. Not surprisingly these readings are often the same. Sometimes the terms preferred reading and dominant reading are used interchangeably.

The preferred or dominant readings are not the only way to read representations. They can also be read resistantly, as the following work sample shows.

WORK SAMPLE

Representation of Aboriginality in *Cloudstreet*

In this work sample, the student shows a strong understanding of the preferred reading but argues that it is also possible to read the text resistantly. The student does this partly by pointing to gaps and silences in the novel and by showing how aspects of the novel can be read differently from that encouraged by the preferred reading.

Topic for this work: Texts reveal particular attitudes and values through the way in which they represent social groups. Discuss with reference to one or more novels.

Tim Winton's <u>Cloudstreet</u> represents the values prevalent in the late twentieth century liberal middle classes, reflecting a perceived sense of respect for Aboriginal heritage, culture and desire for reconciliation. This is achieved through the construction of Aboriginal Australians as possessing greater spiritual awareness and appreciation for the natural environment. However, the text can also be read as representing an entrenched racism which constructs Aboriginal people as 'other', and as different to the implied reader of the novel. Its representation of contemporary Aboriginal life is highly partial and selective, excluding or trivialising the irrefutable social inequalities. Further, the text endorses the displacement of Aboriginal people, accepting European expropriation of land as 'given'.

The preferred reading of <u>Cloudstreet</u> presents a criticism of the inequitable treatment of Aboriginal people in the past through the celebration of Aboriginal culture, society and environmental understanding. This is achieved through Winton's sympathetic portrayal of the Aboriginal girls forced to live in the house under the rule of the old woman, indicating a strong criticism of the removal of Aboriginal children from their families and of forced assimilation. <u>Cloudstreet</u>'s chief representative of Aboriginality is the unnamed Aboriginal man, who is portrayed as more spiritually aware than non-Aboriginal Australians. This is exemplified in narrative sequences such as 'Lester saw his eyes suddenly widen ... roving about all the time', which presents the Aboriginal man as sensing evil in the house where others cannot. This suggests that Aboriginal people in general are greater advocates of the spiritual world, a message that is habitually repeated throughout the text through his appearance at the sight of miracles. Similarly, the Aboriginal man's chief dramatic function in the text is to instruct the Lambs and Pickles to remain together at Cloudstreet, guiding Quick back to his home and urging Sam not to sell the house. This characterises Aboriginal people as possessing a greater awareness of the importance of family and place. This ideology comes to a climax during the Aboriginal man's discussion with Sam, which concludes in 'Places are strong, important', articulating the primary ideology of the novel itself. These elements suggest that non-Aboriginal

Australians have much to learn from Aboriginal people in terms of cultural and spiritual understanding.

While the surface reading of <u>Cloudstreet</u> reflects a sense of respect for Aboriginal culture, the novel can be read as stereotyping and marginalising Aboriginal people, constructing them as 'other'. Winton's construction of Aboriginality is highly partial and selective, maintaining a total absence of ordinary, real Aboriginal characters. His portrayal of the race as highly spiritual and mystic dehumanises the characters, constructing them as different to the implied reader. This is reinforced by the habitual comparison of the Aboriginal man to various animals, characterizing him as 'as much bird as he was man', further portraying Aboriginal Australians as 'other'. The only representatives of Aboriginality in the text are in the form of ghosts or spirits, and thus the text is totally silent about the real social inequalities faced by Aboriginal people at that time. Where the text does touch upon actual social conditions, these issues are glossed over, trivialised or ignored. The reality of the discriminatory racial policies in Australia such as the exclusion of Aboriginal children from public schools, lack of employment, public housing and voting rights, confinement of Aboriginal communities to reserves and appalling health conditions are largely ignored in the text or trivialised through the dialogue. A prime example of this is the discussion between Rose and Sam following his confrontation with the Aboriginal man during Election Day. Following Rose's assertion that 'Blacks haven't got the vote', Sam simply replies 'Jesus, that's a bit rough, isn't it. They need a union.' While Winton draws attention to the Aboriginal community's political exclusion from Australian society, there is no exploration of the reasons for this, thus trivialising the matter and presenting Aboriginal disadvantages as 'given'. Similarly, the disparate economic conditions between the indigenous minority and non-Aboriginal majority are mentioned, yet are trivialised through the absence of exploration into the social issues that cause them. This is exemplified during Quick's first encounter with the Aboriginal man. While it is recognised that he has 'never seen an Aborigine in a pinstriped suit before', no disclosure is made as to why this is so. While Winton correctly identifies Aborigines as economically poorer than other Australians, no exploration is made as to why this is the case or who is responsible.

Another facet of <u>Cloudstreet</u>'s inherent racism is the Aboriginal man's displacement within the Australian community. While Winton emphasises the importance of the Lamb's and Pickles' attainment of a sense of place and belonging, there is a blatant disregard for the Aboriginal man's total lack of belonging anywhere within Australian society, portrayed through his appearing and disappearing without mention of any home he might have. Furthermore, the novel's portrayal of the Aboriginal man's acceptance and celebration of their realisation of a sense of belonging completely disregards the fact that Cloudstreet itself is built on land once owned by Aboriginal people. This trivialises the political concern of Aboriginal land rights, and can be read as endorsing the displacement of Aboriginal people by non-Aboriginals. While _Cloudstreet_ superficially reflects the late twentieth century liberal progressive attitudes towards Aboriginal heritage and culture, the novel can also be read as representing traditionally racist attitudes towards Aboriginal people through the construction of Aboriginality as 'other', and European expropriation and domination of Australian land as 'given'.

Tim Winton's _Cloudstreet_ outwardly represents the values prevalent in the late twentieth century liberal middle classes, reflecting a perceived sense of respect for Aboriginal heritage, culture and desire for reconciliation. This is achieved through the portrayal of Aboriginal Australians as possessing greater spiritual insight and appreciation for the natural environment. However, the text can also be read as representing a deeply entrenched racism which constructs Aboriginal people as 'other', and as different to the implied reader. Its representation of contemporary Aboriginal life is highly partial and selective, excluding or trivialising the vast social inequalities. Furthermore, the text can be read as endorsing the displacement of Aboriginal people by non-Aboriginals, accepting European expropriation of Australian land as 'given'.

Work sample supplied by Sarah Salvidge

Activity

Discuss to what extent you find the reading above a convincing and fair interpretation of the novel.

Popcorn can also be read resistantly. While _Popcorn_ criticises films for their portrayal of violence, it can be read as portraying violence in exactly the same way.

- The novel criticises films for using violence as a source of entertainment but it can be argued that this is exactly what the novel is doing.
- The novel criticises films for making murderers and psychopaths attractive, but it can be argued that the novel does this too. Note the following description of Scout, one half of the killer duo: 'She was beautiful, with her big eyes and thin face. If ever Disney decided to do a stage version of Bambi they would be looking for a girl like her.' Scout describes Wayne, her partner as,

the coolest, most beautiful guy that ever was. Better than everything. You could take Elvis and Clint Eastwood and James Dean … and I don't know … all those other cool guys, and mix 'em up, and you wouldn't get no one half as cool as him.

The novel's portrayal of Wayne can also be read as highlighting his 'coolness' by the way in which it frequently draws attention to his muscular body, a traditional symbol of masculine attractiveness. In addition, Wayne is clever, witty and more than capable of holding his own intellectually with Bruce Delamitri.

- *Popcorn* criticises films for violence as a source of humour (see page 153 of the novel) but it can be argued the novel does this too, especially in the scene where the guard's head is impaled on a lava lamp.
- The novel criticises films for trivialising violence, but presents one murder in this way: 'The young man was so offended he shot the storekeeper anyway' (page 76 of the novel), itself an example of trivialisation of murder.
- It also criticises the voyeurism of films that involve making violence entertaining while exploiting the pain and suffering of others: 'Don't you use the terrible sick mental condition that afflicts psychopaths like me just to give people a thrill,' says Wayne to Bruce Delamitri. Is Ben Elton not doing the same thing?
- The novel criticises stereotyping and class prejudice in films, but the novel's portrayal of Wayne and Scout can be read as participating in the same forms of stereotyping and class prejudice.

In summary, it is possible to read *Popcorn* as reproducing the very attitudes and practices it purports to criticise.

CASE STUDY

24

'Neighbours' by Tim Winton

This case study will allow you to apply some of the skills and concepts covered so far in this chapter. The following short story, set in Australia, was published in 1985.

When they first moved in, the young couple were wary of the neighbourhood. The street was full of European migrants. It made the newly-weds feel like sojourners in a foreign land. Next door on the left lived a Macedonian family. On the right, a widower from Poland.

The newly-weds' house was small, but its high ceilings and paned windows gave it the feel of an elegant cottage. From his study window, the young man could see out over the rooftops and used-car yards the Moreton Bay figs in the park where they walked their dog. The neighbours seemed cautious about the dog, a docile, moulting collie.

The young man and woman had lived all their lives in the expansive outer suburbs where good neighbours were seldom seen and never heard. The sounds of spitting and washing and daybreak watering came as a shock. The Macedonian family shouted, ranted, screamed. It took six months for the newcomers to comprehend the fact that their neighbours were not murdering each other, merely talking. The old Polish man spent most of his day hammering nails into wood only to pull them out again. His yard was stacked with salvaged lumber. He added to it, but he did not build with it.

Relations were uncomfortable for many months. The Macedonians raised eyebrows at the late hour at which the newcomers rose in the mornings. The young man sensed their disapproval at his staying home to write his thesis while his wife worked. He watched in disgust as the little boy next door urinated in the street. He once saw him spraying the cat from the back step. The child's head was shaved regularly, he assumed, in order to make his hair grow thick. The little boy stood at the fence with only his cobalt eyes showing; it made the young man nervous.

In the autumn, the young couple cleared rubbish from their backyard and turned and manured the soil under the open and measured gaze of the neighbours. They planted leeks, onions, cabbage, brussels sprouts and broad beans and this caused the neighbours to come to the fence and offer advice about spacing, hilling, mulching. The young man resented the interference, but he took careful note of what was said. His wife was bold enough to run a hand over the child's stubble and the big woman with black eyes and butcher's arms gave her a bagful of garlic cloves to plant.

Not long after, the young man and woman built a henhouse. The neighbours watched it fall down. The Polish widower slid through the fence uninvited and rebuilt it for them. They could not understand a word he said.

As autumn merged into winter and the vermilion sunsets were followed by sudden, dark dusks touched with the smell of woodsmoke and the sound of roosters crowing day's end, the young couple found themselves smiling back at the neighbours. They offered heads of cabbage and took gifts of grappa and firewood. The young man worked steadily at his thesis on the development of the twentieth century novel. He cooked dinners for his wife and listened to her stories of eccentric patients and hospital incompetence. In the street they no longer walked with their eyes lowered. They felt superior and proud when their parents came to visit and to cast shocked glances across the fence.

In the winter they kept ducks, big, silent muscovies that stood about in the rain growing fat. In the spring the Macedonian family showed them how to slaughter and to pluck and to dress. They all sat around on blocks and upturned buckets and told barely understood stories—the men butchering, the women plucking, as was demanded. In the haze of down and steam and fractured dialogue, the young man and woman felt intoxicated. The cat toyed with severed heads. The child pulled the cat's tail. The newcomers found themselves shouting.

But they had not planned on a pregnancy. It stunned them to be made parents so early. Their friends did not have children until several years after being married—if at all. The young woman arranged for maternity leave. The young man ploughed on with his thesis on the twentieth century novel.

The Polish widower began to build. In the late spring dawns, he sank posts and poured cement and began to use his wood. The young couple turned in their bed, cursed him behind his back. The young husband, at times, suspected that the widower was deliberately antagonizing them. The young wife threw up in the mornings. Hay fever began to wear him down.

Before long the young couple realized that the whole neighbourhood knew of the pregnancy. People smiled tirelessly at them. The man in the deli gave her small presents of chocolates and him packets of cigarettes that he stored at home, not being a smoker. In the summer, Italian women began to offer names. Greek women stopped the young woman in the street, pulled her skirt up and felt her belly, telling her it was bound to be a boy. By late summer the woman next door had knitted the baby a suit, complete with booties and beanie. The young woman felt flattered, claustrophobic, grateful, peeved.

By late summer, the Polish widower next door had almost finished his two-car garage. The young man could not believe that a man without a car would do such a thing, and one evening as he was considering making a complaint about the noise, the Polish man came over with barrowfuls of woodscraps for their fire.

Labour came abruptly. The young man abandoned the twentieth century novel for the telephone. His wife began to black the stove. The midwife came and helped her to finish the job while he ran about making statements that sounded like queries. His wife hoisted her belly about the house, supervising his movements. Going outside for more wood, he saw, in the last light of the day, the faces at each fence. He counted twelve faces. The Macedonian family waved and called out what sounded like their best wishes.

As the night deepened, the young woman dozed between contractions, sometimes walking, sometimes shouting. She had a hot bath and began to eat ice and demand liverwurst. Her belly rose, uterus flexing downward. Her sweat sparkled, the gossamer highlit by movement and firelight. The night grew older. The midwife crooned. The young man rubbed his wife's back, fed her ice and rubbed her lips with oil.

And then came the pushing. He caressed and stared and tried not to shout. The floor trembled as the young woman bore down in a squat. He felt the power of her, the sophistication of her. She strained. Her face mottled. She kept at it, push after push, assaulting some unseen barrier, until suddenly it was smashed and she was through. It took his wind away to see the look on the baby's face as it was suddenly passed up to the breast. It had one eye on him. It found the nipple. It trailed cord and vernix smears and its mother's own sweat. She gasped and covered the tiny buttocks with a hand. A boy, she said. For a second, the child lost the nipple and began to cry. The young man heard shouting outside. He went to the back door. On the Macedonian side of the fence, a small queue of bleary faces looked up, cheering, and the young man began to weep. The twentieth century novel had not prepared him for this.

Tim Winton, *Scission*, Penguin, Ringwood 1985 pp. 81–4.

Activities

For discussion:

1. What is the central problem on which the story is based?

2. What are some of the ways in which this problem can be read in terms of context?

3. What readings of the resolution can be constructed in terms of what it suggests about the nature of the central problems and how these can be resolved?

4. What social groups and institutions are represented in this story? How are they represented?

5. If you read the story in terms of European migrants, how are they represented within the text? Consider conceptions of normality and otherness and why, though the ethnic origins of the neighbours are mentioned, the ethnic origins of the young couple are not. Why is this?

6. If you have read *Cloudstreet* how might it influence your reading of this story?

Normality and otherness

One of the ways in which ideology functions through binary opposition is by constructing ideas of normality and otherness. This involves thinking about certain types of people, behaviours and ideas as the norm and other types of people, behaviour or ideas as 'other' or different from the norm. Sometimes the norm is seen as 'better' or superior in some way than the other. Another way of saying this is that the norm may be centred and the other marginalised. Some texts may challenge or subvert ideas of normality and otherness. Still other texts may do both at the same time.

Tim Winton

Activities

1. Choose a novel with which you are familiar and list the main social groups, institutions and societies represented in the novel.
2. Discuss the way these are represented.
3. Consider possible different ways of interpreting the novel's representation by discussing what seems to be the preferred reading and whether it is possible to construct resistant readings. In doing this you may find it helpful to consider representations of the same subject in other texts, including novels, films and television.
4. Choose one of the social groups, institutions or societies represented in the novel and use your notes and discussion as the basis for a written discussion of its representation.

Genre

Examining genre in a novel is not simply a matter of identifying the genre to which a novel belongs or the various genres on which it draws, but of looking at the effects of the novel's use of genre. This involves examining the way in which a novel draws on and manipulates generic conventions and how this contributes to the beliefs and values reflected in the novel and the reader's acceptance of them. Genre also plays a large role in the pleasure and entertainment provided by a text, a subject dealt with in the next chapter.

Cloudstreet draws on and blends the conventions of a variety of very different genres:

- the popular literary tradition of the family saga
- the tradition of working class anecdotes and yarns
- the biblical tradition, with its parables and stories of miracles
- the gothic novel, which revolves around a house with a character of its own and a mystery at its centre
- the postcolonial genre of magical realism.

The family saga genre usually traces the history of a family over a number of years, sometimes generations. In exploring and promoting the importance of family life it promotes the view that individuals can best be understood in terms of their family origins and interactions. It thus promotes the importance of the family as a social institution and emphasises family loyalty over individual desires, views that *Cloudstreet* clearly endorses. Family sagas traditionally portray wealthy or high status families and follow their attempts to maintain their social status and wealth. In focussing on working class families, *Cloudstreet* departs from this tradition. It can be seen as intervening in its literary and social contexts to give value to 'ordinary' families, a reading that can be further supported by examination of its use of the Australian tradition of yarns and anecdotes.

Cloudstreet's use of the Australian tradition of anecdotes and yarns allows the novel to be read as promoting the valuing and celebration of working class experience and of the resilience of working class people, an appreciation of 'battling' and 'battlers'. This valuing of working class experience is particularly highlighted by the celebratory ending of the novel, with its valuing of 'how we've all battled in the same corridor time makes for us'.

> We do have a strong oral tradition in Australia, and that is a tremendous advantage to us as storytellers … In an oral tradition, events just unwind, moving first here and then there, perhaps without any particular logic. [*Cloudstreet*], then, is seeking to capture the spirit of the first white Australian storytellers who sat around the campfire.

Tim Winton quoted in David Butstone, 'Spinning Stories and Visions', *Sojourners*, 21, 8, 1992, pp. 18–21.

The final three genres on which *Cloudstreet* draws have in common a belief in the supernatural and a rejection of the idea that experience can always be explained in rational terms. The use of conventions from these genres allows *Cloudstreet* to be read as endorsing this belief. In *Cloudstreet* there is a powerful sense of some extrahuman force present, sometimes intervening in human affairs, sometimes acting as an observer of and counterpoint to human experience. The pentecostal pig and the Aboriginal man can be read as pointers to another world, one which involves something beyond literal human comprehension.

> … this is true realism: the supernatural and the natural accepted as one thing, as inclusive … The weird things that happen in my books aren't devices. For my money, this is the kind of world where pigs speak in tongues and angels come and go. And I'm not speaking metaphor here. The world is a weird place.

Tim Winton quoted in Beth Watzke, 'Where Pigs Speak in Tongues and Angels Come and Go: A Conversation with Tim Winton', *Antipodes*, December 1991, pp. 96–8.

Cloudstreet's use of the biblical tradition, especially when read in conjunction with the epigraph (see page 53), allows the novel to be read as proposing the Christian view of life as a pilgrimage in which people begin life in a state of dissatisfaction and ignorance but eventually arrive at a state of grace, receiving God's favour. This state of grace is achieved by people battling against the difficulties and evils of life, achieving a knowledge of their place in the scheme of life by accepting God's plan and thus experiencing a 'rebirth'. The narrative of *Cloudstreet* can be read as a pilgrimage in that the characters journey from a state of dissatisfaction and ignorance. Along the way they encounter many difficulties. The state of grace they achieve is their acceptance of each other as a family community and the place where they live as home, all of which brings happiness. This acceptance is most clearly

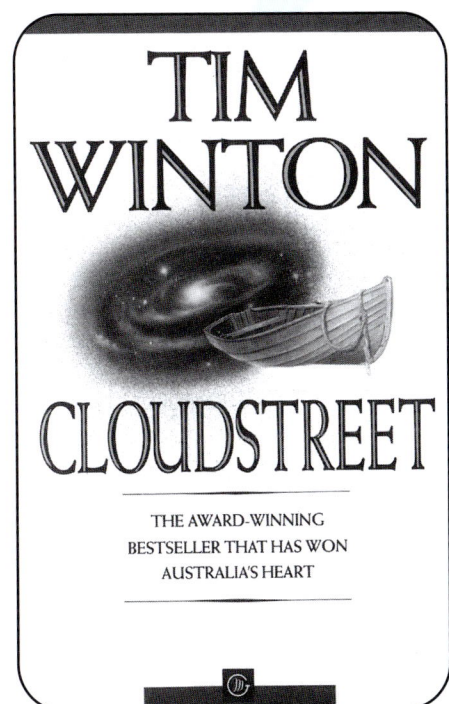

TIM WINTON
CLOUDSTREET
THE AWARD-WINNING BESTSELLER THAT HAS WON AUSTRALIA'S HEART

expressed by Rose towards the end of the novel: 'We belong to it, Quick … It's like a village … I want the life I have'. The importance of belonging is further emphasised by Rose's rejection of independence: 'When I want to be independent I retire. I go skinny and puke … I want to be with people'. Significantly Rose describes her decision to stay as similar to a rebirth, echoing the Christian image of the achievement of a state of grace: 'it's like getting another childhood, another go at things'.

This reading of *Cloudstreet* illustrates once again the importance of the reader's context. Readers who are Christians themselves, or have a knowledge of the Christian tradition, are more likely to recognise these aspects of the novel and appreciate the nature of this reading. Those operating outside a Christian framework may ignore the aspects of the novel that make this reading possible.

Activity

The cover of a novel often reflects and encourages a reading of the text within a particular genre. Compare the cover of *Cloudstreet* on page 162 with that on page 179 and discuss the different readings they encourage.

The Handmaid's Tale combines two genres. The first can be called dystopic fiction, a form of writing that projects existing trends in society into a future society as a way of encouraging readers to reflect on the consequences of these trends. Other examples of dystopic fiction, besides those mentioned by Atwood in her interview in this chapter, include the films *Starship Troopers*, *Robocop*, *Blade Runner*, *The Matrix* and *The Truman Show*. *The Handmaid's Tale* can be read as using the genre of dystopic fiction to warn against the dangers of environmental degradation, narrow religious fundamentalism and male chauvinism.

The Handmaid's Tale differs from many other examples of dystopic fiction, however, by presenting the novel in the form of a diary, a genre that usually encourages a high level of intimacy between the reader and the protagonist.

Popcorn can be categorised as a thriller. This term does not have a strict definition but is generally used to refer to novels and films featuring high levels of action and suspense, usually centred on a crime and often involving a race against time. What is different about *Popcorn* is that it uses the thriller genre in order to satirise it. The novel is written in a manner similar to such books as *The Silence of the Lambs* and films like *Natural Born Killers*, which Bruce's film in the novel, *Ordinary Americans*, is clearly based on. Like these thrillers, violence and murder in *Popcorn* are often committed in an offhand manner and sometimes with sexual overtones. The novel can be read as reproducing the thriller genre in order to raise questions about violence in society and the relationship between violence and the media.

Another way in which *Popcorn* departs from the traditional thriller is that it allows the criminals to voice their opinions on how they are portrayed within the genre in ways that sound credible, rather than psychopathic. At one point Wayne, the killer, points out to Bruce:

You got all this luxury … and you pay for it by making films about ordinary, sad, dumb people, people who live in ghettos and projects and trailer parks, and making them look ugly and sick and violent.

At another point he says, 'Don't you use the terrible sick mental condition that afflicts psychopaths like me just to give people a thrill?' For many readers Wayne might have a valid point.

A third way in which *Popcorn* departs from convention is by presenting chapters 12 and 13 and the first part of chapter 39, the climax of the novel, in the form of a film script. This break with the convention of novel writing can be read as suggesting that the killers Wayne and Scout see themselves as starring in a film, in turn suggesting the way in which they have been influenced by Hollywood films and are unable to distinguish between fiction and reality.

Because *The Wife of Martin Guerre* is based on an actual incident, some people might be inclined to argue that it is a nonfiction narrative rather than a novel. It is more accurate to see the text as a novelisation of a historical incident than a record of one. The techniques used by Lewis that reflect the craft of the novelist rather than the historian include:

- the careful structuring of the narrative around exposition, crises, climax and resolution
- the withholding of vital information from the reader until the very end
- the use of a focaliser in Bertrande de Rols, the only character whose thoughts the reader is privy to and which have obviously been invented by the author
- the use of invented dialogue
- the use of symbolism such as the slaughtered dove.

Natalie Zemon-Davis has written a historical account of the incident on which the novel is based called *The Return of Martin Guerre*. The Bertrande that emerges from that account is very different from the hapless victim in Lewis' novel. In Zemon-Davis' book, Bertrande is aware that the man claiming to be Martin is an impostor at a very early point and is complicit in his imposture.

As a novel, *The Wife of Martin Guerre* combines the conventions of two prose fiction genres, the historical novel and the mystery. The novel gains credibility from its status as a historical novel. Readers more readily accept the truth of the story because they know it is based on historical fact. Knowing that characters and the situation actually existed can add to their credibility. Readers might otherwise dismiss the story of *The Wife of Martin Guerre* as highly improbable.

The novel's presentation of the story in the form of a mystery, the truth of which is only revealed at the end, can cause readers to align strongly with Bertrande de Rols as they share her frustration and dilemmas. If you read the novel from a feminist perspective, you might argue that it aligns the reader with the female, Bertrande, because of her ignorance and her treatment by males, especially the lying impostor Arnaud du Tilh.

Of the four novels used as examples in this chapter, *The Wife of Martin Guerre*, apart from its brevity, most closely reflects the conventions of the traditional novel, except in one important respect. Like most novels, it focuses on a single character and a single problem. You learn little about the protagonist Bertrande, apart from what is revealed through her relationship with her husband and the question of his identity. The novel follows a chronologically linear plot with a clear set of crises and a dramatic and surprising climax. Where *The Wife of Martin Guerre* departs from the conventions of both the historical novel and the mystery is in the ending. Although the mystery is solved and the truth is revealed, the novel does not end happily for Bertrande. How this might affect your interpretation has been discussed earlier on page 165.

Point of view

Every novel or short story has a narrator. The most commonly used points of view are:

- first person, where a character in the story is the narrator
- third person limited or sympathetic, where the narrator is outside the story and tells the story from the perspective of one character (the story 'Neighbours' earlier in this chapter is an example of this)
- third person omniscient, where the narrator is outside the story and moves between the perspectives of different characters.

Some novels use multiple points of view, some switch point of view and some have a point of view that does not fit easily into any of the categories above, but seems to be a mixture of two or more.

The point of view encourages the reader to respond to and interpret the characters and events portrayed in particular ways, and through this to adopt certain attitudes and values. Narrators may influence the reader's perspective through direct comment on characters and events, but more often their influence is more subtle than this and works by implication and connotation.

The effects of a particular point of view depend on the novel. Different novels may use the same point of view with very different results. Similarly, different readers respond in different ways. This is because point of view often works in conjunction with the attitudes and values of the character who is the focaliser. Where the attitudes and values of the focaliser coincide with your own, the point of view is likely to reinforce your sympathy for the character. Where the values of the character conflict with your own, the use of the character as focaliser may reinforce your antipathy.

It is possible to generalise about the effect of different points of view, but these generalisations are only a starting point. The nature and effects of point of view in a novel should be examined with close reference to that novel rather than by simply applying generalised categories.

With first person and third person limited narration, you are likely to align with the views and the values of the character who is the focaliser of the story. *The Handmaid's Tale*, for example, is written almost entirely in the first person using Offred as the focaliser of the story, apart from the historical notes at the end. The access this gives to her thoughts and feelings tends to arouse a great deal of sympathy from most readers. As a consequence, readers tend to adopt her attitudes and accept her interpretations.

There are novels written in the first person, however, which have a very different effect. John Fowles' *The Collector* is written in the first person from the point of view of a young man who kidnaps and holds prisoner a young woman, not exactly the sort of person most readers would be likely to sympathise with. Most readers find the narrator's rationalisation and justification for his actions alienating, although some find the first person point of view allows them to feel a degree of sympathy for him or at least to have some understanding of him.

CASE STUDY

25

The Collector

Focus question

The passage below is the opening of The Collector. Discuss your response to the main character and how this response is affected by the use of first person point of view.

When she was home from her boarding-school I used to see her almost every day sometimes, because their house was right opposite the Town Hall Annexe. She and her younger sister used to go in and out a lot, often with young men, which of course I didn't like. When I had a free moment from the files and ledgers I stood by the window and used to look down over the road over the frosting and sometimes I'd see her. In the evening I marked it in my observations diary, at first with X, and then when I knew her name with M. I saw her several times outside too. I stood right behind her once in a queue at the public library down Crossfield Street. She didn't look once at me, but I watched the back of her head and her hair in a long pigtail. It was very pale, silky, like burnet cocoons. All in one pigtail coming down almost to her waist, sometimes in front, sometimes at the back. Sometimes she wore it up. Only once, before she came to be my guest here, did I have the privilege to see her with it loose, and it took my breath away it was so beautiful, like a mermaid.

Another time one Saturday off when I went up to the Natural History Museum I came back on the same train.

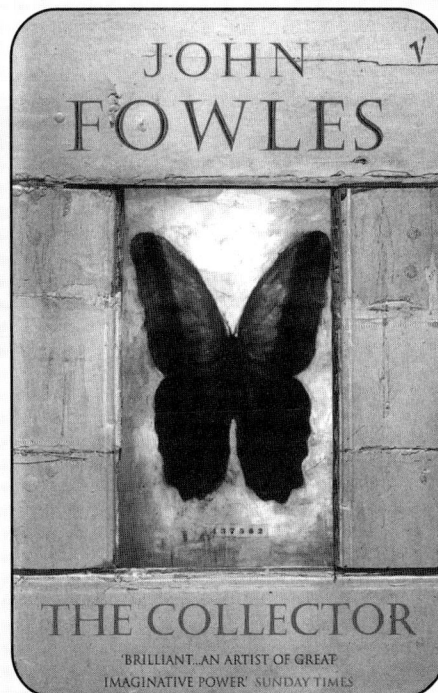

She sat three seats down and sideways to me, and read a book, so I could watch her for thirty-five minutes. Seeing her always made me feel like I was catching a rarity, going up to it very careful, heart-in-mouth as they say. A Pale Clouded Yellow, for instance. I always thought of her like that, I mean words like elusive and sporadic, and very refined—not like the other ones, even the pretty ones. More for the real connoisseur.

The year she was still at school I didn't know who she was, only how her father was Doctor Grey and some talk I overheard once at a Bug Section meeting about how her mother drank. I heard her mother speak once in a shop, she had a la-di-da voice and you could see she was the type to drink, too much make-up etcetera.

Well, then there was this bit in the local paper about the scholarship she'd won and how clever she was, and her name as beautiful as herself, Miranda. So I knew she was up in London studying art. It really made a difference, that newspaper article. It seemed like we became more intimate, although of course we still did not know each other in the ordinary way.

I can't say what it was, the very first time I saw her, I knew she was the only one. Of course I am not mad, I knew it was just a dream and it always would have been if it hadn't been for the money. I used to have daydreams about her, I used to think of stories where I met her, did things she admired, married her and all that. Nothing nasty, that was never until what I'll explain later.

She drew pictures and I looked after my collection (in my dreams). It was always she loving me and my collection, drawing and colouring them; working together in a beautiful modern house in a big room with one of those huge glass windows; meetings there of the Bug Section, where instead of saying almost nothing in case I made mistakes we were the popular host and hostess. She all pretty with her pale blonde hair and grey eyes and of course the other men all green round the gills.

The only times I didn't have nice dreams about her being when I saw her with a certain young man, a loud noisy public-school type who had a sports car. I stood beside him once in Barclays waiting to pay in and I heard him say, I'll have it in fivers; the joke being it was only a cheque for ten pounds. They all behave like that. Well, I saw her climb in his car sometimes, or them out together in the town in it, and those days I was very short with the others in the office, and I didn't use to mark the X in my entomological observations diary (all this was before she went to London, she dropped him then). Those were days I let myself have the bad dreams. She cried or usually knelt. Once I let myself dream I hit her across the face as I saw it done once by a chap in a telly play. Perhaps that was when it all started.

John Fowles, *The Collector*, Vintage, London 1963, pp. 9–11.

CASE STUDY

The Handmaid's Tale

The following passage is from *The Handmaid's Tale*.

Focus questions

Discuss or write a response to the following questions.
1 *What attitudes towards the narrator and her environment does the use of point of view in combination with other aspects of the passage encourage in you as a reader?*
2 *How does your response differ from your response to the passage from The Collector? What reasons can you suggest for the differences?*

A chair, a table, a lamp. Above, on the white ceiling, a relief ornament in the shape of a wreath, and in the centre of it a blank space, plastered over, like the place in a face where the eye has been taken out. There must have been a chandelier, once. They've removed anything you could tie a rope to.

A window, two white curtains. Under the window, a window seat with a little cushion. When the window is partly open—it only opens partly— the air can come in and make the curtains move. I can sit in the chair, or on the window seat, hands folded, and watch this. Sunlight comes in through the window too, and falls on the floor, which is made of wood, in narrow strips, highly polished. I can smell the polish. There's a rug on the floor, oval, of braided rags. This is the kind of touch they like: folk art, archaic, made by women, in their spare time, from things that have no further use. A return to traditional values. Waste not want not. I am not being wasted. Why do I want?

On the wall above the chair, a picture, framed but with no glass: a print of flowers, blue irises, watercolour. Flowers are still allowed. Does each of us have the same print, the same chair, the same white curtains, I wonder? Government issue?

Think of it as being in the army, said Aunt Lydia.

A bed. Single, mattress medium-hard, covered with a flocked white spread. Nothing takes place in the bed but sleep; or no sleep. I try not to think too much. Like other things now, thought must be rationed. There's a lot that doesn't

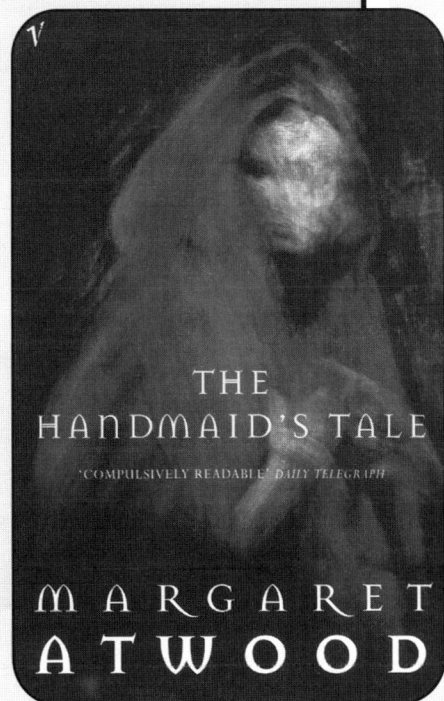

THE HANDMAID'S TALE

'COMPULSIVELY READABLE' *DAILY TELEGRAPH*

MARGARET ATWOOD

bear thinking about. Thinking can hurt your chances, and I intend to last. I know why there is no glass, in front of the watercolour picture of blue irises, and why the window only opens partly and why the glass in it is shatterproof. It isn't running away they're afraid of. We wouldn't get far. It's those other escapes, the ones you can open in yourself, given a cutting edge.

So. Apart from these details, this could be a college guest room, for the less distinguished visitors; or a room in a rooming house, of former times, for ladies in reduced circumstances. That is what we are now. The circumstances have been reduced; for those of us who still have circumstances.

But a chair, sunlight, flowers: these are not to be dismissed. I am alive, I live, I breathe, I put my hand out, unfolded, into the sunlight. Where I am is not a prison but a privilege, as Aunt Lydia said, who was in love with either/or.

The bell that measures time is ringing. Time here is measured by bells, as once in nunneries. As in a nunnery too, there are few mirrors.

I get up out of the chair, advance my feet into the sunlight, in their red shoes, flat-heeled to save the spine and not for dancing. The red gloves are lying on the bed. I pick them up, pull them onto my hands, finger by finger. Everything except the wings around my face is red: the colour of blood, which defines us. The skirt is ankle-length, full, gathered to a flat yoke that extends over the breasts, the sleeves are full. The white wings too are prescribed issue; they are to keep us from seeing, but also from being seen. I never looked good in red, it's not my colour. I pick up the shopping basket, put it over my arm.

The door of the room—not *my* room, I refuse to say *my*—is not locked. In fact it doesn't shut properly. I go out into the polished hallway, which has a runner down the centre, dusty pink. Like a path through the forest, like a carpet for royalty, it shows me the way.

The carpet bends and goes down the front staircase and I go with it, one hand on the banister, once a tree, turned in another century, rubbed to a warm gloss. Late Victorian, the house is, a family house, built for a large rich family. There's a grandfather clock in the hallway, which doles out time, and then the door to the motherly front sitting room, with its fleshtones and hints. A sitting room in which I never sit, but stand or kneel only. At the end of the hallway, above the front door, is a fanlight of coloured glass: flowers, red and blue.

There remains a mirror, on the hall wall. If I turn my head so that the white wings framing my face direct my vision towards it, I can see it as I go down the stairs, round, convex, a pier-glass, like the eye of a fish, and myself in it like a distorted shadow, a parody of something, some fairytale figure in a red cloak, descending towards a moment of carelessness that is the same as danger. A Sister, dipped in blood.

Margaret Atwood, *The Handmaid's Tale*, Vintage, London 1996, pp. 17–19.

The Wife of Martin Guerre is written in the third person sympathetic using Bertrande de Rols as the focaliser. Most readers find themselves aligning themselves with and feeling sympathy for her and this appears to be the reading encouraged by the novel. Some readers, however, especially those holding strong feminist values, find it very difficult to sympathise with Bertrande, seeing her as a character who too willingly submits to the patriarchal ideologies of her society.

Point of view in *Popcorn* seems to be somewhere between third person sympathetic and third person omniscient. Events and characters are presented from Bruce Delamitri's perspective in scenes in which he is present—this is the third person sympathetic point of view and the major perspective of the novel.

The novel also presents scenes involving Wayne and Scout in which Bruce is not present. In these scenes, the perspective is not that of Wayne and Scout because the reader is not given access to their thoughts: It is that of a detached narrator—the third person omniscient. The point of view is complicated by some scenes towards the end being presented from the perspective of the chief of police. There is another complicating factor. Although the reader shares Bruce's perspective for much of the novel, most readers are unlikely to align themselves with him or his values. Access to Bruce's thoughts is more likely to lead readers to construct him as vain, arrogant, self-centred and amoral. Perhaps the real focaliser of this novel is the cynical narrator, who, as well as revealing Bruce's thoughts, stands outside him and judges him for the reader.

Point of view in *Cloudstreet* is also quite complex. Many people believe that *Cloudstreet* is narrated by the spiritual Fish, the part of him that was separated from the physical Fish during the drowning incident. But it is also possible to argue that there is no dominant point of view in *Cloudstreet* and that the narration shifts between an anonymous omniscient third person narrator and the first person of the spiritual Fish.

The main point to note about *Cloudstreet* is that the reader is given access to the thoughts of a wide range of characters, with the thoughts of Rose and Quick being given more attention than others as the novel progresses. For example, the novel presents both Sam's superstitions and Lester's shaky Christianity from their own perspectives and without judgements and therefore as equally valid and understandable approaches. Similarly it accepts Dolly's promiscuity and drunkenness as well as Oriel's puritanism and hard work ethic from their perspectives and without judgement. You can read this use of point of view as challenging the dominance of the individual point of view and the narrow judgement that often accompanies it which is found in many novels, and endorsing in contrast an acceptance and valuing of the diversity of human experience and understanding.

In relation to this, it is significant that in *Cloudstreet* there is no real villain. Even the mass murderer is eventually reconstructed as not aberrant at heart: '... there's no monsters, only people like us', Quick says of him.

In those parts of the novel where it is clear that Fish Lamb is the narrator, point of view can be read as contributing to the meaning of the novel in a number of ways. First, by using a narrator who is a spiritual entity, it can be seen as reinforcing the existence of a spiritual world closely connected and interacting with the physical world. This idea pervades the novel and forms part of its ideology. Second, it can be seen as reinforcing another major theme of the novel, the continuing presence of the past in the present, for the use of Fish as narrator means that the events of the novel are presented as happening both in the past and now, as Fish drowns and narrates them: 'I know my story for just that long, long enough to see how we've come … as long as it took to tell you all this'.

Fish is an interpretive narrator. He comments and judges, thus inviting the reader to share his judgements. This can be seen most clearly in his comments on Rose's mistaken affair with Toby Raven, which Fish invites the reader to see as an abandonment of her family. At the end of the novel, Fish articulates a major ideology of the novel: the vision and celebration of life as a battle 'in the same corridor that time makes for us'.

CASE STUDY

27

The Great Gatsby

The following passage is from *The Great Gatsby* by F. Scott Fitzgerald published in 1926. The passage is set on Long Island just outside New York City in the early 1920s. The case study and the activities that accompany it are intended to show the way in which point of view in prose fiction can be read in different ways.

The narrator of the story is Nick Carraway, who has just moved to New York from the midwest. He has rented a house on a peninsula called West Egg, which is across the bay from a similar peninsula called East Egg. The houses on West Egg are less fashionable than those on East Egg.

Focus questions

1 *Read the passage accepting Nick Carraway as a reliable narrator and discuss the reading of Tom Buchanan encouraged by Nick within this approach.*

2 *Read the passage resistantly. Focus not on what Nick's narration reveals about Tom but what it reveals about him. To what extent is it possible to read Nick's portrayal of Tom as reflecting his own sense of inferiority?*

Across the courtesy bay the white palaces of fashionable East Egg glittered along the water, and the history of the summer really begins on the evening I drove over there to have dinner with the Tom Buchanans. Daisy was my second cousin once removed, and I'd known Tom in college. And just after the war I spent two days with them in Chicago.

Her husband, among various physical accomplishments, had been one of the most powerful ends that ever played football at New Haven—a national figure in a way, one of those men who reach such an acute limited excellence at twenty-one that everything afterward savours of anti-climax. His family were enormously wealthy—even in college his freedom with money was a matter for reproach—but now he'd left Chicago and come East in a fashion that rather took your breath away: for instance, he'd brought down a string of polo ponies from Lake Forest. It was hard to realize that a man in my own generation was wealthy enough to do that.

Why they came East I don't know. They had spent a year in France for no particular reason, and then drifted here and there unrestfully wherever people played polo and were rich together. This was a permanent move, said Daisy over the telephone, but I didn't believe it—I had no sight into Daisy's heart, but I felt that Tom would drift on forever seeking, a little wistfully, for the dramatic turbulence of some irrecoverable football game.

And so it happened that on a warm windy evening I drove over to East Egg to see two old friends whom I scarcely knew at all. Their house was even more elaborate than I expected, a cheerful red-and-white Georgian Colonial mansion, overlooking the bay. The lawn started at the beach and ran towards the front door for a quarter of a mile, jumping over sundials and brick walks and burning gardens—finally when it reached the house drifting up the side in bright vines as though from the momentum of its run. The front was broken by a line of french windows, glowing now with reflected gold and wide open to the warm windy afternoon, and Tom Buchanan in riding clothes was standing with his legs apart on the front porch.

He had changed since his New Haven years. Now he was a sturdy straw-haired man of thirty, with a rather hard mouth and a supercilious manner. Two shining arrogant eyes had established dominance over his face and gave him the appearance of always leaning aggressively forward. Not even the effeminate swank of his riding clothes could hide the enormous power of that body—he seemed to fill those glistening boots until he strained the top lacing, and you could see a great pack of muscle shifting when his shoulder moved under his thin coat. It was a body capable of enormous leverage—a cruel body.

His speaking voice, a gruff husky tenor, added to the impression of fractiousness he conveyed. There was a touch of paternal contempt in it, even toward people he liked—and there were men at New Haven who had hated his guts.

'Now, don't think my opinion on these matters is final,' he seemed to say, 'just because I'm stronger and more of a man than you are.' We were in the same senior society* and while we were never intimate I always had the impression that he approved of me and wanted me to like him with some harsh, defiant wistfulness of his own.

We talked for a few minutes on the sunny porch.

'I've got a nice place here,' he said, his eyes flashing about restlessly.

Turning me around by one arm, he moved a broad flat hand along the front vista, including in its sweep a sunken Italian garden, a half acre of deep, pungent roses, and a snub-nosed motor-boat that bumped the tide offshore.

'It belonged to Demaine, the oil man.' He turned me around again, politely and abruptly. 'We'll go inside.'

* A senior society is an exclusive university club.

F. Scott Fitzgerald, *The Great Gatsby*, Penguin, Ringwood 2000, pp. 11–13.

Pleasure and reader involvement

This chapter has largely focussed on how you can read novels to examine their relationship to context and the way in which they participate in the circulation of values, attitudes, beliefs and ideologies within society. But novels and short stories are not social tracts. Readers read them for pleasure. Pleasure partly derives from becoming involved in the world of the novel. The extent to which this happens depends partly on whether readers can relate to the central problem on which the novel is based. The more involved readers are, the more they are likely to accept the values, attitudes, ideologies or beliefs reflected or expressed by the novel.

As this suggests, ideology and enjoyment are closely related. There are, however, a number of other factors that affect the enjoyment readers gain from a text. These are discussed in the following chapter. Although it focuses on feature film, many of the concepts and analytic skills can be applied to prose fiction.

Feature film

9

Because prose fiction and feature film are both forms of narrative, many of the concepts and skills used in examining them are the same. The first section of this chapter discusses some topics discussed in the previous chapter, such as genre and narrative structure, but in relation to film rather than prose fiction and from a different perspective. Rather than simply examining how these features contribute to the meanings you make of a text, they are also examined in terms of how they contribute to your enjoyment of a text and your involvement in it, in other words how they contribute to the entertainment value of the text. Just as many of the concepts and skills explained in the previous chapter can be applied to film, so many of the concepts and skills explained in this section can be applied to prose fiction and indeed stage drama.

The second section of this chapter focuses on a topic peculiar to feature film, film language.

The chapter concludes with a discussion of realism. While the focus is on realism in film, many of the concepts also apply to prose fiction and stage drama.

This chapter uses two films as the basis for detailed explanation and illustration, *The Truman Show*, released in 1998 and directed by Peter Weir, and *Rabbit Proof Fence*, released in 2002 and directed by Phil Noyce.

These films were selected for a number of reasons. First, they are relatively recent. Second, *The Truman Show* was selected because it is a product of the American film industry, the dominant force in film. *Rabbit Proof Fence* was selected because it is Australian and represents an alternative to the American film industry tradition. Third, the films are dissimilar in many ways, thus offering useful points of contrast. The many things the films have in common, however, help to illustrate some of the basic features of many films. On occasion, other films are also used as examples.

Film as entertainment

Examining what makes a film entertaining can help you to learn about how films are constructed, about society and about yourself. What makes a film entertaining? To answer this question, you can examine at least six things:

- thematic relevance
- genre
- sympathetic protagonists
- antagonists
- narrative structure
- film language.

This section discusses the first five of these and the following section discusses the entertainment value of film language as part of a more general discussion of film language.

How a film entertains depends on the audience. Different people find different things entertaining depending on their context. Factors such as nationality, age, gender, generic preferences and social interests all play a role. Historical context is important as well. This can be seen by how the films people find entertaining have changed over time. The discussion of the different aspects of film below is intended to help you identify those things that make a film entertaining for you and consider why other people might find a film entertaining.

Thematic relevance

Audiences are more likely to find films entertaining if they deal with subjects related to their own lives. Thematic relevance can be read on a number of levels. Audiences may find relevance in terms of a current social issue or they may find it on a more personal level in terms of the way the film relates to their own lives. This may

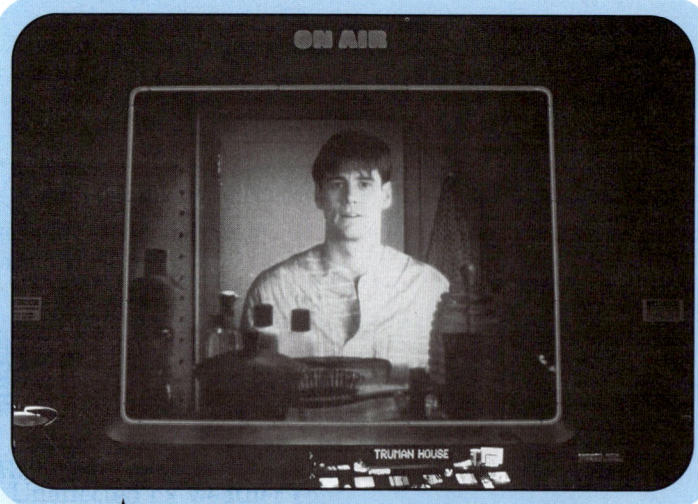

From *The Truman Show*

involve reading the film in terms of archetypal themes, issues that have been relevant to people at many times throughout history, such as the struggle of the individual against authority.

The Truman Show, like other films, can be read thematically on a number of levels. On the most obvious level, *The Truman Show* can be read as reflecting concern in technologically advanced societies about the increasing power of the media to dominate and control people's lives for the purpose of entertainment. It is significant that *EdTV* and *Wag the Dog*, which reflect similar concerns, were released at about the same time as *The Truman Show*.

The Truman Show can also be read as reflecting the debate in the late 1990s and early years of the twenty-first century about the public's increasing taste for reality television and the morality involved in this. Reality television includes shows such as *Survivor*, *Temptation Island* and *Big Brother*. *The Truman Show* can be seen as taking reality television to its ultimate limit by portraying a television show which telecasts the whole life of an individual from birth to death in order to highlight this debate.

> More than anything else, Weir seems determined to make his thoughts about the irony of the world's media clear. As the final moments draw to a close, we realize that there will always be an audience for the next *Truman Show*, and that the people who cheered for his freedom are the same who supported the show over its many years.

Luke Buckmaster, '*The Truman Show*', *Infilm Australia*, http://infilmau.iah.net/reviews/truman.htm

This concern about the power of the media reflects a more general concern about the power of technology and its use and misuse. This was foreshadowed in Mary Shelley's *Frankenstein* in the early 1800s. It has been a strong feature of Western societies since the late nineteenth century, reflected in the birth and development of the science fiction genre.

On another level, *The Truman Show* may reflect many people's perceptions of modern life. Truman finds his supposedly perfect world stifling in its repetitiveness and shallowness. Behind his happy-go-lucky nature in the early scenes, it is clear that Truman desperately seeks excitement. This is indicated initially in his conversation with his reflection in the opening scenes and reinforced in his telephone call to Fiji and his subsequent conversations with his friend Marlon. It is not surprising that Truman wishes to escape: his life is dominated by a nine-to-five routine and an emphasis on shallow consumerism, exemplified in his wife's product placement advertising. Many people may find that Truman's life resembles their own or that of people they know. As one critic puts it, '*The Truman Show* is so compelling because we're all, like Truman, starving for authentic experience'.

At its most fundamental level, *The Truman Show* reflects the desire most people have to control their own lives rather than be controlled by the power of others.

Rabbit Proof Fence is relevant to Australian audiences at the beginning of the twenty-first century on a political and social level because it deals with a topic of considerable political debate: the stolen generation.

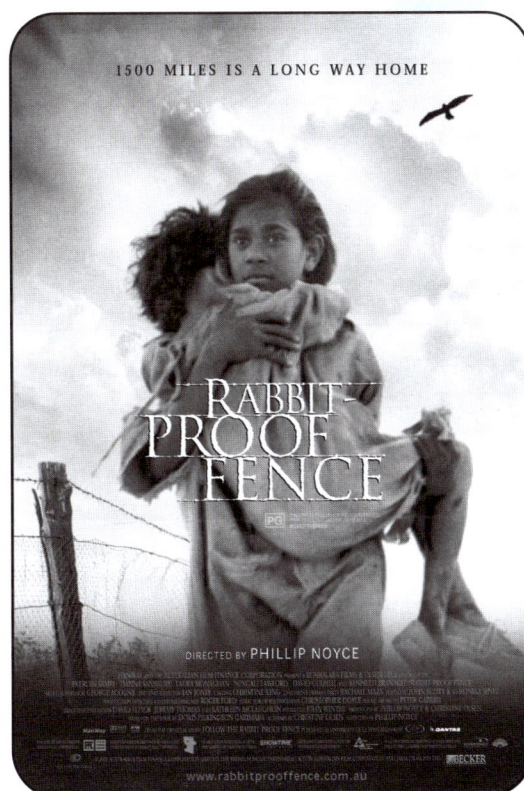

1500 MILES IS A LONG WAY HOME

RABBIT-PROOF FENCE

DIRECTED BY PHILLIP NOYCE

www.rabbitprooffence.com.au

> I could feel in the wind that white Australia wanted a vehicle—whether it was a movie, whether it was a book or whatever—that got beyond the slogans and allowed them to come to terms with the history of race relations in this country. What I'd hope this film might encourage is for all Australians to understand the deeply felt emotions that have fuelled some of the debates on the stolen generation issue and on reconciliation in general.

Phil Noyce quoted in Garry Maddox, 'The long way home', *Sydney Morning Herald*, 15 February 2002.

193

As Noyce's comment indicates, the stolen generation issue is part of a broader issue of relationships between races which has been an ongoing issue in Australian society since white settlement and is of concern and interest to many societies throughout the world. It hasn't always been an issue Australians have liked to confront, however. With the sole exception of *Jedda* in 1955, films dealing with Aboriginal subjects and race relations have not succeeded in attracting Australian audiences, despite the fact that since *Jedda* over twenty such films have been made. Even the highly acclaimed *The Chant of Jimmie Blacksmith*, made in the 1970s, was not successful. The producers of *Rabbit Proof Fence* were taking a large risk in making a film that dealt with race relations in Australia.

At the time of writing this book, it appears that *Rabbit Proof Fence* has been successful in attracting large audiences. This may indicate changing attitudes in Australian society. On the other hand, the film's success may be attributed to its massive marketing campaign and the manner in which it exploits other aspects of audience appeal. One of the most important of these is its construction of the film around a topic of personal significance to most people: the love of children for their parents and the horror of being forcibly separated from them. Phil Noyce, the director, explained this appeal in the following way:

> In terms of the stolen generation issue, it reduces all the rhetoric to something that everyone can understand. Our children have been taken from us, we've been separated from our mothers, we want to go home, we want them back. That's simple, primal.
>
> Phil Noyce quoted in Garry Maddox, 'Success Critical', *Sydney Morning Herald*, 3 January 2002.

Attempts to encourage viewers to connect with the film on this level can be seen in the slogan used in some of the marketing for the film:

> You are in the middle of a desert 1500 miles from home.
> You are hot and tired
> And pursued
> And you are only a child.

Note that this slogan does not say, 'And you are an Aboriginal person'.

The thematic relevance of *Rabbit Proof Fence*, therefore, can be seen to exist on both a political level and a personal level. Audiences may relate to the film on either or both of these levels.

As with a novel, a film is most likely to be successful if it offers the audience a variety of ways of relating to the subject matter—this broadens the potential audience.

Activity

If you have seen *Rabbit Proof Fence*, discuss to what extent you think its success in attracting audiences can be attributed to its political relevance and to what extent its success can be attributed to its appeal on a personal level.

Genre

People are likely to find a film entertaining if it works within a genre they are familiar with. This is because they know the conventions and will be able to read the film more easily. If you follow trends in film-making you will notice that when a film of a particular genre proves popular, it is quickly followed by other films within the same genre. Following the enormous success of *Saving Private Ryan* came a number of other films set during the Second World War, such as *The Thin Red Line* and *Enemy at the Gates*. Working within a currently popular genre does not automatically guarantee success, however. *Pearl Harbour* also tried to cash in on the popularity of the Second World War genre but failed to attract audiences.

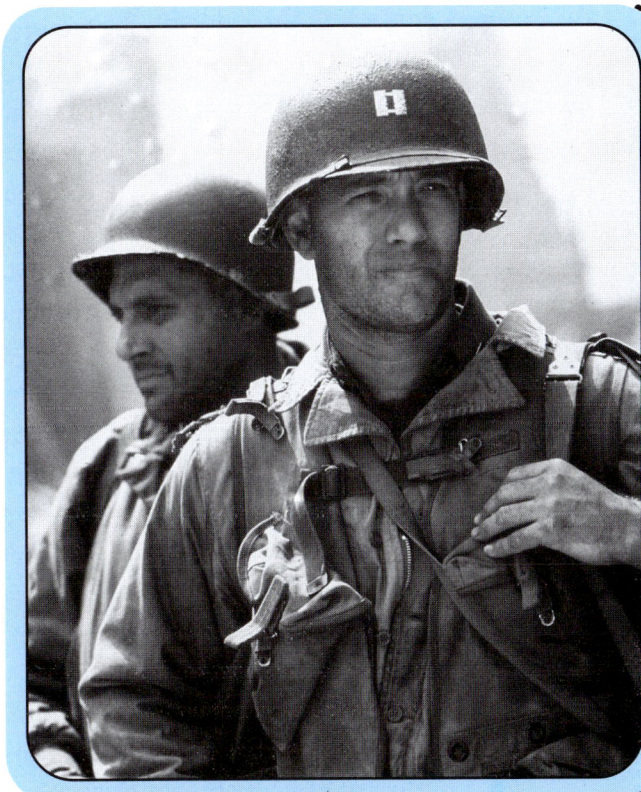

From *Saving Private Ryan*

A film cannot simply repeat the conventions or techniques used by other films. It needs to do something different. Audiences desire a mixture of familiarity and difference in their films. Some of the most successful films have been ones that take a well-known genre and do something surprising or unexpected with it. One of the ways of doing this is to take a well-known genre and change the gender of the protagonist to female. Examples of this include the thriller *The Silence of the Lambs*, Ridley Scott's use of the science fiction genre in the *Alien* series of movies and the same director's use of the road movie or buddy genre in *Thelma and Louise*. As well as creating innovation within a familiar genre, these films reflected the changing views of the capacity of females to be more than helpless victims and thus appealed to the changing attitudes of Western audiences. They combined generic innovation with thematic relevance.

The following extract from a film review shows that the reviewer understands the need for innovation within a genre in order for a film to be entertaining.

> *The Matrix* is undeniably science fiction, but, unlike most pictures claiming that association, it never falls into the boring, expected patterns of space battles and laser gun shoot-outs. Instead, it ventures into territory that, while not virgin, is sufficiently interesting to provide an involving, invigorating backdrop … The die-hard science fiction fan will discover a plot that mixes and matches both new and old conventions of the genre in a compelling fashion. Action aficionados will find that there's no shortage of electric excitement, whether it's in the form of hand-to-hand kung fu-type fights or shoot-outs with seemingly limitless ammunition.

> James Berardinelli 1999, 'The Matrix: A Film Review', *Reelviews*
> http://movie-reviews.colossus.net/movies/m/matrix.html

The Truman Show has been acclaimed for its 'startling originality', with one reviewer saying, 'viewers will be justified in feeling that they've never seen anything quite like it. And how often can you say that in this derivative age?' If you look closely, however, you will see that it shares elements with quite a few genres.

First, because of its presentation of an imperfect future society it falls within the dystopic fiction genre that includes books such as *Nineteen Eighty-four*, *Brave New World* and *The Handmaid's Tale*. Although not as popular as other film genres, the dystopic fiction genre has a long and respected history in films stretching from Fritz Lang's *Metropolis* in 1926 to *Total Recall* in 1990. A new print of *Metropolis* with a rock music soundtrack is available and worth looking at, even if you don't watch the whole film, to gain an appreciation of the genre.

A modern subset of the dystopic fiction genre with which *The Truman Show* shares similarities is what has been called the 'false worlds' genre. This genre portrays characters who learn that their everyday taken-for-granted world is not what it appears to be. Examples include *The Matrix*, *Dark City* and *Total Recall*.

Another subset of the dystopic fiction genre with which *The Truman Show* shares similarities has been mentioned in the discussion of thematic relevance. This is the genre of media satires such as *Wag the Dog* and *EdTV*. The interesting thing about these films and *The Truman Show* is that no attempt is made to situate them in an obviously future society. The message seems to be not that these things could happen in the future if certain trends continue, but that they are possible right now.

The Truman Show also draws on the quest genre. Initially, Truman's quest is to discover the truth about his world and himself. Towards the end, the quest becomes a more archetypal one as he attempts to escape Seahaven. In this respect, it shares elements with many of the escape movies, both prisoner of war films and films such as *The Shawshank Redemption* and *Rabbit Proof Fence*.

In portraying a person at the mercy of powerful forces he does not know about or understand, *The Truman Show* shares similarity with texts such as Franz Kafka's *The Trial*, a novel that portrays the plight of a man arrested and put on trial without being told why he is on trial. Like *The Trial*, *The Truman Show* can be read as reflecting modern fears about the power of large organisations to control our lives while keeping us in ignorance at the same time.

Rabbit Proof Fence is more generically conventional than *The Truman Show*, working largely within the quest genre, like the last part of *The Truman Show*. The quest genre is a much more straightforward and simple genre than many and is thus likely to increase the potential audience for the film. The invitation for audiences to

read the film in terms of this genre is evident in the tagline on many of the posters for the film: '1500 Miles is a Long Way Home'.

In *Rabbit Proof Fence*, however, a degree of innovation is added to the genre to expand the entertainment possibilities. The quest genre in *Rabbit Proof Fence*, as in *The Truman Show*, is combined with the chase genre, a recent example of which was *The Fugitive*. The combining of the girls' quest to return to their mothers with the drama of the attempts to recapture them adds an extra dimension to the suspense and drama of the film. It adds the central question of the chase genre, 'Will they be caught?' to the central question of the quest genre 'Will they achieve their goal?'

Another thing that makes *Rabbit Proof Fence* different to many other quests is its manipulation of the archetypal struggle between the apparently small powerless individual and the forces of authority. In most films portraying characters fleeing from the police or other figures of authority, the characters tend to be constructed as less powerful than their pursuers, but in *Rabbit Proof Fence* this is intensified by the fact that the characters concerned are young girls from an oppressed social group. Richard Kimble in *The Fugitive*, in contrast, was a wealthy middle-class doctor with many contacts among people in positions of authority and influence. Compared to Molly, Gracie and Daisy, Richard Kimble had it easy.

Activities

1. Make a list of the genres on which both *The Truman Show* and *Rabbit Proof Fence* draw. Next to each, brainstorm other films that draw on that genre. Discuss similarities and differences between the films.
2. Identify other genres or films with similarities to *The Truman Show* and *Rabbit Proof Fence*.
3. Choose another film and identify genres it draws on to appeal to audiences.

Sympathetic protagonists

Audiences want someone to be involved with in the film narrative. If they care about and identify with the protagonist they are more likely to become involved in the narrative and be interested in the outcome. Characters with whom the audience becomes involved are referred to as sympathetic characters. The term sympathy in regard to narratives like films does not mean feeling sorry for someone, although this might be one way of arousing sympathy for a character. Sympathy is usually created by a combination of pity, identification and admiration. Pity usually arises because of the suffering or misfortune of the character. Identification can be evoked when the audience can relate to the experience a character is undergoing or the feelings of the character. Admiration is usually aroused because of the character's attempts to fight back against misfortune.

In *The Truman Show*, sympathy is initially encouraged through knowledge of Truman's entrapment within his artificial world. The opening scenes reinforce this by focussing on his dissatisfaction with his life. The first time the audience sees him he is standing before his mirror engaged in an imaginary conversation about climbing a mountain. This suggests a character seeking excitement and an alternative to his routine lifestyle, an attitude many members of the audience might identify with. His dissatisfaction is further underlined soon after through his ambivalent response to the question by an announcer on his car radio, 'How do you feel today?' In addition, Truman's cheerful interactions with other characters seem forced and insincere. His desire to escape is expressed openly in the scene where he is playing golf with his friend, Marlon, on a bridge which significantly goes nowhere:

> I'm thinking about getting out, Marlon … out of my job, off this island … out … Don't you ever get antsy, itchy feet?

Jim Carrey as Truman in
The Truman Show

Truman's description of Fiji to Marlon suggests that its attraction lies in the fact that it is as far away from where he is as it is possible to be. The following scene with his wife makes clear that his desire to get away and see some of the world is related to his fear of being trapped into family life and repetitive routine, a repetitiveness emphasised in the scenes of Truman going to work in the morning by the recurrence of the musical theme and of Truman's greeting and farewell to his neighbours.

The film encourages further sympathy for Truman when the audience learns of his grief and guilt over the death of his father and the fact that his attraction to Fiji is associated with his romantic longing for Lauren/Sylvia, the young woman who infiltrated the set as a cast member some years before.

All this is established before the first turning point or crisis in the film, which is Truman's hearing his movements monitored on the car radio. Before the plot begins in earnest then, the film has gone to considerable trouble to encourage audience sympathy for the protagonist so that when he commences his struggle against the forces that control him, the audience will take his side.

From this point on the audience's sympathies are likely to be associated with Truman's confusion as to the real nature of his world, his failed attempts to escape, the audience's knowledge that in his attempts to fathom his predicament his best friend is deceiving him and the manipulation involved in the return of his father.

As the film moves to its conclusion, the audience's response is likely to shift towards admiration for Truman's determination to escape, especially as this means overcoming his artificially induced fear of crossing water, and fear for Truman's life. Truman is symbolically linked to the great explorers of the past through the name of the boat he uses to try to escape Seahaven, the *Santa Maria*, which was the name of the boat used by Christopher Columbus in discovering the new world.

In *Rabbit Proof Fence*, Molly is created as a sympathetic character early in the film through her separation from her mother. The audience's response to this is likely to be strengthened by the violence associated with the separation, the disturbing nature of which is reinforced by the use of a hand-held camera for this scene. Molly's youth is also likely to intensify audience sympathy because it makes her suffering even greater and her determination to reach home even more admirable.

Molly also invites admiration from the audience for her protective behaviour towards Gracie and Daisy and her intelligence and cunning in covering the girls' tracks to avoid capture by the tracker. It is significant that the audience's attention is drawn to both her intelligence and her determination by the tracker himself in the two sentences which are his only lines of dialogue in the film. Molly's determination and intelligence are complemented by her emotional strength—she does not shed tears until her return home.

Everlyn Sampi as Molly in *Rabbit Proof Fence*

Everlyn Sampi's performance as Molly plays a large role in influencing the audience's reactions. She has little dialogue, so her body language is especially important in conveying her determination and inner strength. As one reviewer commented, 'Molly is quite terrific with the set of her jaw and her steely gaze'.

Antagonists

Just as audiences want someone to side with in a film, so they often want someone to dislike. This person is the antagonist. The presence of an antagonist in a film can arouse the emotions of a viewer and enhance their involvement in a film, making it more entertaining for them. An antagonist is likely to be most effective in entertaining the audience if his or her motivation to stop the protagonist from succeeding is as great as the protagonist's motivation to succeed. This makes the outcome more uncertain and adds to the suspense.

Both Christof in *The Truman Show* and Neville in *Rabbit Proof Fence* are strongly committed to their beliefs. Christof is committed to the continuation of *The Truman Show*. His belief in the show is reflected in his final speech to Truman when he describes it as bringing 'hope and joy and inspiration to millions'. Christof truly believes that the world he has created for Truman is preferable to the real world and cannot conceive why Truman would want to leave. 'There's no more truth out there than there is in the world I created for you, the same lies, the same deceit. The difference is in my world you're safe,' he tells Truman.

Ed Harris as Christof in
The Truman Show

Kenneth Branagh as
A. O. Neville in
Rabbit Proof Fence

The Christof of *The Truman Show* is a peculiarly loving fascist, a self-styled patriarch who has convinced himself that the tidy '50s TV universe he has fabricated is superior to the real one—and that Truman, his 'son', is lucky to have so attentive a god.

David Edelstein 1998, 'Peep Show: Are *you* Big Brother?', *Slate*, http://slate.msn.com/?id=3255

Similarly, it is clear in *Rabbit Proof Fence* that Neville strongly believes that 'half-caste' children should be separated from their parents as part of his ideology of breeding out the Aboriginal race. It is interesting in this respect to compare Neville with the tracker Moodoo, who at times does not seem fully committed to recapturing the girls. Neville's commitment to his beliefs and his determination are conveyed by Branagh's performance, especially his steely gaze and his self-assured body language and manner of speaking. The scene in which Neville shows slides and explains his policies to a gathering of society matrons serves to underline the degree to which his actions are occasioned not by malice but by deeply held beliefs.

Rabbit Proof Fence has been criticised for focussing on Neville as the villain because this personalises the issues and does not sufficiently acknowledge that the policy of taking Aboriginal children away from their parents was a widely accepted and officially endorsed policy and just a part of a much wider policy that some people now describe as genocidal. The problem with focussing so much attention on one individual, the argument goes, is that it relieves society of the blame for what happened. While there may be some truth in this argument, film prioritises individuals because audiences generally want to focus on individuals rather than impersonal social forces. If the film had not constructed one individual as a powerful antagonist then its potential to attract audiences might have been at risk.

Audiences normally expect the antagonist to be more powerful than the protagonist, so that when the protagonist finally triumphs the audience can see this as a victory for the underdog which is ideologically reassuring.

Christof is godlike in his power. Symbolically situated in the moon above Truman's world, he has the power to direct the lives of thousands, to make the sun of Truman's world rise and set at his command and to control the weather, which, as the climax shows gives him the power of life and death over Truman.

> The film picked up metaphors as it went along. I was surprised as we began to put it together how it was relaying other meanings. I was rather more drawn to Greek legend. Christof is Zeus, in the sense that he's trying to control the mortals. In my reading, as I recall, the one thing Zeus could not do is interfere with fate. He could do other God-like things, including controlling the weather, but he cannot, as Christof/Zeus does, begin to interfere with the decisions his creature has taken, which is to leave. So Christof/Zeus crosses a line at the end and is punished for it. There are all sorts of other understandings. Somebody gave me a brilliant Buddhist one, with Christof as Siddharta's father, the King, trying to stop him leaving the garden and discovering the pain of life that lies outside the palace walls.

Peter Weir in Paul Kalina 1998, 'Imprisoning Visions', Urban Cinefile and Cinema Papers,
www.urbancinefile.com.au/home/view.asp?a=1593&s=Interviews

While Neville may not be as powerful as Christof, he is extremely powerful in comparison to Molly and the other girls because of his position and his ability to command and direct resources for the girls' recapture. His power is emphasised cinematically in the assembly scene, where Molly is confronted with Neville personally. The scene is composed to place Neville at the top of the slope. As Molly approaches him, his size increases until at one point it fills the frame. His power is further reinforced by the low camera angle that reflects Molly's point of view, constructing her as powerless and Neville as powerful.

The use of motor cars in the film can also be read as a symbol of Neville's power and his ability to direct his forces to appear with great suddenness seemingly out of nowhere. Their noise and speed contrast strongly with the girls' silence and slow progress.

Neville's power and importance is further emphasised in the office scenes where the fact that his control over people's lives extends to approving their choice of marriage partner is revealed by the dialogue and underlined by the shots through the window of groups of people waiting outside his office.

In many films, the antagonist is totally evil and has no redeeming features. Think of Darth Vader in *Star Wars* or the various villains in the *Batman* movies. Such antagonists are likely to be acceptable to audiences of comic-book style fantasy genres and some crime genres because such characterisation is one of the conventions. With other genres, audiences expect the protagonist to be a multidimensional character whose motivation is to a certain extent understandable, if misguided. The complexity and humanity of the antagonist not only intensifies the conflict, it makes the conflict seem all too human and thus more credible.

Neither Christof nor Neville are presented as total villains. Christof is almost fatherly in his concern for Truman. This is reflected in the scene of him stroking the giant screen showing a sleeping Truman which, significantly, mirrors the scene moments before when Sylvia, whom the audience accepts as truly loving Truman, strokes the image of Truman on her television screen. At the very end he reveals his humanity by pulling back from killing Truman when Truman shows that he is willing to die. As his final speech progresses, with its reminiscences of Truman's childhood, Christof sounds more and more like a loving, if misguided, father whose son is leaving home. Like many fathers, it is Christof's blindness to the need for freedom and self-determination that renders him incapable of understanding Truman's need to escape, rather than any inherent malice.

> I think that Christof (Ed Harris) is such an interesting character, he is a kind of artist. He sees himself as a great teacher, doing something very worthwhile. There was a decision early on in talking to Ed that he would not be crazy, insane—in the legal definition. He is certainly a fanatic, but, on the other hand, while making billions of dollars he was doing something that he thought was beneficial to the world and was demonstrating a way to live. That's what makes him truly sinister.

> Peter Weir in Paul Kalina 1998, 'Imprisoning Visions', *Urban Cinefile* and *Cinema Papers*, www.urbancinefile.com.au/home/view.asp?a=1593&s=Interviews

In many ways, Neville is similar to Christof. His attitude is similarly patriarchal and stems from his belief that he knows better than Aboriginal people what is in their best interests.

> Noyce's greatest success is making the villain of the film, A.O. Neville (Kenneth Branagh) completely understandable. As the man implementing the policy, there is a strong sense that Neville truly believes he is doing the right thing, and Branagh plays him perfectly. With an imperious tone and a tight-lipped smile, Branagh gives Neville the frustrated sense of a man genuinely baffled by the indigenous population's rejection of what to him is a perfect solution to a difficult problem. And although Noyce decides to sometimes distort Neville physically as he peers around the settlement, he is never derided as an evil fool, but as a man of good intent consumed by ignorance.

> Mark Freeman at home.vicnet.au/~freeman/reviewsqz/rabbitproof.htm

It is also possible to read Christof as nothing more than a tool of the media machine and the audiences whose demands created *The Truman Show*. In his televised telephone conversation with Sylvia, there is a hint of regret and dissatisfaction in Harris' performance of Christof. There is also a hint of tiredness as though Christof himself is locked into something from which he cannot escape.

These are just some possible readings of Christof and Neville. For those who prefer their villains totally evil, it is possible to ignore these aspects of the films or interpret them in very different ways. There is plenty in *The Truman Show* for those who wish to read Christof as a total villain: his black clothing, his cold demeanour and his surroundings all construct him in line with the techno-villains of many James Bond films. His callous, offhand response to the complaint that they can't allow Truman to die in front of a live audience, 'He was born in front of a live audience', adds to this construction. Similarly, you might argue that Neville, as portrayed in *Rabbit Proof Fence*, lacks any redeeming features and that his commitment to his racial ideologies makes him less rather than more human.

Activities

Choose two or three antagonists from films you are familiar with.

1. What qualities make them powerful in comparison to the protagonist?
2. How is their commitment to their cause shown?
3. To what extent are they multidimensional characters?

Narrative structure

Plot is what happens in a story. Narrative structure is how the events are arranged. Narrative structure is crucial to a film's entertainment value. A producer may have a film that is thematically relevant to its target audience, uses generic conventions in innovative ways and has a highly sympathetic protagonist with a worthy antagonist, but if the story is not told in such a way as to engage the audience then it will not attract one.

At the heart of narrative structure is suspense. The ability to create suspense depends on creating desire within the audience to see the film through to its end in the hope of finding out something. There are two forms of suspense. First is the desire to find out what will happen. This is the most commonly used form of suspense in most films, but it is sometimes assumed that it is the only kind. The other kind of suspense arises from the desire to know what has gone before. Many murder mysteries are based on this second form of suspense.

The Truman Show deploys both forms of suspense. Initially, it relies heavily on the second form of suspense. For first-time viewers, *The Truman Show* can be initially confusing. The fact that Truman is appearing in a television show is hinted at in the opening, but the full nature and history of the show are only gradually revealed throughout the film. Audiences may be encouraged to engage with the film in the hope of receiving answers to questions such as:

- How would it be possible to stage such a program?
- How could Truman not know that he was performing in a television show?
- Where did Truman come from?
- Why is Truman so dissatisfied with his life?
- Why has Truman not tried to leave the island before?

It is not until after Truman's failed escape attempt and just before his final quest for freedom that the complete history of the show is revealed to viewers. To reveal too much before would be to destroy this form of suspense.

At the same time as this form of suspense is being established, so is the first form of suspense: 'What is going to happen?' This question is not of itself enough to keep audiences engaged. The question has to be placed in the context of a specific incident or problem. The question audiences are engaged with might be better phrased as 'What will happen next as a result of … ?'

In *The Truman Show*, this form of suspense is initially related to the audience's awareness of Truman's dissatisfaction with his life. The question it encourages is 'Will Truman succeed in leaving the island?' The suspense is intensified when Truman hears voices on his car radio tracking his movements and in the following scenes as he begins to suspect that there is something strange about his world. Audiences might be encouraged to ask questions such as 'How will this affect his behaviour?', 'Will he discover the truth?' and 'Will this intensify his desire to escape?' Once Truman's determination to leave is established, the final section of the film relies heavily on a traditional form of suspense about how and whether he will achieve this goal.

Rabbit Proof Fence relies on the same form of suspense, the central question being whether the girls will reach their goal and how they will do it. Information about how the situation portrayed in the film arose is provided in the text at the beginning of the film where the nature and origins of Australia's racial policies at the time are described. The film does not, therefore, depend on suspense related to what has gone before. This allows the audience to focus on the girls and their journey.

Activities

1. List the two forms of suspense described above.
2. Next to each brainstorm the titles of books and films that make use of each kind.
3. Discuss your findings.
4. Can you observe any similarities in the texts using each form of suspense?
5. Are there ways in which different texts employ the same forms of suspense in different ways?

Narrative structure is often described as being built around a sense of complications or crises. These are key events that act as obstacles to a protagonist achieving his or her goals and thus increase the suspense. In most narratives, each complication becomes increasingly challenging and makes it seem even more difficult for the protagonist to succeed—there are ever-higher walls to climb over. As a result, the suspense builds. The final complication usually provides the most difficult challenge of all and the one where it seems that all the character's previous efforts have been in vain and he or she will finally be defeated. It is the character's triumph over this final challenge that provides the climax of the film and the satisfying end.

The complications Truman faces in his quest to learn the truth about his world and to escape from it gradually rise to the climax of the storm scene where he must conquer the greatest challenge of all, the possibility of death.

In *Rabbit Proof Fence*, the nearer the girls get to home, the greater the possibility that they will fail or be recaptured as the physical proximity of their pursuers increases. This builds to the situation where it seems their hopes will be destroyed by the Jigalong police officer, until he is vanquished by the girls' mother and grandmother.

Another important aspect of narrative structure is the editing of the film. Editing affects the sequence in which events are presented. During the girls' journey home in *Rabbit Proof Fence*, tension is enhanced through the juxtaposition of scenes of the girls with scenes of their pursuers. This enhances tension by building up the audience's sense that the girls are succeeding and then counterpointing this with information that suggests they will be caught. As the film moves towards its conclusion, scenes of the girls are juxtaposed with scenes of their family at Jigalong expecting their return. This juxtaposition serves to emphasise the spiritual bond between the girls and their family.

Narrative structure and values

Narrative structure does not just involve conflict between the characters, but also involves conflict between the values the characters represent. The audience's pleasure in seeing the character they have identified with throughout the film succeed is complemented by their pleasure in seeing values they adhere to triumph. In *The Truman Show*, the values of knowledge and freedom represented by Truman triumph over the values of ignorance and tyranny represented by Christof. In *Rabbit Proof Fence*, the values of freedom and familial love triumph over the values of control and unfeeling racial ideology represented by Neville.

Film language

The elements of film language in feature film are the same as those for documentary discussed on pages 71–3 under the headings Shot construction, Soundtrack and Editing. In addition, dialogue and performance should be considered part of film language in feature films, as these are creations of the film-makers. Film language can play an important role in contributing to an audience's response to the film and the meanings it constructs of the film. Examination and discussion of film language needs always to be related to the audience's response and the meanings it constructs, rather than studied in isolation.

Discussions of film language might take one of two forms, close examination of a sequence of the film or discussion of the patterns of film language over the film as a whole. Even in a brief sequence of film there is so much film language at work that it is not possible to examine every aspect in detail. Rather, you should focus on those aspects which are important in your reading of the film and the meanings you construct. The work sample below provides an example of close examination of the opening of a film.

WORK SAMPLE

Close examination of opening scenes in *Pretty Woman*

Pretty Woman was released in 1990 and starred Richard Gere and Julia Roberts. It was the film that made Roberts a major star. While the film is somewhat dated, this work sample provides a useful model for how you might discuss a short sequence of film in some detail. Notice how the opening paragraph establishes the writer's reading of the film by describing the themes of the film and what the writer believes the main character learns over the course of the film. This allows the writer later in the essay to focus on those aspects of film language which are relevant to this and how they can be seen as contributing to this reading.

Topic for this work: Making detailed reference to one or more scenes of a feature film, discuss the way in which film language contributes to the audience's understanding of theme, character and plot.

Pretty Woman, like many films, deals with the relative importance of material wealth and human relationships and the respective roles of men and women in relationships. The narrative of Pretty Woman concerns the discovery by the main male character, Edward Lewis, that in spite of his wealth, his life is unsatisfying without a female partner. Edward learns, however, through his relationship with the character of Vivian, that in contrast to the rest of his life, which is dominated by business, women cannot be bought or treated like property. Rather Vivian teaches him that successful relationships between men and women must be based on mutual respect, rather than the dominance of women by men.

The early scenes establish the world of Edward Lewis. The film opens with a close-up of a male hand placing money into female hands and the voice of a male character saying, 'No matter what they say, ladies, it's all about money'. This scene serves to highlight for the audience one of the features of the world in which the main character, Edward Lewis, lives, its belief in the power of money and the use of money by males to attempt to control females, thus drawing attention to one of the themes which will be explored in the film.

As the camera zooms back and tracks we find ourselves witnessing a party scene on a balcony overlooking Los Angeles. The people are well-dressed and apparently successful business people. The appearance of the people, the glorious view, the sumptuously laid tables and the musical group in the background emphasise the wealth and sophistication of the setting. The dialogue establishes that the party is being held in honour of Edward thus indicating his importance and also implying that the wealth and sophistication the audience sees are qualities associated with him. On being asked where Edward is, a character replies, 'If I know him he's probably off in a corner somewhere charming a very pretty lady' suggesting that Edward is a successful ladies man.

The scene then shifts to Edward himself and provides an ironic contrast to the preceding dialogue. Rather than charming a pretty lady, he is alone and on the telephone. In the conversation of which we hear both sides, Edward's girlfriend is breaking off their relationship because she refuses to be at his 'beck and call'. While Edward denies he makes such demands, his response to her comment, 'I have my own life too, you know' suggests that he is focussed on his own needs and ignorant of hers. During the conversation the camera shows Edward looking at his reflection in a window, an image which can be read as indicating his self-centredness and vanity. Shortly after, Edward is shown leaving the party. Thus these scenes establish the fact that, rather than being a successful ladies man, Edward Lewis is, despite his wealth, unsuccessful in terms of relationships with women because he expects them to serve his needs and ignores theirs. This point is reinforced in a conversation Edward has with a former lover as he is leaving. The dialogue reveals that she, like his current girlfriend, spent more time communicating with his secretary than with him which establishes Edward as a man who treats women as an aspect of his business dealings.

As Edward is shown driving down the hill, the credits role and we hear a song on the soundtrack which we can interpret as reflecting Edward's feelings. The song is an ironic statement by a male about breaking up with his lover. While claiming he will get over it, the singer admits the reverse by describing himself as 'the king of wishful thinking'. The notion of wishful thinking is picked up immediately as the camera provides a long shot of the 'Hollywood' sign above Los Angeles. While serving partly to identify the setting of the film, the shot can also be read as evoking the connotations associated with the world of Hollywood. Often called the dream factory, Hollywood is seen, because of its association with the movie industry, as a place where dreams can come true and anything can happen. The audience is thus prepared to accept that Edward may find his dream, a woman. The notion of Hollywood as the dream factory is reinforced shortly after by a close-up of the name of the 1930s film actor Carole Lombard in a star on the footpath of Hollywood Boulevard and the explicit comment by a minor character on the street.

Thus the opening scene of Pretty Woman uses a variety of cinematic techniques, or film language, to reveal the character of Edward, establish the themes of the film and foreshadow the plot.

Activity

Choose a short sequence that you believe plays an important role in a feature film and produce a detailed examination of the scene, using the above work sample as a model.

Below is an example of a discussion of the patterns of film language in a text.

From *The Matrix*

Stylistically, *The Matrix* is much like *Bound*. Both films are visually stunning, with images painstakingly constructed and action sequences choreographed to excite the eye and quicken the pulse. The Wachowskis use a varied pallette that includes shadows, slow motion, quick cuts, and offbeat humor to paint a unique portrait. Like in *Dark City*, theirs is a grim world, where darkness and gloom seemingly always hold sway. Everything from the set design to the costumes (lots of black, lots of sunglasses) is intended to contribute to an overall look. When it comes to shoot-outs, the Wachowskis show that John Woo isn't the only director capable of doing interesting things with familiar devices. The shots of Keanu Reeves streaking down a hall with guns blazing all around him and the air thick with shattered bits of concrete is only one of many snapshots that lingers in the mind's eye long after they have vanished from the screen. The special effects, which are not as numerous as those in many science fiction pieces, are flawless.

James Berardinelli 1999, '*The Matrix:* A Film Review', *Reelviews*, http://movie-reviews.colossus.net/movies/m/matrix.html

When looking for patterns of film language over the course of the film as a whole you could focus on such things as:

- the way in which certain characters, groups or institutions are represented through dialogue, camera angles, lighting, costumes and body language
- the way in which contrasts are established between characters, groups or institutions using the same techniques
- the use of recurring musical themes or symbols
- the patterns revealed by an actor's performance.

A number of examples of the use of film language in *The Truman Show* have already been mentioned in this chapter. One example is the manner in which Jim Carrey's performance in the opening scenes reveals Truman's dissatisfaction with his world through his insincere forced cheerfulness. It is worth noting the contrast between Carrey's manner in the opening scenes and his manner in later scenes. In the middle of the film, during his first escape attempt, Carrey's performance is much more manic, suggesting a Truman who is on the edge of hysteria and possibly insanity. In the final scene, Carrey's body language and performance portray Truman as relaxed and at ease with himself and his new found certainty of purpose.

Another example of film language is the recurring dialogue and musical theme that accompanies the start to Truman's working day, suggesting the repetitive nature of his superficially perfect and cheerful life. Truman's refrain of the line 'In case I don't see ya, good afternoon, good evening and good night' at the end of the film can be read as Truman finally taking control of his own life because for the first time he is using the lines consciously and deliberately, rather than as part of an unthinking routine. These lines and Carrey's bow to the audience at the end portray Truman's final attainment of knowledge of himself as an actor. His departure signifies his rejection of this role.

Other aspects of the use of film language in *The Truman Show* include the contrast between the brightness and strong colours of Truman's world and the darkness of Christof's. While the darkness of Christof's world is consistent with the portrayal of the antagonist in many films, it can also be read as suggesting Christof's dark, obsessive nature and his immunity to normal human feelings. The brightness and colour of Truman's world can be read as suggesting not that it is a pleasant, cheerful environment, but rather that it is artificial, an idea reinforced by Truman's almost clownlike costume in the scene of him gardening.

Earlier discussion of *Rabbit Proof Fence* has mentioned Everlyn Sampi's performance in conveying Molly's determination and Kenneth Branagh's performance in conveying Neville's commitment and determination. The similarity between these performances contributes to the sense of conflict in the film by establishing them as equally committed adversaries and by suggesting the similarity in strength of the values each represents, despite the disparity in power between them.

Another example of the use of film language in *Rabbit Proof Fence* is the way in which cars are used as a symbol of Neville's power. The rabbit proof fence itself can also be read symbolically. As the girls get closer to home, cuts to members of their family touching the fence establish it as symbolic of the strong spiritual link between them and the girls.

Rabbit Proof Fence makes extensive use of aerial, wide angle and long shots to convey the immensity of the landscape the girls must traverse in order to reach home and the harshness of the environment, thus underlining the immensity of their quest and the magnitude of their final victory. This is reinforced by lighting, especially in the desert scenes, which, as in many Australian films, is harsh and washed out and conveys the effect of shimmering sun.

Innovation in film language

Another way of examining film language is to consider the way in which a film uses film language differently to other films and the effects of this.

The Truman Show is cinematically innovative in a number of ways. It begins in the form of a promotional documentary with interviews with Christof and the cast members of the television show. This was actually shot with a different film stock to enhance the resemblance to documentary. The opening credits are not those of the film *The Truman Show*, but of the television show *The Truman Show*. Both of these can be read as contributing to the sense of realism of the film.

The interviews with the actors in the documentary contribute to the portrayal of them as totally committed to the concept of the show they are starring in and unable to step outside and question the morality associated with it.

Rabbit Proof Fence is unusual in comparison to most films in that it relies much less on dialogue. The lack of dialogue, especially from the girls, has been criticised by some reviewers who argue that it inhibits audience identification with the girls. Others argue that this is compensated for by the musical soundtrack which can be read as adding an epic quality to the girls' journey.

Film language and pleasure

Film language can also be a major source of entertainment and pleasure for audiences. Indeed some people argue that they can enjoy the visual and aural experience of a film quite apart from its themes or narrative. This is the approach taken by the following work sample.

WORK SAMPLE

Starship Troopers

This work sample was produced by a Year 12 student in an examination.

Topic for this work sample: Many films rely for their success more heavily on special effects than they do on the presentation of serious ideas and issues. Discuss the extent to which you think this is true, making reference to at least one feature film to illustrate your argument.

Starship Troopers is an eye-candy feature film whose success is based purely on the litres of blood, big guns and computer image bugs contained therein. I can admire the political satire made through the Sweet Valley High in space characters but I wouldn't pay money to see it. But brains being sucked out, flying limbs and huge explosions are definitely worth it.

I'd normally use this paragraph to outline the basic premise of the film, but I honestly don't think SST has one beyond, 'Lets get soap stars to fight super-combat bugs in space with knives!' But the lack of a storyline isn't important. I don't care why director Paul Verhoeven put Casper Van Dien on an asteroid with spiders the size of buses, as long as I get to see his well muscled body spattered with gore and dressed in a skin tight combat fatigues. Do I care what's motivated the bug war? No.

That this film relies heavily on special effects is perhaps demonstrated by the poor script writing. It may seem stupid for Earth destroyer-class ships to fly so close together they collide, but the explosions produced are some of the best I've ever seen. They also take up about ten minutes in screen time. Given that disaster special effects are the most visual ones, making pea brains the commanders of huge lumbering ships is a brilliant idea.

To say that this movie is not relying on special effects is ridiculous. The grouchy cockroaches humankind is waging war on are completely computer generated. The army sergeant's advice to shoot anything with more than two legs may be speciesist, but bile-green blood and arachnid legs flying about the landscape is why you go to see this movie, not to analyse the socio-species implications.

If you sat down and thought about it, sending mobile infantry into space armed only with their knives to fight bugs that are 86% combat capable even after the loss of limbs is a little stupid. The fact that a bug would only allow a grossly underarmed human near it if it was dead becomes peripheral during a scene where Carmen Ibanez slices off a clawed appendage. So the only chances of it happening are Buckley's and more. So what? I wouldn't have missed the following blood spray for the world.

Seeing Doogie Howser MD in a Rommel style trenchcoat may fall a little short on the 'serious socio-political comment on neo-fascism' scale, but the special effects of his surroundings mean I don't really care.

From *Starship Troopers*

'We're going back to pee,' may not be the most stimulating line of all time, but the panorama of space through warp drive means I'm not actually listening to him anyway.

Huge lumbering bugs shooting fluorescent flatulence at orbiting ships and the following chaos is probably a metaphor for something as is men being bitten in half and covering their comrades with blood. But watching this I'm not concerned with indepth analysis. I'm wanting 3D virtual reality gear with 'real blood effects!'. 'Be splattered like you're there!'

This film does make some cutting political comments. The world is run by the Federation whose insignia is like Hitler's eagle. Only citizens can vote or procreate, and to be a citizen you have to be a soldier. All joking aside, the commentary about political extremism is biting. Candidates stand in rows under flags chanting in unison, 'I do this of my own free will'. But if I wanted to see a mind expanding film I could rent <u>Kundun</u> or a biography on Mohandas Ghandhi. As good as it is, *the political criticism doesn't go far enough and really can't cut the mustard against the special effects, and political satire really needs a plot base, and to say this film has no plot is perhaps overly kind.*

Watching <u>Starship Troopers</u> as I mentioned before it sometimes feels like the poor script is deliberate in order to focus attention on the special effects. But deliberate or not this is what has happened, and without big bad scary bugs, bloody dismembered limbs and superhuge explosions some of the $100m budget might have had to have been spent on people who could act, which is always a dicey investment. Better to hire clothes-horse actors and spend big on special effects which are a winner. Serious issues? Who cares? The average audience will go for the blood and guts every time.

Work supplied by Claire Pullen

Activities

For discussion

1. To what extent do you agree with the arguments put forward in this essay?
2. Do you agree that most people are not interested in films that deal with serious issues?
3. To what extent does your enjoyment of a film rely on special effects and spectacular cinematography?
4. Compare this work sample with the one on *Starship Troopers* on page 59. Which do you find more convincing? Why?
5. Which is the more entertaining piece of work? Why?

Realism

For some people, 'It was so unrealistic' is one of the strongest criticisms that can be levelled at a film. But films like *Star Wars* are completely unrealistic and this certainly doesn't stop them from attracting audiences. Because films make more extensive use of visual and aural language than other texts, they can seem more realistic. But if you think about it for a few seconds, all films are totally unrealistic. They jump from scene to scene in a way that is nothing like the experience of real life. The audience's perspective in a film involves aerial shots, close-ups and wide angles—all quite unlike the way people experience real life. Background music at key moments in a film swells to a crescendo—if that happened in real life you would look around for the boom box or ghetto blaster.

Realism in film is a complex concept and has little to do with a film's similarity to real life. First, what most people mean when they say that a film is realistic is that it is absorbing or that it involved them strongly at an emotional level. Thus realism is produced by some of the factors discussed earlier in this chapter: thematic relevance, sympathetic characters, worthy antagonists and narrative structure.

Second, realism depends partly on learnt textual conventions. The audience accepts the abrupt changes of scene, the unusual camera perspectives and the background music because they have learnt that these are part of the conventions of film. They are absorbed into the audience's framework of what constitutes realism in a film. Similarly, the audience's knowledge of generic conventions allows them to accept talking robots, warp speed and all of the unrealistic elements of some science fiction as part of the world of the film. Audiences are willing to suspend disbelief in order to enjoy the film. So realism is genre dependent. What is accepted as real in one genre will not be accepted as real in another.

Third, for many films realism depends not on whether the world of a film resembles the real world, but whether the world of the film is plausible. The audience knows the world of the film is fiction, but usually they are willing to accept it and become involved in it if they see that what is portrayed is a possibility based on their knowledge of the way the world works and the way it is developing. Part of the enjoyment of many films lies in entertaining these possibilities. Films can keep us 'entertained' in both senses of the word.

Peter Weir describes some of the attempts that were made to make *The Truman Show* seem plausible:

Q. What shifts took place during the course of those 10 drafts?

A: [Andrew Niccol's original script] was more what I think you could call Kafkaesque. It was certainly darker. It was a more psychological piece. He had it set in New York City and was going to shoot it there. Truman was more of an everyman. I'd like to have seen his version of it, but, unlike theatre, you can't get to see anyone else's take on [a film]. Andrew wanted to direct the film; he just didn't have any track record and it was too expensive. When I read it, I felt the first problem was New York. More than usual, I had to satisfy the credibility of the idea. You had to believe it was possible. Being set in the near future, you have to relax the area of logic for the audience to join in with the film, so they would not be constantly thinking, 'Could this happen?' I said no producer would build New York!

Also, it wouldn't be an ideal community. Why would you create something that had all the problems of our world? Why not build an idealized world? That led eventually to Seaside, to a pristine community created in the style of the last century. Given that it was set in the near future, this would be the way people would like to live, almost like a holiday brochure really, an ideal island somewhere.

Peter Weir in Paul Kalina 1998, 'Imprisoning Visions', *Urban Cinefile* and *Cinema Papers*,
www.urbancinefile.com.au/home/view.asp?a=1567&s=Reviews

Psychological realism

More important for the sense of realism than what happens or what the world of the film looks like is how the characters behave. This is psychological realism: the audience expects characters to behave in psychologically believable ways and according to motives the audience can relate to or understand. It is for this reason that films featuring non-human characters, like *Babe*, portray the characters as acting according to human psychological motives as a way of enhancing the realism of the film.

What constitutes psychological realism may vary between audiences and members of the same audience and is related to the values and beliefs of the audience. The assertive and often heroic behaviour of female characters in modern films might not have seemed psychologically real to audiences in the 1930s when cinema began.

Activities

1. List some films that you consider extremely realistic and some that you consider unrealistic.
2. Compare your ideas with other students and tease out the definitions of realism you are applying.
3. Write on the topic 'What makes a film real for me' using specific films to illustrate your explanation.

Like to know more?

Visit the Longman website www.longman.com.au for links to a number of sites related to *The Truman Show* and *Rabbit Proof Fence*.
Here you will find reviews of the films as well as comment and information on the cinema and media.

Index

Concepts

Aboriginality, representations of 170–3, *see also Rabbit Proof Fence*
actuality footage 76
Americans, representations of 113–20
antagonist 199–203
archetypal narratives 49–50, 75
archival footage 76
Australia and Australians, representations of 113–20
authorities 127

body image, female 141–55

camera
    angle 71
    distance 72
    movement 72
character development 165–6
characterisation in documentary 89–90, 94–103
children, representations of 31–5
cinéma verité 76, 79, 81
close-up 72
connotation 133
context 1, 2, 8, 61, 70, 77, 83–4, 93–4, 121–2, 129, 159–60, 161–3, 177, 178, 180, 190, 192, *see also* 19–21
constructed footage 76

direct documentary *see* cinéma verité
docudrama 76
documentary 69–110
    construction process 70–3
    narrative structure 74–6
    key terms 76
dominant reading 170
drama, stage 191 *see also* 35–44
dystopia; dystopic fiction 9, 162, 167, 180, 196

editing 73
epigraphs, titles and 53–8
ethnicity, representations of 29–30, 174–7
expository writing 111–156
    types of 112
    construction 125–33
    language 133–6
    structure 137

fables 15–19
fictional documentary 76
film language 205–210, *see also* 71–3
focaliser 74

foregrounding 44–5, 48–9

gender, readings and representations of 6–7, 9, 35–44, 44–5, 92–3, 100, 122–5, 141–5
genre 3–5, 19–21, 59, 75, 77, 81, 168, 178–182, 195–7

ideology; ideologies; ideological readings 3–5, 13, 20, 29–30, 47, 50, 57–8, 77, 81, 83, 90, 92, 95, 121–5, 164, 166, 171–3, 177, 187–8, 190, 200, 202, 205
intertextuality; intertextual readings 3–5, 6–7, 21, 46–60, 100
irony, 61–8

levels of reading, 13–25
lighting 73
long shots 72

narrative
    incursion 137
    structure 73, 74–6, 103–5, 203–5
narratives, archetypal, 49–50, 75
narrator *see* point of view
normality and otherness 177
novels 157–90
    framework for approaching 159
    history and nature of 158

otherness 177

panning 72
persona 125, 142
pleasure and reading 190, 210–12
point of view 182–90
preferred reading 170
problems, central 74, 160–4
prose fiction *see* novels
protagonist 197–9

race, representations of 122 *see also* Aboriginality
reading intertextually 46–60 *see also* intertextuality
reading resistantly 29–30, 170–4
reading
    dominant 170
    levels of 13–25
    preferred 170
readings
    arguing for 11
    constructing 1–12
realism 212–14
reality television 193

reconstructed footage 76
representation 26–45, 170–7, *see also* Aboriginality, Americans, Australia, children, ethnicity, gender, race, teenagers
resistant reading, 29–30, 170–4

science fiction 3–5, 19, 59, 168, 193, 195, 208, 213
soundtrack 73
special effects 73
speculative fiction 168, *see also* science fiction
statistics 130–3
stereotypes, ethnic 29–30, *see also* ethnicity
structure, narrative 73, 74–6, 103–5, 203–5
sympathy 197

teenagers, representations of 19, 26–8, 122–5
theme 166–7, 192–4
titles and epigraphs 53–8
tracking shot 72

values and the audience 141

zoom 72

Authors, directors and texts

10 Things I Hate About You 19
101 Dalmations 49
1984 48
Aesop's Fables 15–17, 19
Alice in Wonderland 55
Alien 49, 195
All Quiet on the Western Front 47
Allende, Isabel 53
Anna's Story 19, 26–8, 55–6
'Ant and the Grasshopper, The' 16
Apocalypse Now 47
'At Sea with the America's Cup' 119–20
A Thousand and One Tales of the Arabian Nights 53
Atwood, Maragaret *see Handmaid's Tale, The*

Babe 214
Barba Kueria 76
Basketball Diaries, The 25
Batman 201
Beauty and the Beast 49